Professional
Office Procedures

Professional Office Procedures

SECOND EDITION

Susan H. Cooperman
Montgomery College

Prentice Hall
Upper Saddle River, New Jersey 07458

Library of Congress Cataloging-in-Publication Data

Cooperman, Susan H.,
   Professional office procedures / Susan H. Cooperman. — 2nd ed.
      p.   cm.
   Includes index.
   ISBN 0-13-979576-6 (pbk.)
      1. Office practice—Vocational guidance.   I. Title
   HF5547.5.C66   1999
   651'.023'73—dc21   98-30199
                                                            CIP

Director of production and manufacturing: *Bruce Johnson*
Managing editor: *Mary Carnis*
Production coordinator: *Ed O'Dougherty*
Editorial/production supervision, interior design,
   and page layout: *Julie Boddorf*
Creative director: *Marianne Frasco*
Cover design: *Miguel Ortiz*
Acquisitions editor: *Elizabeth Sugg*
Marketing manager: *Danny Hoyt*
Editorial assistant: *Maria Kirk*
Proofreader: *Susan Shakhshir*

Trademark Information: Access, FoxPro, Microsoft Network, Microsoft Office, Microsoft Publisher, Microsoft Word, MS-DOS, PowerPoint, Windows 95, and Windows 98 are registered trademarks of Microsoft Corporation. America On-line is a registered trademark of America Online, Inc. Best's Insurance Reports is a registered trademark of Best Insurance & Financial Service. Best Western is a registered trademark of Best Western International, Inc. CompuServe is a registered trademark of CompuServe, Inc. WordPerfect and WordPerfect Office are registered trademarks of Corel, Inc. Dbase is a registered trademark of Borland International. DHL is a registered trademark of DHL Worldwide Express. FedEx and Federal Express are registered trademarks of Federal Express Corporation. Forbes is a registered trademark of Forbes, Inc. IBM is a registered trademark of IBM Corporation. Kinko's is a registered trademark of Kinkos, Inc. Mail Boxes Etc. is a registered trademark of Mail Boxes Etc. Macintosh is a registered trademark of Apple Computer, Inc. The New York Times is a registered trademark of the New York Times Company. Official Airline Guides is a registered trademark of the Reed Travel Group. PageMaker is a registered trademark of Adobe Systems, Inc. UPS and United Parcel are registered trademarks of United Parcel Service. Xerox is a registered trademark of The Xerox Corporation. The names of all other products mentioned in this book are used for identification purposes only and may be registered trademarks of their owners.

Printed in the United States of America

10   9   8   7   6   5   4   3   2   1

ISBN   0-13-979576-6

PRENTICE-HALL INTERNATIONAL (UK) LIMITED, *London*
PRENTICE-HALL OF AUSTRALIA PTY. LIMITED, *Sydney*
PRENTICE-HALL CANADA INC., *Toronto*
PRENTICE-HALL HISPANOAMERICANA, S.A., *Mexico*
PRENTICE-HALL OF INDIA PRIVATE LIMITED, *New Delhi*
PRENTICE-HALL OF JAPAN, INC., *Tokyo*
SIMON & SCHUSTER ASIA PTE. LTD., *Singapore*
EDITORA PRENTICE-HALL DO BRASIL, LTDA., *Rio de Janeiro*

Photo Credits: Photos used courtesy of William Cooperman: Figures 3-2, 6-1, 6-2, 8-1, and 10-1; DHL Worldwide Express: Figure 4-7; IBM Corporation: Figures 1-1, 1-2, 1-6, 5-1, 5-2, 5-3, 5-4, 7-1, 9-1, 12-1, 13-2, and 13-3; Newell Office Products Company: Figure 3-4; Pitney Bowes: Figures 4-8 and 4-9; Reed Travel Group: Figures 8-2, 8-3, and 8-4; and The Xerox Corporation: Figure 10-5.

In memory of my mother, Libby Rosenthal.
She will always be remembered.

And for my husband, Bill.

Their support, encouragement, and dedication
made this second edition possible.

Contents

▼ 3 ▼

COMMUNICATIONS

▼ 4 ▼

PROCESSING THE MAIL

▼ 10 ▼

THE OFFICE

▼ 11 ▼

SEEKING EMPLOYMENT

Preface

Professional Office Procedures will assist, inform, and train people for careers in today's office. An office may be in a large corporation, midsized company, or a small business. In addition, an office can be a personal enterprise working out of one room in a home. Regardless of the size of the organization or the type of the business, all employees from entry level to management need to know office procedures so that they can function effectively in today's workplace.

The information contained in this book will be useful to students entering the world of office employment for the first time as well as for workers currently employed in offices. This material will also be useful to people returning to work after a period of time at home attending to family responsibilities and to persons who have made a career change. With downsizing in many offices, today's workers need the skills to perform a wide variety of job functions. Office employees will find many practical procedures in this book for cross training which will enhance their skills and assist the advancement of their careers.

The purpose of the book is to train people to think, work under stressful and difficult situations, and perform office duties in a professional manner. The focus of the book is to prepare students for the realistic problems and situations they will encounter in a modern office. Instead of reading about a topic, students are directed to practice the skills and discuss the professional office procedures presented in this book. Each chapter contains a series of activities that allow the student to implement the material covered. For example, when discussing business travel, the person is asked to contact airlines for schedules and prices; and when planning a meeting, the student is asked to contact local restaurants and inquire about accommodations and prices.

Special emphasis is given to the development of positive human relations skills. Being able to work as a cooperative member of a team, getting along well with co-workers and managers, and dealing with difficult clients are all vital to a successful office career. Each chapter contains a section on developing human relations skills and includes a section where students are encouraged to analyze problem situations that occur in the workplace and develop their own methods and solutions. The problems are typical situations that occur in an office and often do not have right or wrong answers.

In this second edition, the use of current technology in a constantly changing computerized business world is combined throughout the book with basic office procedures that are always essential to advancement and survival in an office environment. In addition to completely revising the sections on computers and telecommunications, this edition incorporates computers and the Internet into every aspect of the modern office. Facets of the modern business environment such as seeking employment, office security, delivering speeches, and telecommunications have been incorporated into *Professional Office Procedures*.

Since the objective of most workers is to advance from an entry-level position to a position of greater responsibility, the development of decision-making skills is stressed throughout the book. The final chapter, entitled "Tips of the Trade," includes hints to make the office worker's life more efficient and less stressful.

Two hands-on projects are included in each chapter. Additional projects that may be used for testing or timed assigned are included in the instructor's manual. Timed assignments can be used to simulate a chaotic office atmosphere with frequent interruptions and "rush jobs."

At the end of each chapter, there is a punctuation review. The Appendix contains a review of grammar, punctuation, and spelling, which are very important for office employees.

Packaged with the text is a computer disk, which reinforces the skills taught in the course. The student is given projects to complete, job assignments to analyze and research, situations to solve, and punctuation exercises to do as a review.

Professional Office Procedures integrates computer skills, office skills, language skills, human relation skills, life experiences, knowledge of the business world, and organization techniques so that the student may develop into a competent, conscientious, reliable, and dependable office assistant.

Finally, the helpful suggestions and comments of those who reviewed the manuscript for *Professional Office Procedures* should be acknowledged. These people are: Charlotte L. Atkins, Waubonsee Community College; Sue Baldwin, Southwest Texas Junior College; Yolanda V. Foley, Watterson College; Linda Swinter, Rock Valley College; Carolyn B. Webb, Robert Morris College; and Jerry L. Wood, Northern Montana College.

Professional
Office Procedures

▼1▼
The Successful Employee

OBJECTIVES

After studying this chapter, you should:

1. Be able to list the personal traits of an office employee.
2. Understand how to improve listening skills.
3. Be able to list the duties of an office employee.
4. Be familiar with the concept of time management.
5. Understand how to schedule appointments.
6. Be familiar with an organization structure.
7. Know how to become an effective team player.
8. Be familiar with leadership skills.
9. Understand brainstorming.
10. Be familiar with alternative work schedules.

▼ THE OFFICE EMPLOYEE ▼

Technological changes have created an upheaval in the duties and responsibilities of employees. In the past, basic office functions such as placing and answering telephone calls; writing and keyboarding letters, memorandums, and reports; greeting clients; arranging meetings; filing; and numerous other jobs were the responsibility of a secretary, receptionist, or assistant. Today, these duties are handled by all office employees regardless of their level of responsibility. These basic duties are performed by entry-level as well as management-level employees. Knowledge of basic office procedures, therefore, cannot be limited to a secretary, administrative assistant, or administrative aide in today's office.

There are many titles that can be used to describe persons who work in an office. Some of these titles are administrative assistant, administrative aide, personal assistant, coordinator, office manager, office worker, executive assistant, and clerk. At one time many office employees were given the title *secretary*, but that is not true today. Traditionally, the term *secretary* was the office support staff with responsibility for shorthand and typing, which is now called *keyboarding*. The business world is now recognizing that the duties and responsibilities of the secretarial position have grown beyond that of keyboarding and shorthand. Modern offices require mastery of computers and a variety of electronic equipment unavailable just a few years ago. As office jobs have become more complex, the responsibilities of the office support staff have also increased. Professional Secretaries International (PSI) defines a *secretary* as "an *executive assistant* who possesses a mastery of office skills, demonstrates the ability to assume responsibility without direct supervision, exercises initiative and judgment, and makes decisions within the scope of assigned authority."

Reflecting the expansion of the secretary's duties and responsibilities, the title *secretary* is now changing to that of *administrative assistant*. The duties and responsibilities of

FIGURE 1-1   An Executive's Office. (Courtesy of International Business Machines Corporation. Unauthorized use not permitted.)

these positions are the same, and in this book, these terms are used interchangeably.

The person who supervises the office employee can be called by a number of titles. Whether the supervisor is a low-level junior executive or the president of the organization, the supervisor is given the responsibility for overseeing the work of the employees. Any of the following titles are commonly used to refer to a supervisor and are used interchangeably in this book: *manager, supervisor, executive, boss, principal,* or *office manager.*

The office employee field offers a wide range of job opportunities. For a person with skills, there are entry-level and advanced positions in accounting, merchandising, education, government, medicine, social services, law, technology, and many other fields. An entry-level position may eventually evolve into a management position or to a new career in a related profession. The office employee position can be an open door to the future. An opportunity to travel to exciting places, meet interesting people, and grow in your field can all be part of your world of business. With good skills and a professional attitude, you will be able to find a rewarding career.

▼ CHARACTERISTICS OF A GOOD OFFICE EMPLOYEE ▼

Your Abilities

As an office employee, you are hired for your ability to assist your supervisor. The greatest ability you have, and the one most often overlooked, is simply your ability to think. An employee who does not think, solve problems, or show initiative requires continuous supervision by the manager. Usually, the employee who does not assist in solving office problems becomes part of the problem.

As an effective office employee, you should use initiative and accept responsibility. You were hired to assist in solving problems and to develop new and better ways to complete your work. Be sure you always meet deadlines. Do not make excuses. Plan to complete projects early in case there are last-minute problems. Your goal should be to develop a reputation for dependability and reliability.

Do not be afraid of your supervisor. It is difficult to work in an environment where fear is your constant companion. Fear can inhibit your decision-making capability and can lessen your ability to show initiative. If you are fearful, you will not be able to produce the work you are capable of doing. Remember, you were hired because you had the necessary skills to do the job.

Human Relations Skills

An essential skill for all employees is the ability to get along with others. Handling difficult human relations problems is an everyday occurrence in an office. As an office employee, you must learn to handle these problems diplomatically. This does not mean agreeing with everything that others say to you and doing everything that others want you to do. Everyone should be treated with courtesy, respect, and dignity. Treat others as you want them to treat you. Listen to their views, express your views, and then work out a compromise if necessary. Mastery of human relations skills is important to the success of any employee, but it is especially important for the office employee who deals with management and with people from outside the office.

Important Characteristics

The most important characteristics of a good office employee are those required of all good employees. Employers place a high value on these characteristics, but they are rarely included in a job description.

Successful office employees must be able to:

- Think
- Listen to and understand directions
- Handle office situations efficiently
- Handle a crisis in a logical manner
- Express themselves in a clear and concise manner

Think before you speak. To communicate so that others understand you, organize and plan what you are going to say. Obviously, you cannot plan every comment but learn not to blurt out irrelevant remarks.

Throughout this book you will be presented with suggestions and practices that will prepare you to deal with the daily challenges of office situations. Mastering these skills will help prepare you for success in both business and personal situations.

The following list includes some of the essential characteristics of a successful office employee. Some of these are skills that can easily be learned in a classroom, whereas other traits are related to your attitude and personality. If you do not possess the characteristics of a successful office employee, you should work to improve your skills, attitude, or personality. Ask yourself if you currently meet all of these qualifications. If you do not, decide on a *specific plan* to develop them.

A good office employee:

1. Projects a pleasing personality
2. Is dependable
3. Projects a positive attitude
4. Displays initiative
5. Demonstrates organizational skills
6. Has the ability to spell correctly
7. Is knowledgeable of office procedures
8. Is neat in appearance
9. Is loyal
10. Is sincere
11. Is courteous
12. Is reliable

FIGURE 1-2 Working in a Typical Office Setting. (Courtesy of International Business Machines Corporation. Unauthorized use not permitted.)

13. Is honest
14. Is a team worker
15. Is a decision maker
16. Is committed to work
17. Believes in the work ethic
18. Is flexible
19. Possesses a professional demeanor
20. Is interested in and curious about the office
21. Maintains confidences
22. Is punctual
23. Is responsible enough to notify the office when absent
24. Is tactful
25. Follows instructions
26. Asks for clarification of a project when necessary
27. Is confident about his or her own personal abilities
28. Is prepared mentally and physically for the job
29. Has the ability to think
30. Possesses good computer skills
31. Possesses good keyboarding skills
32. Possesses good language arts skills

Personal Traits to Avoid

Some people possess negative personal traits that interfere with job performance. The following list describes some negative behaviors that should be avoided in the office.

A poor employee:

- Has a bossy manner
- Is a gossip
- Displays a quick temper
- Chews gum

- Has poor listening habits
- Cracks his or her knuckles
- Brags
- Uses slang
- Is too aggressive
- Is lazy

▼ EFFECTIVE LISTENING ▼

Listening is a skill much like running or throwing a ball. Anyone can throw a ball, but some people have developed the skill to throw a ball faster, farther, or more accurately than other people. The skill of listening can be strengthened in the same manner. Listening skills are vital in the office because most office instructions are given orally. Excellent listening skills also help you to remember more of what you hear, respond more accurately to what you hear, and understand more of what you hear. When listening, concentrate on what is being said and do not allow your mind to wander. Summarize the important details to yourself so that you will remember them. You should, of course, feel free to request clarification of instructions if you do not understand them. You should also remember that people can become annoyed if they must continually repeat instructions because you were not paying attention.

Suggestions to help improve listening skills

- Be close enough to the person you are listening to so that you can hear clearly what is being said.
- Concentrate on what is being said, and do not daydream. If your mind starts to wander, focus on what is being said.
- If music is played in the office, select relaxing background music. Do not play music that commands your attention.
- Pay attention to what is being said. Also be aware of gestures, facial expressions, body language, and voice tone—they add to the message.
- Focus your eyes on the person talking to you.
- Do not allow the speaker's personal mannerisms to interfere with your concentration.
- Clarify and verify everything that you do not understand by asking questions.
- Be prepared when someone approaches you with instructions; have paper and pen ready to take notes.
- Do research and obtain background information about office projects so that instructions will be clearer to you.
- Identify the main ideas in the instructions given.
- Repeat the important points to yourself.
- Avoid the pitfalls of biases that cloud the message when listening. Some people have difficulty listening to:
  —Members of the opposite sex
  —Members of an ethnic group
  —Persons older or younger than themselves

▼ DUTIES OF AN OFFICE EMPLOYEE ▼

The Job Description

A *job description* is a list of all the duties and responsibilities of a particular job. As a new employee, you should be given a copy of your job description. Study your job description carefully so that you will be familiar with all the duties and responsibilities incorporated in your job. You do not want to be guilty of neglecting a job duty because you were unaware that it was your responsibility.

An example of a typical job description

> The office employee will perform the following duties: greeting clients, answering the telephone, preparing expense and travel reports, organizing and supervising the daily operations of the office, ordering and maintaining supplies, keyboarding, writing reports, researching projects, and additional duties as deemed appropriate by the supervisor.

Most job descriptions end with a phrase such as "additional duties as deemed appropriate by your supervisor." These additional duties can be new and exciting projects, but they may also include making coffee or running personal errands for your supervisor. As the duties of an office employee have changed in the last several years, some office employees have become uncomfortable completing jobs that they feel are *personal* rather than *professional*. The decision to complete these personal tasks will be your own. You should base that decision on the work environment. In some offices, making coffee is shared by all employees. If your supervisor is flexible about how you perform your job duties, you should be flexible about taking on additional tasks.

Listed below are typical administrative assistant duties often found in job descriptions. The type of job and company will determine your exact responsibilities.

Typical administrative duties

- Keyboarding reports, letters, and memos
- Writing letters, reports, and memos
- Answering the telephone
- Screening telephone calls and visitors
- Greeting visitors
- Sorting and routing the mail
- Maintaining time logs for completion of jobs
- Maintaining employee attendance records
- Preparing expense reports
- Maintaining appointment calendars
- Supervising employees
- Ordering supplies and equipment
- Calling vendors for equipment repairs
- Making travel arrangements
- Arranging meetings
- Photocopying
- Filing records manually and/or electronically
- Sending and receiving fax messages
- Working as a team player with other members of the staff
- Prioritizing work assignments
- Solving office problems
- Using online computer services
- Researching on the Internet
- Using computer application packages to create and revise word processing, spreadsheet, and database management documents
- Completing other jobs that are necessary for efficient running of the office

Appointments

As an office employee, one of your responsibilities is to schedule appointments for your supervisor. Know your manager's preferences concerning days and times of appointments.

Monday, September 5	Telephone Number
9:00	
9:30	
10:00	
10:30	
11:00	
11:30	
12:00	
12:30	
1:00	
1:30	
2:00	
2:30	
3:00	
3:30	
4:00	
4:30	

FIGURE 1-3   Page from an Appointment Calendar.

Certain days or times may not be convenient for appointments. For example, the office may have a staff meeting every Monday morning. Compare your appointment calendar with your supervisor's calendar frequently and add appointments that the supervisor may have scheduled without your knowledge. (Even if it is not your fault, it is embarrassing for you to schedule an appointment at a time the supervisor already has an appointment scheduled.)

Today, many offices maintain a computerized calendar. This can be an individual calendar or a shared calendar where the assistant has access to the supervisor's calendar to make appointments.

Consider the following when making appointments

1. What is the name of the visitor? (Always verify the spelling and pronunciation of the visitor's name. You should write a note to yourself if the pronunciation is difficult or unusual.)
2. What is the name of the company where the visitor is employed?
3. What is the reason for the appointment?
4. When does the visitor want the appointment and how much time will be needed?

5. Request a telephone number in case the appointment must be canceled.

6. If the appointment is not going to be held in your employer's office, obtain specific information concerning the location.

7. Know in advance your employer's policy about scheduling appointments. Know who will be seen and who will not be seen. Diplomacy will be required if you are not allowed to schedule an appointment. For example, your supervisor may not be interested in seeing a particular sales representative who is very persistent about making an appointment.

Visitors

Remembering names and faces is an important skill for office employees. Some people have the gift to remember faces and names easily. If you do not possess this skill, make notes to help yourself remember. Think of ways to associate a person's name and face with something you will remember. It may be helpful to set up a 3 x 5 in. card file or a computer note pad system with information about your clients. Clients like to feel they are important to the company, so it is good business policy to address them by name.

All visitors should be greeted in a pleasant and professional manner. Invite the visitor to be seated. If a visitor must wait for your employer, offer a soft drink or coffee if it is the policy of your company. Be pleasant but continue with your work.

Learn your supervisor's preferences concerning visitors without appointments. Will your employer see friends and family members if they stop by the office?

Before a visitor is ushered into your employer's office, notify the employer that the visitor has arrived. This can be done by calling on the telephone or intercom, by taking a note to the employer, or by walking into the employer's office and announcing the visitor. Always close the employer's door when you go into the office to deliver your message so that your conversation will be private.

Interrupting your supervisor during an appointment requires diplomacy. Sometimes you may be required to remind a supervisor that there is another appointment waiting or that the supervisor must leave for a meeting. You should be aware of your supervisor's policy regarding interruptions. The manager's personal preference will determine how you handle each situation. Interruptions can be handled by calling the employer on a private telephone line, by delivering a note to the supervisor during the meeting, or by walking in and speaking with the employer. Interrupting an appointment can also be an effective way of ending an appointment that has lasted too long.

Some offices maintain a log of visitors. The log is useful when it is important to verify that a client visited on a specific date. Some companies maintain a visitor's log for security purposes.

Chronological File

One of the duties of an office employee is to maintain a chronological file, which is a filing system that contains a copy of everything that has been mailed. This file is kept in date order, with the most recent date on top. The chronological file is used as a quick reference or review of a project.

DATE	VISITOR	COMPANY	REASON FOR VISIT
4/5/XX	Joe Martin	Lamps, Inc.	Discuss report
4/7/XX	Bill O'Dell	S & R Limited	Review project
4/8/XX	Sue Larkins	Print Shop	Discuss brochure

FIGURE 1-4   A Visitor's Log.

Policy and Procedures/Desk Manual

When you begin your new job, you may be presented with a policy and procedures/desk manual, which may contain an explanation of company rules and procedures, examples of forms often used in the office with an explanation of how to complete them, and an organization chart of the company. The organization chart will allow you to become familiar quickly with important names and titles. You should consult the desk manual frequently until you become familiar with the operation of the office. Policy and procedures/desk manuals also inform new employees of company policies and goals. Information concerning leave policies, health benefits, and grievance procedures are usually included. The examples and explanations found in a policy and procedures/desk manual will make your job much easier.

If you are not presented with a policy and procedures manual, immediately begin to compile your own.

Items that should be included in the policy and procedures/desk manual

1. Procedures for operating the company telephone system
2. Organization chart
3. Letter and memorandum styles
4. Samples of form letters
5. Location of company facilities
6. Daily routines
7. Due dates of routine matters
8. Payroll procedures
9. Additional information for running the office efficiently

▼ ORGANIZATION AND TIME MANAGEMENT ▼

Peak Time

Do you have a particular time of day when you are more alert and are able to solve difficult problems? Some people have more energy and do their best work early in the morning, whereas other people are most productive in the afternoon. Your peak time is when you are most productive; therefore, use your peak time to your best advantage. Whenever possible, plan your work so that you do the difficult jobs which require problem-solving skills during your peak time, and the routine jobs such as filing during your low times.

Time Management

In an office there is never an end to the work. Most office jobs have a continuous flow of work—there will always be another project once the current activity is complete. For that reason it is important to manage your time carefully so that you can work with maximum efficiency and productivity. Learn to juggle your regular job responsibilities while completing major projects. Set realistic time lines and build contingency plans, because not all plans will be successful.

To manage your time:

1. The first thing to do is to plan. Organize what needs to be done and estimate the time it will take to do those tasks. You should do your planning at least once or twice each day. Although last-minute changes may alter your plans, you should prepare daily and weekly work schedules. You should also prepare a master one-month schedule even if you do not always know in advance what all the jobs will be.
2. Organize your desk. Place the most frequently used items in an easily accessible location.

3. Do not allow others to control your time with interruptions or unnecessary talk.
4. Establish priorities for completing the most important work first. If you do not set priorities, you will have difficulty completing assignments and may disappoint your supervisor because primary tasks are not completed on time.

Do not think that your life in the office is going to be calm—everything will happen at once.

Wasting Valuable Office Time

It is very easy to waste time in an office. Your time is valuable to you and the company, so you must not allow others to waste your time. Ten minutes wasted three times a day becomes a half an hour of misused time each day. By the end of a week, you have wasted 2 1/2 hours. Think of what you could have accomplished in those 2 1/2 hours.

To avoid wasting time in the office:

- Organize your desk and supplies.
- Delegate work to others.
- Keep telephone conversations to a minimum. Do not let yourself get stuck on a long nonproductive telephone call.
- Process the daily mail efficiently and rapidly.
- Have the back of your chair face the door. This will discourage people from stopping by to chat.
- Have only one or two chairs in your office. This will discourage people from sitting and wasting your time.
- Stand when people are in your office. (Hopefully, that will discourage them from staying too long!)
- Be concise and to the point when answering questions.
- Make appointments for people to meet with you and stick to your time schedule.
- Be friendly with co-workers but socialize with them in places other than at your desk. You then have the option of walking away when you want to get back to work.
- If you must attend meetings, diplomatically encourage leaders to adhere to the agenda.
- Use E-mail, which is discussed in Chapter 3, to avoid playing telephone tag.
- Use E-mail to avoid lengthy telephone calls.

Organize Your Desk

Design your desk so that you have an in-basket, an out-basket, a pending file, bring-up file, and a signature file. An *in-basket* is for incoming materials. Your manager and other employees can leave work for you in the in-basket. The *out-basket* is for documents that you have completed. A *pending file* is for items that you are processing and for which you need additional information. Depending on the workload, it may be helpful to have several pending files in a horizontal file holder on your desk. The *bring-up file* is used for items that you need to discuss with your manager. A *signature file* is used to hold documents until the supervisor has time to sign them. The use of a signature file eliminates interrupting the supervisor to sign a document.

At the end of the day, clear your desk. Place all working papers in a locked drawer designated for that purpose.

Reminders

A *desk calendar* is an important item for everyone in an office to use to remember meetings and appointments. Traditional desk calendars are the size of a book and are usually kept open on the top of a desk for quick access. There are numerous styles of desk calendar, many of which are designed to aid in organizing work. Today, many people use computer calendars which can be revised easily and printed. Also, computer calendars can be set to give an audio reminder of an appointment. Use your calendar, whether kept in a book or on the computer, as a planning device to organize your day. Include on the calendar vacations for yourself and other employees, deadlines for projects, and where a traveling employee is going to be on a specific date. In some offices, computer calendars have almost replaced desk calendars. If an office assistant has access to everyone's computer calendar, the availability of a meeting time can be found without ever talking to anyone. Further information on computer calendars is given in Chapter 5.

A *tickler system* is a reminder system for due dates. A tickler system can be set up on a daily desk calendar, computer calendar, large wall-planning calendar, or on 3 x 5 in. cards indicating due dates of items. The card box would contain a separate *guide* for each day of the month. A 3 x 5 in. card with a description of the project and the due date is placed behind the appropriate guide. For example, the payroll reminder card is placed each month behind the date the payroll is *prepared*. A card may be used once or many times. Tickler systems are also available on desktop computer programs that bring up reminders automatically at the beginning of each day.

Organization Chart

An organization chart is a chart that shows the relationship between employees in an office. It is the structure of the business, and it identifies who reports to whom. The relationship between departments is also well illustrated by an organization chart. The first day on a new job, request a copy of the organization chart and study it carefully. It is important for you to be aware of the structure of the company so that you can follow the chain of command and the relationship among departments.

In the organization chart shown in Figure 1-5, the business manager, production manager, and sales manager report to Roberta Wilkins, president. Clifton Daniels reports to the business manager and Patrick Anthony reports to the sales manager.

▼ GROUP DYNAMICS ▼

Team Players

Teams are the rage in business today. Your career and job opportunities may depend on your ability to work as a member of a team. Team members may come from a variety of departments with members at many job levels. Teams are formed to complete projects, create new ideas, reengineer company policies, and perform many other functions.

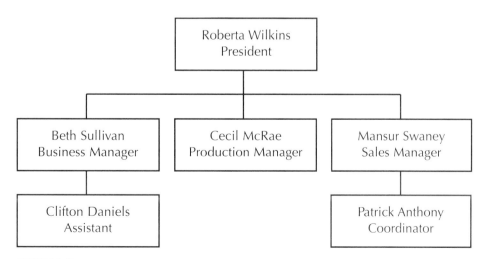

FIGURE 1-5 An Organization Chart.

Suggestions for team members

- Keep project team members focused.
- If possible, select your own team members. Select persons whose ideas are compatible with yours and who will work well with you.
- The team should secure top management's agreement before beginning a project.
- One advantage of working in a team is to showcase your talents to upper management and members of other departments.
- By contributing your ideas at team meetings, you increase your visibility. Of course, you could risk alienating a high-level executive who does not agree with you.
- Before you join a team, research the project and the team's members. Is one member the dominant member of the team? Become an expert on the project's background before the first meeting.
- Be diplomatic when you express your opinions.
- When representing your team to other employees, always use the term we, not I.

Leadership Skills

Employees at all levels need leadership skills. Depending on the circumstances, an employee may function as a leader or as a team member. The leader is the person who guides organizations or projects through new and innovative enterprises. Also, the leader must motivate the other team members. An effective leader looks to the future and analyzes the current and long-term aspects of the project. In addition, effective communications is essential to a leader because poor communications can doom any project. Since the leader cannot and should not complete the project alone, the leader must be able to delegate responsibilities to others. A leader must have organization skills because time is a precious quantity. The leader must also accept the responsibility for the project while meeting the goals of the project.

Brainstorming

Brainstorming is a technique used to develop ideas on solving a problem. Since one person's idea will stimulate ideas in others, brainstorming is frequently used by a group of people. It can be used by a single person as well. In brainstorming, people try to think of any possible solution to a specific problem. All ideas are written down. No idea is dismissed or belittled, no matter how silly or outlandish it seems. As one idea builds on another idea, several possible solutions usually develop. Those ideas are then explored, and additional information may be gathered before a solution is reached.

▼ WORK SCHEDULES AND LOCATIONS▼

Today's office employee is no longer restricted to a work schedule with a fixed number of hours, five days a week. Work schedules and places of employment have become flexible in response to the demands of modern businesses, employees, and society at large. Many employees have the opportunity to schedule their hours according to *alternative work schedules, flextime,* or *job sharing.* Some workers have the opportunity to change their workplace and work from home or alternative work sites via *telecommuting.*

Alternative work schedules permit the employee to work other than the traditional five days a week. With an alternative work schedule, an employee may work four 10-hour days a week to satisfy a job requirement. Another way for implementing alternative work schedules is to operate on a two-week schedule of longer days with alternate Fridays or Mondays off. In some businesses, all the employees work the same alternative work schedule; in others, the schedules are staggered, for example, so that only half the employees are off on any Friday. Alternative work schedules allow flexibility for the employee, save commuting

FIGURE 1-6 A Home Office. (Courtesy of International Business Machines Corporation. Unauthorized use not permitted.)

costs, and reduce traffic and air pollution; but they may cause scheduling problems for the employer.

Flextime allows employees to decide on their own starting and ending times. Usually, the company establishes a two- or three-hour time frame from which the employee may select the start or end of their workday. There are usually *core hours* when all employees must be present in the office. Employees must work every day during the normal workweek. When flextime is an option, absenteeism and tardiness are usually reduced, production is increased, employee satisfaction is higher, and employee moral is improved. Flextime allows an employee greater flexibility in scheduling personal appointments and meeting personal needs such as child care and elder care.

As business has become more amiable to the needs of the employee, job sharing has become popular. *Job sharing* is one job shared by two persons. Both workers may receive full or partial benefits. The major advantage for the workers is a part-time job that allows the employee to have time to pursue personal interests. A major disadvantage for the employer is increased record keeping and costs. A shared job often has one employee working in the morning and another in the afternoon. Some companies require that there is some overlap time where both employees are at work at the same time to discuss shared projects.

Telecommuting or *teleworking* allows the employee to work from outside the office with the assistance of communications equipment. There is a definite increase in the number of persons working at home. Some employees can work from home a few days a week, a few days a month, or when working on a special project. Some employers are establishing *satellite offices* where employees can work several days a week in their own region rather than commuting across large metropolitan areas.

Working from a home or satellite office has become easier with the widespread availability of the fax machine, computer, and access to the Internet. Telephone services using paging, voice mail, and conference calling allow more people to work from home. Computer groupware software allows employees at home to share E-mail, calendars, and assignments. Also, companies now have internal computer sites that allow home workers to access company files in the same way that they access information from the Internet. Voice communication is managed over the telephone, with the home office an extension of the office telephone system. While decreasing the number of people commuting to work improves air quality and reduces traffic congestion, all workers are not productive while working from home. There may be too many distractions for some employees, whereas others are unhappy without the social contact an office environment brings to the workday. To maintain continuity on projects, employees occasionally commute to the office for meetings.

The benefits of telecommuting for the employee include less commuting time and lower commuting costs, more flexible job hours, lower expenses for an office wardrobe, and being at home with young children or elderly parents. Companies believe that they benefit from telecommuting by being able to hire employees who may not be able to work in a traditional office setting, and the employer can also save the cost of office space for those employees who work out of their homes.

It is very easy to waste home business time by allowing your personal life to interfere with your business life. If you work out of your home, establish regular office hours and adhere to them. Inform business associates and friends of your work hours. A home office may interfere with your family life or be limited by the availability of space. You should designate a specific area of your home as your office. Keep this area professional in appearance. If you are visited by business associates, dress in a professional manner. If you have your own business or use the telephone frequently, you should have a separate telephone line for business.

CONCLUSION

An office employee is a well-rounded person who possesses the skills and personal traits to succeed in an office environment. As you progress through this book, you will develop and expand the skills and traits required for you to reach your goal of being the best office employee you can possibly be.

CHAPTER REVIEW

1. List 10 characteristics of a good office employee.
2. List five negative personal traits.
3. Why is listening important?
4. List four suggestions to improve your listening skills.
5. What is a job description?
6. What is a policy and procedures/desk manual, and what should be included in it?
7. What is the purpose of an organization chart?
8. List three suggestions for team members as discussed in this chapter.
9. Describe brainstorming.
10. What are the employee advantages of telecommuting?

ACTIVITIES

1. Contact five businesses and find out what job titles are used for support staff in their company.
2. Ask three employees:
   a. To name the three most important things they have learned since they have been employed.
   b. To describe three positive aspects and three negative aspects of their particular job.
   c. How often they have changed jobs.

d. How they handle difficult situations on the job.
   (Ask any additional questions that you feel important.)

3. Write a one-page paper explaining why you want to become an office employee.

4. Write a one-page paper explaining the duties of the job you expect to hold five years from now.

5. Introduce yourself to two new people this week, and think of a way to remember their names and how to recognize them.

6. Keep detailed records for one week, showing how you spend your college-related time. Indicate assignments and deadlines for college projects. Did you meet the deadlines? How much time was spent on each? Do you feel you used your time efficiently? Did someone else interfere with your ability to use your time efficiently? How should you have handled that situation? What changes would you make in your time management techniques?

7. For three days keep a list of the times when you are full of energy and the times when you are tired. Discover your peak time and learn how to plan important activities around that time.

8. Invite an office employee who you know to speak with your class.

9. Write a two-paragraph report with many important facts. Read the report to the class, and ask questions about the report to determine the level of listening skills of the class.

10. Read a detailed article to a partner. The listening partner should write a summary of the article. Compare the details in the article with those in the summary. (For additional listening practice, the partners can swap roles.)

11. Request policy and procedures/desk manuals from three companies and review them. Make lists of the contents of each manual and compare them.

12. Ask three companies for a job description for an entry-level support staff job. Review the job descriptions and determine your qualifications.

13. Write a job description for the position you hope to obtain when you leave school.

PROJECTS

Project 1

Key in the following document.

POLICY AND PROCEDURES MANUAL

L. Levy and Company

Revised June 1, XXXX
By Zev F. Carlton

Topics
- Telephone System
- Company Locations
- Organization Chart
- Letter Styles
- Memorandum Styles
- Payroll Procedures
- Project Due Dates
- Employment Procedures
- Grievance Procedures

Project 2

Create the following notice. If possible, include a graphic similar to the one shown.

Time Management Seminar

Monday

December 9

Administration Center, Room 247

9 – 4

Learn Time Management Techniques

Prepare for a New Job

To register, call Katie at 2477

HUMAN RELATIONS SKILL DEVELOPMENT

Functioning as a Member of a Team

Working as a member of a team requires that all members be able to work together even though they have different viewpoints. Learning to respect the thoughts of others and to listen to the views of others encourages a good working relationship. Completing your part of a project by the due date is a team *requirement*. One member of the team who does not complete an assignment on time may hamper the progress of other members of the team.

- What would you do if a member of your team did not complete an assigned project on time?
- What would you do if a member of your team took credit for an idea that you developed?
- What would you do if two members of your team had an argument and refused to work on a project?
- What would you do if a member of your team always needed extra help to complete projects?

Complaints

When employees gather at lunch, during breaks, or at staff meetings, the conversation can quickly turn into a complaint session about the job. While complaint sessions may allow the airing of personal feelings, they are rarely productive in solving job-related problems. Sometimes people try to outdo each other with complaints, which results in increasing employee aggravation and lowering morale. If lunch or office breaks have routinely become gripe sessions, find another way to spend your time. If staff meetings frequently become gripe sessions, try to focus the group on the objective of the meeting.

- What would you do as a member of the support staff if a question-and-answer session at the end of a staff meeting turns into a gripe session?

- What would you do in your role as a *supervisor* if the question-and-answer session at the end of a staff meeting turns into a gripe session?
- What would you do if your supervisor hears you make negative comments about the supervisor?
- What would you do if you are the supervisor and you hear negative comments about yourself?

SITUATIONS

How would you handle each of the following situations?

- You have a confirmed reservation at a hotel hosting a convention. When you arrive at the hotel, you are told that they do not have your reservation and that the hotel is completely filled.
- Your flight from Boston to Miami was delayed. When you arrived at the Miami airport, you discovered that your car rental agency was closed, although you were informed that the agency is supposed to be open 24 hours a day.
- You are a receptionist in an office where Phil and Bill both work. When you transfer a telephone call to either one of them, you always seem to transfer the call to the wrong person.

ROLE PLAYING

Act out the following situations to demonstrate how you would handle each problem.

1. Assume the role of a receptionist. Greet the person sitting next to you and ask if the person has an appointment.
2. Give a firm businesslike handshake to the person sitting across from you.
3. Ms. Yee has just arrived for her 10:30 appointment. Your supervisor has been called out of the office on a personal emergency. You do not know when the supervisor will be back. Explain the situation to Ms. Yee.
4. Your supervisor told you that she does not want to talk to Mr. Bern, an important client. Mr. Bern called to talk to your supervisor at 10:30. At 1:00 he called again, and at 3:00 he called back a third time. What would you tell Mr. Bern each time?
5. Your manager had intended to return a telephone call from Mr. Morales, an important client, but neglected to do so and has left for a business trip. What do you say to Mr. Morales when he calls? Mr. Morales says that it is urgent.
6. An irate person arrives at your office and insists upon seeing your employer, who is in a conference with an important client. What would you do?
7. You neglected to tell your supervisor that Mr. Colony called, and now he has called again and is upset.
8. Your supervisor has forgotten his lunch meeting with Ms. Stevens. Ms. Stevens has been waiting at the restaurant for an hour and now she is on the phone. Your supervisor went to lunch with someone else. What would you tell Ms. Stevens?

PUNCTUATION REVIEW

Punctuate each of the following sentences.

1. Jerry who was hired last year has received a promotion
2. Because the machine was broken the report was late

3. Our stockholders have earned large dividends and our brokers have been helpful

4. Therefore a conscious decision was made to build up the reserves in the bond fund mutual fund and trust fund so that future generations of the family would be financially secure

5. I cannot work late tonight however I can work late tomorrow

6. Zero-coupon bonds pay interest upon maturity but stocks pay dividends quarterly

7. On Friday July 12 the commission intended to vote on the budget for the year but the attorney received a telephone call that called a halt to the vote

8. George Williams Jr an accountant teaches part time at the college

9. Industrial companies on the other hand benefit in the longer term from a dollar that has been stabilized

10. The mortgage rate has risen 1 percent a year but the selling price of most homes has risen 10 percent a year

11. The Dow Jones Industrial Average lost 25 points on Friday but gained 35 points today

12. Du Pont General Motors and IBM are blue chip stocks but Florida Power and Lights price earning ratio was better

13. Paul said Bertha wrote the last report

14. Anna said the process of changing the passwords is very complicated

15. Employees from the center met August 23 September 28 and October 15

▼2▼

Document Preparation

OBJECTIVES

After studying this chapter, you should be able to:

1. Write business letters and memorandums.
2. Write a news release.
3. Write the minutes of a meeting.
4. Research and write a report.

▼ BASICS ▼

Written communication is vital to all businesses, nonprofit organizations, and government agencies. A written communication may be the only contact that an individual or company has with your office. The communication will shape the reader's opinion of the company and of the writer in a positive or negative way.

Depending on the situation, an office employee may be asked to keyboard, rewrite, or compose a letter, memorandum, or report. The assistant may write or design the company newsletter, which is a weekly, monthly, or quarterly document describing the events, news, or announcements of the company.

Although computer sent electronic mail, *E-mail*, which is discussed in Chapter 3, has changed written communications in the office, preparation of memos sent by E-mail requires the same writing techniques as those used in the preparation of printed memos.

The success of your writing will depend on your ability to make the reader understand your message. Face-to-face conversation allows you to use hand and facial gestures to help convey your thoughts. Your vocal inflections and tone of voice can change the meaning of a sentence. Written communication, however, does not have the benefits of these techniques to convey your message.

Your documents should be:

- Clear
- Concise
- Correct
- Complete
- Courteous
- Concrete
- Conversational

A good writer will express thoughts *clearly* and *concisely* so that they will not be misinterpreted. When creating documents, come to the point quickly. Also, use direct, simple language and sentence structure to express your thoughts.

Verify that the facts in your letter or report are *correct*. The surest way to lose credibility is to include inaccurate information in your document.

A *complete* document will contain all the facts necessary for the reader to respond to it. However, the document should not contain unnecessary information that would overwhelm, confuse, or mislead the reader.

Always be *courteous*, even if you disagree with the person who will receive the document. Personalize letters by using the reader's name in a sentence. Be careful, however, not to overuse this technique. If you are angry, do not allow your anger to influence your writing. Angry people often write in a sarcastic manner. Avoid writing when you are upset. If you must write when angry, do not mail the document immediately. Set your document aside for evaluation when you are calm.

Write in a friendly, *conversational* tone, as though you were talking to the reader.

If you are asking the reader to take some explicit, *concrete* action, clearly state the action that you are requesting.

Answer letters and memos within two days. Important business transactions are at stake.

Some business executives feel it is bad taste to end a letter or memo with a thank you for a future action. Their rationale is that a writer does not know if the reader is going to perform the requested action. People who end a document with a thank you believe that it is positive reinforcement that encourages the requested action. Company policy and your personal opinion will help you decide if a thank you should be included in your communication.

▼ CORRECTING COMMON WRITING PROBLEMS ▼

Clarity

The primary goal of all writing is to convey a message clearly to the reader. Incorrectly placed words or phrases are a common cause of misunderstandings. How would you rewrite these sentences to make them clear?

> Driving a car, the office only was five minutes from the house.
> Office desks are on sale in every store with printer stands.
> Barry ate an ice cream cone walking down the street.

Misused pronouns are another source of misunderstandings. When using pronouns, make sure that the pronoun refers to the noun it is replacing—not another noun in the letter. The reference may be obvious to the writer but confusing to the reader. The following are examples of confusing sentences:

> June told Kathy that she was late. (Who was late?)
> Linda and Peggy went shopping. She bought a computer. (Who bought the computer?)

Friendliness

In oral communication the voice indicates the tone of the sentence. In written communication, the words alone must convey a friendly and helpful tone. Here are some examples of a friendly tone:

> We are very happy to be of service to you.
> We greatly appreciate the time you have devoted to our civic project.
> We are truly sorry that we will not be able to be with you to share your joy on the occasion of your daughter's wedding.

Interesting Language

Outdated Words or Phrases with Their Current Equivalents

The English language has changed over the years and expressions that were correct many years ago are now considered stiff and formal. Listed below are outdated words or phrases with their current equivalents.

Words to avoid	Words to use
forward	mail
peruse	review
enclosed herewith	enclosed is
enclosed please find	enclosed is
attached please find	enclosed is
beg to advise	[omit this phrase]
investigate	check
endeavor	try
acknowledge receipt of	received
terminate	end
permit	let
obligation	responsibility
ascertain	find out

Inappropriate or Redundant Words

Many phrases that are commonly used in oral communications are inappropriate in letters. The following is a list of phrases that are inappropriate or redundant and should be avoided in written business communications.

good as gold	very complete
upon receipt of	seldom ever
each and every	close up
awfully good	terribly good

Transitional Words

Transitional words carry the reader from one thought to the next. If transitional words are not used, the sentences do not flow and the letter sounds choppy. Varying the length of the sentences helps in writing a letter that reads smoothly. The following is a list of transitional words that should be used in business communications.

accordingly	also
and	as
because	consequently
for example	furthermore
however	if
in addition	since
so	therefore
thus	yet

Rewrite and improve the following paragraph by using transitional words:

We would like you to speak at the meeting. It will be January 17 at 8:00. The topic is "Foods in the Office." We hope you will come. Write me soon.

Vary Your Language

Repeating the same phrases or beginning every sentence with the same word is boring. People writing about themselves frequently begin sentences with the word *I*. Avoid the *I* syndrome.

Use a variety of descriptive words to add interest to a letter. Every sentence should not contain the same adjectives and adverbs. A thesaurus will help you to select *synonyms* (words similar in meaning to the words you normally use). A thesaurus, which is contained in most computer word processing packages, should be used when writing documents.

Gender Bias

Correspondence should be free of gender bias. If the gender of a person is not known, use nongender words. Instead of using "her" or "him" to express general concepts, use nongender nouns.

If the gender of a person is not known:

Do not say:	Send the material to him.
Say:	Send the material to the manager. (Manager does not imply a gender.)
Do not use the salutation:	Gentlemen
Use the salutation:	Ladies and Gentlemen or Dear Sir or Madam

Moving the Reader to Action

Moving the reader to action requires tact so that the reader is not alienated or offended. When people are told to do something, they often react in a negative way. Accordingly, people are more receptive to suggestions than to demands.

Dear Ms. Mendez:

We are very happy that you have enjoyed the service that we have provided you. As you know, our customers are very important to us.

We received your letter of June 12 and have considered your request carefully. Unfortunately, we cannot extend the payment time on your account. Our credit policy is that a minimum payment of only $10 must be made within 30 days of the statement closing date. The remaining balance may then be carried over until the next month. Once the outstanding balance is below your credit limit, you will be able to make additional charges.

We hope that you will resume your visits to our store so that we can continue to serve you as we have for the last 20 years.

Sincerely,

R. E. Pazirandeh

skc

FIGURE 2-1　A Letter with a Negative Response Placed between Two Positive Remarks.

Always write from the reader's point of view, which is the "you" point of view, and convey what the reader wants to hear. A letter should be *reader oriented*, emphasizing what is important to the reader.

If a negative message must be delivered, accent the positive aspects of the situation. If you must deny a request, place the denial after a positive comment. Always end a letter on a positive note.

Never write "you are wrong" or "you made a mistake." This may anger the reader. Instead, write "there is a problem" or "there is a mistake." If this approach is used, no one must accept the responsibility for the error. *Never imply that the reader is stupid.*

▼ LETTERS ▼

Before you start writing a letter, define the letter's objective and prepare an informal outline. This outline will help to organize your thoughts so that the letter meets your objectives. An outline of the letter should consist of the following three main sections.

1. Introduction   A short paragraph explaining the purpose of the letter.
2. Body   Includes all the details necessary for the reader to understand the situation.
3. Conclusion   The closing paragraph of the letter. It should summarize the entire letter and end the letter on a cordial note. Any action the reader must take should be included in this section.

A letter should:

- Be clear and easily understood
- Have an attractive visual appearance
- Contain no errors
- Be pleasant in tone
- Be truthful
- Be sincere
- Be concise but include sufficient information
- Contain no outdated or overused expressions
- Be well organized

Letterhead

Business letters are usually keyboarded on letterhead stationery, but a business letter may also be keyboarded on plain paper. Letterhead stationery contains the name, address, city, state, and ZIP code of the sender. Many companies also include a telephone number, a facsimile (fax) machine number, and an E-mail address on the letterhead. If plain paper is used, the return address must be keyboarded about 1.5 in. from the top of the letter.

Letter Margins

Standard paper is 8 1/2 in. wide by 11 in. long. Paper used for some legal documents is 8 1/2 in. wide by 14 in. long. Some firms have converted to paper sized in metric measurements, which is slightly smaller than the sizes mentioned.

A letter should have equal margins on each side of the text. The size of the margins will depend on the number of words in the letter. Word-processing software makes margin changes easy to do. Most packages have a *fit-to-page feature* which adjusts the text to the page, which is helpful if a document has only one line carried to another page. A letter with balanced margins makes an attractive presentation to a reader.

Number of words	Left and right margins should each be:
0–100	2 in.
101–200	1 1/2 in.
201–up	1 in.

Letter Styles

Word-processing packages have made document creation easier by the use of a *letter template* feature. The letter template feature leads the writer through the parts of the letter and automatically formats the letter to a specific style. Using a word-processing template, the user enters only the specifics of the letter. While some offices use the word-processing letter template feature, others use letter templates created specifically for their company.

If the writer does not use a computer template, a letter style must be selected. The letter style defines the placement of the parts of the letter on the page. There are several letter styles. In the *block*-style letter, all parts begin at the left margin. In the *modified-block*-style letter, the date and closing begin at the center of the paper, the remaining parts of the letter are placed at the left margin. Modified block letters can have block paragraphs, which begin at the left margin, or paragraphs indented to the first tab location. See Figures 2-2 and 2-3.

Letters may have open or mixed punctuation. *Open punctuation style* omits punctuation after the salutation or closing; the *mixed punctuation style* includes a colon after the salutation and a comma after the closing.

Parts of a Letter

Most of the work in writing a letter concentrates on the text of the introduction, body, and conclusion. The entire letter, however, actually includes several additional parts. Some of these parts are essential to all letters, while others are used only when there is a special need for them. An office employee must be familiar with the proper placement of each of these parts.

The essential parts of a letter are listed below in the order in which they appear. These are followed by a list of the optional parts of the letter. Information on each of these parts follows or is self-explanatory. Review the sample letter styles for placement of each part of a letter.

Essential parts of the letter

- Date
- Inside address
- Salutation
- Body of the letter (including introduction, body, and conclusion)
- Complimentary close
- Writer's name
- Initials

Optional parts of the letter

- Special notation
- Attention line
- Subject line
- Company name in closing lines
- Title of writer
- Initials of writer
- Copy notation

- Enclosure
- Postscript

Date

Depending on the length of the letter, the date may be 1/2 to 2 1/2 in. from the top margin; the shorter the letter, the lower the date is placed on the page. The date is keyboarded a couple of lines below the company letterhead.

Special Notations

Special notations indicating CERTIFIED MAIL, REGISTERED MAIL, or HOLD FOR ARRIVAL are placed a double space below the date, at the left margin, and in all capital letters.

Inside Address

The inside address includes the name and address of the person receiving the letter.

Attention Line

An attention line is used when a letter is addressed to a company but the writer would like the letter directed to a particular person. Keyboard the attention line as the second line of the inside address and keyboard the envelope in the same style. It is preferable to address the letter to a specific person.

Professional Computer Services
Attention Ms. Karen Thornton
7800 West Fall Lane
Rochester, NY 46219

Ladies and Gentlemen:

Subject Line

The subject line, which quickly explains the purpose of the letter, is keyboarded a double space below the salutation. In a block-style letter, it is keyboarded at the left margin. In a modified-block-style letter, the subject line may be indented or centered. The subject line has increased in importance because people are busy and glance at mail to determine its value to them.

Body

The body of the letter, including the introduction and conclusion, is single spaced with a double space between paragraphs.

Complimentary Close, Company Name, Writer's Name, and Title

The complimentary close includes a closing and the writer's name. It may also include the company name and writer's title. After keyboarding the complimentary close, depress the Enter key four times (three blank lines) before keyboarding the writer's name. If the company name is used in the complimentary closing, Enter twice after the closing (Very truly yours), key in the title, then Enter four times, and key in the writer's name. The company name is keyboarded in all capital letters.

Sincerely,

Charles F. Wood

or

Very truly yours,

JOHNSON & BROWN CORPORATION

Martha Wilson
Assistant Director

An office employee may have the authority to sign a letter in the supervisor's absence. The two most frequently used methods of signing the supervisor's name are as follows.

Very truly yours,

Victor M. Crawford/BL

Victor M. Crawford
Assistant Director

The office employee would sign the name Victor M. Crawford and then write the employee's initials.

or

Very truly yours,

Barbara M. Larkin

Barbara M. Larkin
Assistant to Victor M. Crawford

Writer's and Typist's Initials

The typist's initials are placed at the left margin a double space below the keyboarded writer's name or title. If the writer's initials are used, they are keyboarded in all capital letters before the typist's initials.

shc
LLR:shc   or   LLR/shc

Enclosure Notation

An enclosure notation is used if items are sent with a letter, and it is keyboarded at the left margin a double space below the initials. There are several styles that may be used.

Enclosure
Enclosures (3)
Enclosures
    Report
    Check #3456

Copy Notation

A copy notation is used when a copy of the letter is sent to another person, and the notation is keyboarded at the left margin a double space below the initials. If an enclosure is used, the copy notation is keyboarded a double space below the enclosure.

The following copy notations are used:

cc	Used for *carbon copy*. Carbon paper is no longer used, but cc is still used by some people.
pc	Used for *photocopy*.
c	Used for *copy*.
bcc or bpc	Used for a *blind carbon copy* or *blind photocopy*; this notation is used when a copy of a letter is sent to someone without the knowledge of the addressee. To create a blind copy, print a separate version of the letter for the person receiving the blind copy and keyboard bcc at the bottom of the letter.

Examples of copy notations

* Carbon copy sent to one person

    cc: Michael Walker

* Copy sent to one person

    c   Tillie K. McNeal

* Photocopy sent to several persons

    pc   Mary D. Johnson
    Rodney H. Gibson
    Rhonda L. Hunter

If there are several copies, a check mark may be placed beside the pc or cc listing to indicate to whom it is being sent.

    c   Kirk Kong
    c   Deanna D. Liggett
    c   Jill R. Wood ✔

Postscript

A postscript is used to emphasize an idea. It is the last item keyboarded on the letter and is a double space below the preceding section. The postscript may be keyboarded at the left margin or indented to align with the paragraphs. Postscripts are normally used only in sales letters.

Postscript We hope to see you soon.

or

P.S. We hope to see you soon.

Two-Page Letter

The first page of a business letter is usually printed on letterhead stationery. Subsequent pages are printed on plain paper and will use the same margins as were used on the first page. There are two styles that may be used for the heading, and they are created by using the header feature in a word-processing package. All pages of a letter except page one have 1 in. top margins.

THE MARKETPLACE INC.
467 Meritor Drive
Cleveland, OH 45678-0923

May 15, XXXX

CERTIFIED MAIL

Ms. Catherine Linder
Linder & Peterson Limited
8009 Jefferson Road
Suite 200
Joplin, MO 64801-1265

Dear Ms. Linder:

Our sales representative, Steven Goldstein, will be in Joplin in the middle of June to demonstrate to you our new computer software. As we discussed at the Computer Expo in Kansas City, we have several new software application packages that will simplify your office management problems. The packages range from $1,250 to $5,000 in price and will be available by the end of the summer. As part of each package, we provide two days of training for your employees.

Mr. Goldstein will call you next week and arrange a convenient time to meet with you.

I will be at the Computer Expo in Dallas in September and hope to see you there.

Very truly yours,

THE MARKETPLACE, INC.

Ted J. Nicholas
Marketing Manager

skr

FIGURE 2-2   A Block-Style Letter with Mixed Punctuation.

The following heading is keyboarded at the left margin.

Ms. Janie B. Elliott   (the person receiving the letter)
2   (page number)
September 1, XXXX   (date)

The second heading style begins at the left margin, the page number is centered, and the date is right justified.

Ms. Janie B. Elliott   2   September 1, XXXX

THE MARKETPLACE INC.
467 Meritor Drive
Cleveland, OH 45678-0923

May 15, XXXX

Linder & Peterson Limited
Attention: Ms. Catherine Linder
8009 Jefferson Road
Suite 200
Joplin, MO 64801-1265

Ladies and Gentlemen

Subject: Software Demonstration

Our sales representative, Steven Goldstein, will be in Joplin in the middle of June to demonstrate to you our new computer software. As we discussed at the Computer Expo in Kansas City, we have several new software application packages that will simplify your office management problems. The packages range from $1,250 to $5,000 in price and will be available by the end of the summer. As part of each package, we provide two days of training for your employees.

Mr. Goldstein will call you next week and arrange a convenient time to meet with you.

I will be at the Computer Expo in Dallas in September and hope to see you there.

Very truly yours

Ted J. Nicholas
Marketing Manager

skr
c Desi Perez

P.S. I know that our software package can solve your application problems.

FIGURE 2-3   A Modified-Block-Style Letter with Open Punctuation.

▼ INTEROFFICE MEMORANDUM ▼

An interoffice memorandum (memo) is correspondence to be delivered within the same company or organization, not mailed to a client or member of the public. An interoffice memorandum may be less formal than a letter; but the same writing rules of clarity, tone, and organization are applicable.

The tone of interoffice memos can vary from casual to very formal. Memos written to your co-workers can be written in an informal manner, whereas memos intended to be sent outside your immediate office or to company executives should use the same tone as a letter. If you know the reader well, write as though you are talking to that person. When writing the memo, consider the recipient's personality, interests, likes, dislikes, and needs.

If bad news must be given, deliver it in person rather than in a memo. Consider the implications of any memo that you write. A verbal comment may be forgotten, but the written word lasts forever.

Although the specific format for a memo varies from office to office, the headings of interoffice memos include four basic items:

To:
From:
Date:
Subject:

A memo is a quick and informal way of sending messages and information within an office. A memo can be attached to E-mail, which will be discussed in Chapter 3.

When writing a memorandum, do not repeat the subject line in the first line of the memo because this information is already in the document. Memos should be concise, so it is better to limit them to one page. After the body of the memo, the memo concludes with the same sections as letters regarding initials, enclosures, and copy notation. As an alterna-

---

TO: Sid Bartow

FROM: Joann Henderson
             Director of Employee Relations

DATE: September 30, XXXX

SUBJECT: Physical Fitness Center Opening

Mr. Napali will be out of town on October 15, and he has requested that we postpone the grand opening of our Employee Physical Fitness Center from October 15 to October 17. He also suggested that we include a demonstration of physical fitness techniques by the Senior Fitness Group, which meets at the Grace Community Center. Information about this group is enclosed.

I indicated to Mr. Napali that we would review the plans for the grand opening by the close of business tomorrow and get back to him with our recommendation.

Please prepare a status report on the plans for the grand opening. We will meet in the conference room tomorrow at 2 P.M. to review what adjustments must be made to reschedule the grand opening to October 17.

jpg

Enclosure

c Arnold Hardy
   Sally Moore

FIGURE 2-4　An Interoffice Memorandum.

tive to keying the memo format, a memorandum template may be used. A memorandum sent to several persons uses Distribution instead of the recipient's name. The recipients' names are listed at the bottom of the memorandum similar to a copy notation.

▼ MINUTES OF MEETINGS ▼

A written summary of a meeting is called the *minutes of the meeting*. The preparation of the minutes of a meeting requires the combination of highly developed listening skills, concentration, and note-taking ability. During the meeting, an assistant must be able to listen, take notes, and summarize the points being discussed while discussion continues.

Since the minutes must be accurate, the person taking the minutes must be alert and must concentrate on the subjects discussed. Also, familiarity with the participants is essential because the minutes of a meeting indicate the names of the people who attended the meeting, participated in the discussions, and made and seconded motions. When taking minutes, quickly record all important comments, discussions, motions, and resolutions. To eliminate uncertainty concerning what was said at a meeting, tape recorders are often used to record the entire meeting. When the minutes of the meeting are prepared later, information not essential to the minutes can be omitted.

Each organization uses its own preferred format for minutes of a meeting, so you should review past minutes to determine the standard format used by your organization. Usually, the minutes include the date, time, place of the meeting, names of those attending,

---

MINUTES OF THE ORLANDO BUSINESS ASSOCIATION

March 1, XXXX

The monthly Board of Directors meeting was held at Mike's Seafood House. The Board of Directors meeting was called to order at 7 P.M. by Vice-President Sue Phong.

Present: Stephanie Coffman, Eli Stone, Najar Pooser, Marcia Pearce, Sue Phong, and Earl Button

Absent: Stella Meyer, Anita Bradford, Mike Beller, and Libby Wayne

Minutes of the February meeting were read and approved.

Treasurer's report showed that $300 was raised by the calendar sale.

Eli Stone moved, seconded by Marcia Pearce, that an honorarium of $200 be approved for guest speakers. The motion passed unanimously.

Stephanie Coffman moved, seconded by Earl Button, that July 25 be selected as the date of the art auction. The motion passed unanimously.

Stephanie Coffman moved, seconded by Najar Pooser, that the president appoint a committee to plan the fall fund raiser. The motion passed 3 yes, 2 no.

Meeting was adjourned at 9 P.M.

FIGURE 2-5   The Minutes of a Meeting.

and names of absent members. The minutes are routinely written in the past tense, and they include a summary of the discussions and actions taken.

Minutes may be taken at informal staff meetings and business gatherings or at formal business meetings such as those held by a board of directors. Minutes are usually prepared immediately after a meeting. Prior to the next formal meeting each member of the organization should receive a review copy of the minutes of the previous meeting. At the next meeting, members vote either to approve the minutes as written or to make corrections. The approved version of the minutes are usually signed by the secretary of the board or the president of the organization.

▼ NEWS RELEASE ▼

A news release is publicity or news that is given to the news media. News releases are often used to announce the promotion of an employee, election of officers, introduction of a new product, or the hiring of a new employee.

Requirements of a news release

1. Double space
2. Two-inch side margins
3. Suggested headline
4. Date of the release
5. Notation at the top regarding whether the information is for *immediate release* or whether it must be held until a specific date and time for release

---

Serobus Incorporated
3500 Executive Drive
Kingsland, GA 31548
Telephone 912-670-8900
FAX 912-670-8901
E-Mail Sero.cgo.com

May 16, XXXX

Hold for Release: 10 A.M. May 21

Director of Marketing for Serobus Incorporated

Patricia Sanez has accepted the position of Director of Marketing for Serobus Incorporated. Her duties begin on June 1. Prior to her move, Ms. Sanez was Assistant Director of Marketing for Taylor Markets in Tacoma, Washington. Serobus Incorporated, which is located in suburban Mayfield, manufactures door locks and hardware. Serobus Incorporated projects sales of $10 million for next year.

#

For further information, contact: Greg H. Castleman
                                    Public Affairs Office
                                    (912) 555-6666

FIGURE 2-6   A News Release.

6. Person and telephone to contact for further information
7. "More" to indicate the news release is continued on another page
8. "#" to indicate the end of the news release

▼ REPORTS ▼

Writing a Report

Report writing is a common office activity. Reports may be directed to potential customers, stockholders, the general public, or senior management. Some reports are based on information internal to a business, such as describing a company project, presenting findings of a research study, or reviewing the progress the business has made in meeting targeted goals. Information for internal reports is usually available in the company's files. Other reports, such as background papers on an industry or information requested by a client, may be based on information from outside the company. The process of researching and writing reports may be long and complex, and an office employee may be involved in this process at several stages.

Whatever your duties in the preparation of reports, whether you are doing research or are keyboarding the report, you should be familiar with the process of writing a report. The process is the same whether the information is gathered from within the company or from outside sources.

The first step in writing any report, after the subject is chosen, is to prepare an informal outline that helps organize your thoughts by listing the points you want to discuss. In the beginning of the project, you may not know what you want to discuss because you are not familiar enough with the topic. The outline should help identify those areas where additional information is required. Also, try to identify sources of information for the report. List people in your office whom you would contact in the search for information. If the report relates to company business activities, your supervisor should be able to help you identify the best sources for the information required.

The source of information for internal reports may be other employees or departments directly involved in the specific projects covered by the report. The larger the organization, the more difficult it may be to gather the relevant information for a report. An office telephone book and organization chart are useful when trying to locate the people who have the information required for a report. A good assistant is persistent in following leads from one office to another until the proper person is located. Do not be surprised if people are not eager to provide the information you require. Gathering information for your report may be seen as an interruption to another person's busy schedule. A polite but persistent approach may be needed—stressing how important the information requested will be to the report and to the ongoing business of the company.

Gathering information for internal reports based on company files can be easy if the files are available and other staff members are helpful. Researching information for reports from outside your company's files, however, may be a major task. If you are unfamiliar with the subject, research the topic with the use of books, magazines, newspapers, periodicals, pamphlets, statistical reports, research dictionaries, and other research materials. Information for these reports may be available from references located in your company's research library or information may have to be sought from outside sources, including public libraries, the Internet, governmental agencies, or other businesses.

The Internet allows businesses to search for information without leaving the office. Since the Internet is updated frequently, it may be easier to obtain current information from the Internet than from printed sources. If you find a Web site that is helpful, mark it for future reference by using a *bookmark*, which is built into Internet software. The Internet and bookmarks are discussed in greater detail in Chapter 5.

Research Materials

The following are examples of research books and periodicals that are available in a library.

- *ABA Journal*
- Almanacs
- Atlases
- *Best's Insurance Reports*
- *Books in Print*
- *Business History Review*
- *Columbia Journal of World Business*
- Commerce Clearing House publications
- *Consumer Guide*
- Dow Jones News Retrieval Database
- *Electronic News*
- Encyclopedias
- *Facts on File Yearbook*
- *Guide to Venture Capital Sources*
- *Harvard Law Review*
- *Industrial and Labor Relations Review*
- *Journal of Research*
- *Journal of Advertising*
- *Justice Quarterly*
- *Moody's Public Utility News Report*
- *Moody's OTC Industrial Manual*
- *Moody's Transportation Report*
- *Moody's Bank and Financial Manual*
- *Nation's Business*
- *New York Times Index*
- *Organizations Master Index*
- *Polk's Work Bank Directory*
- *Reader's Guide to Periodical Literature*
- *Sales and Marketing Management*
- *Standard and Poor's Register of Corporations*
- *The International Who's Who*
- *The Monthly Catalog of U.S. Government Publications*
- *Toll Free Telephone Number Directory*
- *Who's Who in America*

After you have developed the outline, you are ready to begin the research. As you do the research, you should review your outline and revise it to reflect the new information you have found. You should develop your own method of organizing your research. Keep good records that include the name of the book or magazine, date of publication, author, publishing company, and pages used. (Some researchers like to use index cards with notes on one side of the card and reference information on the other.)

To save time, instead of handwriting research information while away from the office, a notebook computer can be used. Then the data can be transferred from the notebook to the office computer system.

Write the report from your notes using your outline as the guide. Where appropriate, use *footnotes* to cite sources of information or to give credit for quotations or ideas gathered from documents researched. Word-processing packages have removed the drudgery of keyboarding footnotes because most software packages automatically place the footnote at the correct location on the page. Another way to simplify the keyboarding of footnotes is to place the notes on a separate page at the end of the report and call them *endnotes*. The completed report may be edited and revised several times to refine the copy and delete errors before it is finalized. As a precaution, create several backup diskettes and keep them at alternate sites. When the report is completed, it should be printed and distributed.

Report Organization

The following format is often used in reports:

Summary	Includes the recommendations or conclusions of the report and is helpful to a busy person who does not have the time to read the entire report. Most reports begin with a summary.
Table of contents	Indicates where particular information is located in the report.
Introduction	Explains what the report is about.
Body	Develops the important topics in the report.
Conclusion	Reviews the important points and recommendations of the report.
Bibliography	Lists references used in preparing the report.
Endnotes	Lists sources of direct quotes or the ideas of others placed at the back of the report. If these are placed at the bottom of their page of citation, they are referred to as *footnotes*.

Keyboarding Reports

The style of the report will depend on whether the pages are to be *loose* (unbound), *left-bound* (as in a book), or *top-bound* with a single staple.

Guidelines for Keyboarding Reports

Margins

Unbound manuscript margins	
Top margin	
Page 1	2 in.
Subsequent pages	1 in.
Side margins	1 in.
Bottom margins	1 in.
Left-bound manuscript margins	
Top margin	
Page 1	2 in.
Subsequent pages	1 in.
Side margins	1 1/2 in. left and 1 in. right
Bottom margins	1 in.

If the pages are to be printed on both sides in a book, the side margins should alternate so that a 1 1/2-in. margin is on the left side for odd-numbered pages and on the right side for even-numbered pages.

Top-bound manuscript margins	
Top margin	
Page 1	2 1/2 in.
Subsequent pages	1 1/2 in.
Side margins	1 in.
Bottom margins	1 in.

Page Numbering.   Begin all page numbering on page 2.

Footnotes.   References for footnotes must be keyboarded on the same page as the quoted material. Endnotes are keyboarded at the end of the report. To create a footnote or endnote, use the feature in the word-processing package. This software automatically renumbers when notes are added or deleted.

CHAPTER REVIEW

1. What is a *conversational* tone?
2. List six transitional words.
3. Explain how gender bias is avoided in writing.
4. When is an office memorandum used?
5. What should be included in the minutes of a meeting?
6. What are the requirements of a news release?
7. List six examples of research books and periodicals.
8. Show one example of how an assistant would sign a letter for an executive.

ACTIVITIES

1. Save 20 business letters. Analyze each letter, and on a separate sheet of paper, indicate the good points and the bad points of each letter. Select the five worst letters and prepare a revision to correct or improve them.
2. Attend a meeting of a local organization (college, social, garden, political, etc.) and take minutes of the meeting. Prepare a copy of the minutes in the correct format.
3. Consult four of the reference books listed in the chapter. Write a paper describing the items found in each reference book. Indicate under what circumstances a researcher would use those reference books.
4. Visit a library and consult four reference books not listed in the chapter. Write a paper describing the items found in each reference book. Indicate under what circumstances a researcher would use those reference books.
5. Research two topics on the Internet. List the Web addresses used and write a summary of each topic.
6. Use a word-processing template to create a letter.
7. Use a word-processing template to create a memorandum.

WRITTEN ASSIGNMENTS

Supply any information needed to complete the letter assignments and write your response to each of the following situations.

1. Write a letter congratulating a colleague on receiving a promotion.
2. Write a letter explaining that there is an incorrect charge of $50 on your account.
3. Write a letter to a well-known member of your community inviting the person to speak at a luncheon. Include all necessary information about the event.
4. Assume that you are the invited speaker in assignment 3 and accept the invitation.
5. Assume that your are the invited speaker in assignment 3 and decline the invitation graciously.
6. You received a book order for *Working Keeps Me Happy*. The letter indicates that the check was enclosed, but it was not enclosed. Write a courteous letter stating that the company policy will not permit shipping a book without receiving payment in advance.

7. Write a letter to a computer store in your area and request that a sales representative visit your office to demonstrate a new line of computers.

8. Write to a local office supply store requesting a copy of their latest catalog.

9. Order a subscription to *Working in the Modern Office* for yourself and three of your friends. Enclose a check for each subscription. (Include each person's name and address in your letter.)

10. Your employer stayed at the Miami Hotel the nights of December 6, 7, and 8. While reviewing the travel records, you noticed the following: your employer checked out on December 9 at 9 A.M.; the bill showed a room charge for December 9. Write a letter requesting a credit to the American Express card for the room charge of December 9.

11. Write a letter purchasing a product by mail order from a newspaper or magazine advertisement. Charge the purchase to a major credit card.

12. Write a news release for your local newspaper announcing that you and two other students have won the local Business Association Scholarship. Include names, information about each person, and the criteria for winning the scholarship.

13. Write a memorandum inviting everyone in your office to the annual company picnic. Everyone should bring a covered dish. The company will provide sandwiches and drinks. Include all details.

14. Answer the following letters after reading the comments in the margins.

Dear Peter,

Our annual stockholders meeting is scheduled for January 15 at 9 A.M. in the Mirror Room of the Charleston Hotel. The hotel is located at 8900 Cosmo Drive, so take the Cosmo Drive exit from Interstate 170.

Write a letter indicating that I will attend

I will need a reservation for Jan. 14 & 15

After the meeting, the officers of the company will get together for lunch and a discussion of our next project.

We hope you can attend. Let me know what time you expect to arrive and if you plan to stay overnight. I will be glad to make a hotel reservation for you.

Dear Ms. Lighter:

I plan to be in Washington November 7, 8, 9, and 10 for the annual Broadcasters Convention. I will be staying a few additional days to meet with some colleagues. While I am in Washington, I would like to talk with you about the agenda for the next association meeting.

Write a letter.

OK, meet in my office.

Will you be available to meet with me on November 11 at 9 A.M.? We could meet either at your office or at the Association Building on 7th Street. Either location is fine with me.

Please let me know soon if this date and time are convenient for you.

PROJECTS

Project 3

Send this letter to Ms. Penny J. Bowman, 9907 Mead Drive, Roanoke, VA 22804. Use a block letter style. Make a file copy. Use an appropriate closing and sign the letter from yourself as Consumer Specialist.

Thank you for contacting our Consumer Services Department.

As I mentioned to you on the telephone, I contacted the manufacturer concerning the delay in your receiving the replacement parts. They informed me that their plant has been closed for the last two weeks so that their employees could enjoy a well-deserved vacation.

I apologize for the inconvenience that you experienced. Please accept the enclosed gift certificate as a token of our concern for you.

Thank you for bringing this matter to my attention.

Project 4

Send this memo to the staff and supply all necessary information. The memo is from Alice Garrison, Public Relations Director.

We need your help on a project to honor the 100th birthday of our company. Your help, creativity, and ideas are needed to make our birthday a wonderful celebration.

Put on your thinking caps and decide on a plan for our celebration. Send your suggestions to Walter Mason. Four checks of $25 each will be given to employees with the best suggestions.

The deadline for suggestions is February 14, so start thinking.

HUMAN RELATIONS SKILL DEVELOPMENT

Working with People of All Ages

Although you may be most comfortable working with people your own age, in the typical office your co-workers will probably range in age from those who have just graduated to those reaching retirement. Your supervisor may be older or younger than you. If the supervisor is older than you, you may be reminded of your parents; or if the supervisor is younger than you, you may be reminded of your children. Some people have difficulty following the directives of a younger person. When you are in the office, disregard the age factor and remind yourself that the company is paying for the supervisor's expertise in the field, not for the supervisor's age. Above all, you must remember that as an employee you must adhere to the guidelines established by your supervisor.

- How are you going to handle the situation if your supervisor reminds you of your father or mother and you do not get along with your parents?
- How are you going to create a good working relationship with a supervisor who is 15 years younger than you are?
- How would you develop a good working relationship if you and your supervisor are the same age?
- How would you develop a good working relationship if your supervisor reminds you of your younger sister and your sister is a brat?

Money in the Office

Plan your budget so that you always have money with you at the office. You may be asked to attend a last-minute luncheon with a client or another employee, or you may be asked to contribute to a collection for a condolence, going-away party, birthday, or wedding gift. The more employees in an office, the more frequently you may be asked to contribute to an office collection. You should control decisions about how you spend your money, but be aware that office collections are a common occurrence. It is not prudent to have a reputation as a person who never gives to anything, but you may have to learn the knack of saying no without offending others in your office.

- How are you going to handle the situation if you are approached to contribute to the going-away gift for a member of another department?
- How are you going to handle the situation if you are approached to contribute to the baby gift for your supervisor's daughter?
- How are you going to handle the situation if you are approached to attend the fifth luncheon in two weeks?

SITUATIONS

How would you handle each of the following situations?

- You sent an envelope to Mrs. Rose and just discovered that your assistant did not include the letter. What action would you take?
- A sales representative, who will be working with your office for a few weeks, annoys you by making snide remarks.
- Your supervisor has asked you to talk to Joyce about her clothing. The supervisor feels that Joyce's skirts are too short and tight for an office. Plan your conversation with Joyce. Also, indicate the tone you would use in the conversation.

PUNCTUATION REVIEW

Punctuate each of the following sentences.

1. Ellen was the elevator working when you arrived today
2. After a closed door meeting the company announced that Ms Sheldon the president resigned
3. The attorney entered a guilty plea and everyone went home to celebrate
4. The trade deficit fuel economy and bank failures were all discussed at the convention
5. The Dow Jones Average rose 5.8 percent therefore the stockholders were pleased
6. Sarah said that she is happy in her new job
7. Yes the report was hand delivered
8. The dues that all members pay allow us to fund our scholarship programs
9. As you mentioned the report was late
10. Our manager Mr Lander was sick yesterday
11. Is the photocopier broken again Ted asked
12. Julie said I always attend the department meetings
13. Under a Chapter 13 filing International Footwear will reorganize and reschedule debt payments to its creditors
14. The #5345 womens dress will be available in the following colors peach avocado mauve and lemon
15. Yes we use FedEx

▼**3**▼
Communications

OBJECTIVES

After studying this chapter, you should be able to:

1. Use voice mail.
2. Use E-mail.
3. Use a fax machine.
4. Speak on the telephone in a professional manner.
5. Make long-distance domestic and foreign telephone calls.
6. Understand the use of specialized telephone services.
7. Understand audio and video teleconferencing.

▼ COMMUNICATIONS ▼

Excellent oral communication skills are needed on a daily basis by each office employee. We speak daily with people whose knowledge of our company and projects vary greatly. It is a mistake to assume that each listener always understands everything that is being said. Oral communications demand exactness and clarity. If the spoken word is not understood, there is no written reference to consult. Expressing yourself so that others understand you may take practice. Before you speak, organize your thoughts so they flow in a logical sequence. When speaking, pronounce each word correctly, talk loudly enough to be heard, and pause to indicate oral punctuation. While speaking, you must look for feedback from the listener in the form of facial expressions and gestures. By observing the listener you will learn how well your message is being received, so you can then rephrase thoughts that were not clearly expressed or cite examples to clarify your ideas.

Semantics and perception are barriers to effective communications. Misunderstandings often occur because two people may hear the same words but interpret them differently. For example, a supervisor may ask you if you are going to return a telephone call soon. If you answer "yes," the supervisor my interpret your statement to mean that the phone call will be returned within a few minutes, whereas you may have meant the next day.

Another barrier to effective communications is the withholding of communications. One staff member may not tell other employees important information, thereby causing problems in the office. Information may not be communicated due to busy schedules, forgetfulness, or a desire to withhold information from others. Learn to recognize a breakdown in communications before it causes misunderstandings that will be difficult to resolve.

During the past decade, there have been major innovations in communications technology and the future will bring additional communication changes to the office. In this chapter we explain many communications technologies that affect the workplace.

▼ VOICE MAIL ▼

Voice mail, which is available in most offices, is a sophisticated telephone answering system that records a caller's voice for later playback. A central voice-mail answering system serves an entire office instead of having an answering machine for each telephone. A voice-mail system does not require the *caller* to use any special equipment since the caller is simply dialing a phone extension. If the person being called does not answer, the caller is asked to leave a message, which is recorded on the voice-mail system. The receiving party uses a regular touch-tone telephone to open a private *mailbox* assigned to that person. The mailbox is opened by using an individual access code to ensure privacy, and then the recorded message is played. Voice mail can be used from home as well as the office by entering the user's access code. Voice messages can be stored in an archive for later use. After listening to a voice-mail message, you can send a reply to the caller automatically if the caller is using an extension on the voice-mail system.

Suggestions for using voice mail

- Never chew food or gum when leaving a voice message.
- Speak slowly and distinctly.
- Leave your name and telephone number. Your voice may not be recognizable, and your call cannot be returned if your telephone number is unclear.
- Organize your thoughts before you leave the message.
- Leave a short concise message; do not ramble.
- Indicate why you are calling.
- Indicate when you will be in the office to receive the return telephone call.
- If you are leaving a long message, repeat your telephone number at the end of the message.
- When recording your voice-mail greeting, sound professional and enthusiastic. Do not make a cute or joking voice-mail greeting.

▼ E-MAIL ▼

Electronic mail, E-mail, is a system for sending written messages over phone lines directly from one computer to another. E-mail is the electronic version of having a short conversation in the hallway with someone. It also allows the sender to talk with someone who would normally not be approached. For example, it is easy to use E-mail to congratulate someone for receiving an award. Use E-mail to your advantage.

E-mail will work with a computer in the same office or with a computer across the world. With an electronic mail system, the receiving computer will receive and store a message automatically. Each employee has an assigned *mailbox*. The sender directs a message to the mailbox of the recipient, where the message is stored. When the recipient returns to the office, the system is checked for messages. The messages can be read on the computer screen, printed, or forwarded to another mailbox. A major advantage of electronic mail is that recipients can respond to a message quickly and return an answer to the sender's mailbox, which can speed up business decisions. The turnaround time for electronic mail messages can be a matter of minutes; the same message sent by traditional mail could take weeks.

Some companies have their own electronic mail system for internal mail and subscribe to commercial electronic mail services to exchange messages with other companies. E-mail can also be sent directly over the Internet to another computer. The capabilities of electronic mail systems vary greatly. Many computers can dial the telephone automatically to access the electronic mail system, and most systems provide directions on the screen to assist the user. As in voice mail, to ensure that the message remains confidential, each user can be assigned an individual access code.

Unfortunately, there are few directories of E-mail addresses. If employees want to use E-mail, they usually have to give their E-mail address to people with whom they are doing business. E-mail addresses can be included on letterheads, placed on business cards, or included in the body of a letter. You should also create your own directory of E-mail addresses of people with whom you are dealing.

There is software available to allow employees who are out of the office to obtain their E-mail. Travelers can check their E-mail using portable computers that connect with the office E-mail system or connect to a central E-mail server. Other software can actually translate E-mail into voice format so that users can dial into their office computers and listen to audio versions of their E-mail over the telephone.

E-mail details

- E-mail is sent by keyboarding the recipient's name, E-mail address, and message.
- Mail can be sent to one person or to a *distribution list*, which is sending the same E-mail message to several persons at one time.
- E-mail may take less time to create than a mailed letter because E-mail does not contain all of the parts that a letter contains.
- E-mail is less formal than mailed communications.
- E-mail allows the sender to attach a long document to the E-mail message. A letter, memo, or report can be attached to the E-mail.
- Instead of sending a printed memo to office employees, an E-mail message with a memo attachment has become common.
- E-mail can be sent at all hours. Therefore, sending communications to a person in a foreign country or other time zone is not restricted by the local time.
- E-mail programs show a list of incoming messages. To read a message, select it and give the read command. After reading the message, there are four options: *reply, save, print,* or *delete*. The recipient may select one or more of the options. E-mail programs have a *reply* command that automatically addresses the mail to the person who sent it. Replies can be sent to one person or to an entire distribution list.
- If the computer is on, most E-mail systems can be set to flash a message or beep so that the user will know that a message has been received. The user can be working with any software package, not only E-mail, when the flash or beep is received.
- Always include a subject line and keep the length of the message short. Some E-mail users decide which messages to read by reading the subject line.
- Always verify the E-mail address before you send a message. If the message is received by the wrong person, it could be very embarrassing.
- Do not use all capital letters when composing a message because the impact is shouting the message.

Situations that should be communicated by telephone, not E-mail

- When negotiating a contract, raise, or similar situation
- When security is an issue
- When several people have input into the conversation
- When personal feelings are involved
- When it would be better not to have a written copy of the communication
- When a problem needs to be resolved
- When the sender is angry
- When the topic should remain confidential

Since words cannot convey hand or facial gestures, E-mail users use symbols, which are called *smileys*, to convey emotions. Smileys are cute but should be used only sparingly in business communications.

Examples of smileys

:)	smile
;)	wink
:-o	surprise
:-(	frown
:-O	shock
<Grin>	grin

▼ FAX ▼

A *facsimile machine* (often called a *fax* machine), which is standard equipment in most offices, sends exact copies of reports, letters, graphics, and so on, over a telephone line. A photocell or laser scans a page and converts an image (print or graphic) into electronic signals. Information is not rekeyed, so time is saved and the accuracy of the transmission is assured. Graphic and hand-signed materials can be transmitted as easily as typed or printed material. A document, converted into electronic signals, is sent to a receiving facsimile machine. When the document is received, a copy is printed. Some machines send the signals to a computer instead of a fax machine, and the document is stored on a disk.

Most fax machines conform to international standards and can send a document to a foreign country at the cost of a telephone call. Fax machines that are connected to their own telephone line can answer the telephone automatically and receive the information transmitted. Using a fax machine can solve the problem of a time difference between countries. A fax can be sent by an employee during normal working hours in one country and received by a machine in another country where the time is the middle of the night.

The speed with which facsimile machines can transmit documents over long distances is a tremendous increase in office efficiency. The use of facsimile machines is very efficient when sending a short document to one location. A bad telephone connection can result in illegible copy at the receiving location. Unless the receiving machine has a computer attached, only the hard copy is available when received—nothing is saved on tape or disk.

When using a fax machine, remember that anyone at the receiving end can read the document. Obviously, confidential material should not be faxed. Some fax machines have mailboxes that store documents until a personal access code is entered. If the document you are faxing is urgent or contains sensitive information, it is wise to notify the receiver that a fax is coming.

Frequently, a cover sheet is used when a document is faxed. Review the sample fax cover sheet shown here.

FACSIMILE

To:	Clifton P. Woodrum
Of:	B & W Enterprises
Fax:	513-882-7740
Phone:	513-882-9924
Pages:	1, including this cover sheet.
Date:	September 1, XXXX

FIGURE 3-1   A Fax Cover Sheet.

You can fax a document directly from many word-processing programs, such as WordPerfect and Microsoft Word, without first having to print the document on paper. If your computer or network is connected to a fax modem and has the proper software, it is easy to fax a message to one person or to 100 people. You can set up a series of address lists and then fax a document to all people attending an upcoming meeting or to all sales persons in a particular region. This method of faxing is referred to as *broadcast fax* and is a timesaving way of sending faxes to many people. A broadcast fax is an efficient method of distribution when using a computer. When a broadcast fax is distributed by a regular fax machine, it can be scheduled to send the faxes overnight or during weekends when the fax machine is not otherwise in use.

To obtain a fax number, use a fax directory, which is similar to a telephone directory and lists the company name and fax number. Fax directories are also available as part of online Internet services.

Fax-back capability permits a phone caller to receive a fax automatically, without human intervention. A phone call is answered by a computer which responds with recorded messages. The caller may have a prepared list of publications available or the computer may recite a listing of information available through the service. Using the telephone keypad, the caller enters the number of the item requested as well as the phone number of the fax machine that will receive the document. The computer then automatically faxes the information to the caller's fax machine or computer. Fax-back capability is a service for the distribution of information on demand and is available any hour of the day without the need for live staffing.

▼ THE TELEPHONE ▼

Answering the Telephone

When you answer the telephone in your office, you are giving the caller an image of yourself and your company. If you speak with a pleasant voice, you create a courteous image for yourself and create goodwill for the company. However, if you are abrupt or rude, you make a poor impression for yourself and your company. We have all experienced rude people. Usually, rude people make us angry, and we are reluctant to patronize a company if the people we deal with are rude.

To portray the image of a helpful person

- Speak clearly.
- Vary the tone of your voice.
- Speak directly into the telephone.
- Use a friendly and helpful voice.
- Use professional words, not slang.
- Speak slowly.
- Project a pleasant manner.
- Be courteous.
- Use the caller's name.
- Be alert; give the caller your full attention.
- Talk naturally; use your own words.
- Speak in a pleasant voice.
- Project an enthusiastic personality.

When you talk on the telephone, speak loudly enough so that you can be heard, particularly if you normally speak softly. It is difficult to talk into the telephone mouthpiece and be heard if you have the telephone receiver wedged between your shoulder and your chin. People who frequently speak on the telephone use headsets, which free their hands

FIGURE 3-2   Answering the Telephone.

for other uses, such as keyboarding the information they are hearing. Never talk on the phone if you have food or gum in your mouth.

When answering the telephone, pronounce the name of the company and the person whose phone you are answering so that they can be understood—for example: "Epson and Epson, Ms. Wood's office." If the call was first answered by the switchboard, you may say "Ms. Wood's office" or "Alicia Wood's office." In some instances you may wish to include your name—for example: "Ms. Wood's office, Barbara Rosen speaking." Do not overwhelm the caller with a long speech, such as: "Good morning. This is the Epson and Epson Company, Ms. Alicia Wood's office. I am Barbara Rosen. May I help you?"

If you must ask the caller to wait, speak so that the caller hears you. Often people answer the phone, and slur "please wait." If additional information is necessary or another telephone rings, say, "May I place this call on hold for a moment?" or "Please hold." As soon as possible, return to the caller and say, "I am sorry to have kept you waiting." Then talk with the caller. Do not keep the caller on hold for a long time. If you cannot get back to a caller quickly, ask if you may return the call.

If you do not have voice mail and you must leave your desk (even for only a couple of minutes), ask someone to answer your telephone. An unanswered telephone does not promote goodwill for the company.

Frequently, you will screen telephone calls for your employer. The employer may be too busy to talk or may not wish to speak with someone. You must be very clever and skillful when screening calls. The caller knows that the call is being screened and some people are offended by that. Do not say, "Who is this?" Instead, say, "May I tell Ms. Wood who is calling?" or "May I ask who is calling?"

Taking Messages

Taking messages is a very important aspect of office work. If the person being called is not available, ask if the caller would like to leave a message. Unfortunately, many people do not know how to take messages. Always have a pencil and paper available when the telephone rings. Do not say, "Wait—I have to get pencil and paper." Begin writing notes as the caller speaks. It is easier to write information as it is given rather than to try to remember a comment a few minutes later.

Write the required information on a message pad immediately. Some companies use a message pad that prepares a copy of the message automatically. If it is difficult to read your

```
                        Messages

To      _____

Date    _____

Time    _____

Caller  _____

Company _____

Telephone No. _____

Return the Call _____

Will Call Again _____

Message Taken By  _____


Message
        _____

        _____

        _____

        _____
```

FIGURE 3-3   A Telephone Message Form.

scribbling, write your notes on scrap paper and immediately rewrite the message on the message pad. As soon as the call is completed, deliver the message or place the message where the recipient will pick it up.

Today, messages may be recorded and distributed via computer systems. Many office E-mail systems have templates designed to record telephone messages. These templates are electronic message forms and will help you record information regarding an incoming phone call. If you have primary responsibility for answering the phone and taking phone messages, you should have a phone message form open on your computer and enter the information directly in the computer. Distributing phone messages by E-mail is a quick and easy way and provides a computerized record of the call.

Telephone messages should include the following:

- Caller's name. (Verify the spelling of the caller's name.)
- Telephone number, including area code and extension if applicable.
- Reason for the call.
- Indicate if the person receiving the call should return the call.
- Message, if any.
- Date of the call.
- Time of the call. The exact date and time can be very important.
- Name or initials of the person who took the call. (This is needed if a question arises concerning the call.)

Before ending the conversation, verify the telephone number and caller's name. It is impossible to return a telephone call if the telephone number on the message form is incorrect. Not returning a telephone call creates a bad image of your office. For example, you might say "Thank you, Mr. Bouquet, for calling. I would like to verify that your telephone number is 202-555-5555. I will have Ms. Henson return your call as soon as possible."

Every person who answers the telephone should have a copy of the corporate directory with names and telephone numbers of employees. This eliminates the need to ask important officials of the company to spell their names and give you their telephone numbers.

Placing Telephone Calls

When you are placing a telephone call, first identify yourself by saying, "I am Ms. Scott from American Systems" or "I am Katie Scott from American Systems." Then state with whom you would like to speak.

Before making a telephone call:

- Verify the telephone number.
- Plan what you are going to say. Prepare a short outline of the points to cover.
- Have reports and letters available for quick reference.
- If the call is long distance, compute the time difference and decide if it is a reasonable time to place the call.
- Plan what action you would suggest if the caller is not available. Do you want to leave a message, have the call returned, or speak with someone else?

Personal Telephone Directory

It is important that you keep a personal directory of telephone numbers that you and your supervisor may call. Maintaining a personal telephone directory of frequently called telephone numbers increases your efficiency and reduces the number of searches for unknown telephone numbers. There are several ways that you can create a personal telephone directory. Record a new phone number you receive on a small card kept in a loose card file hold-

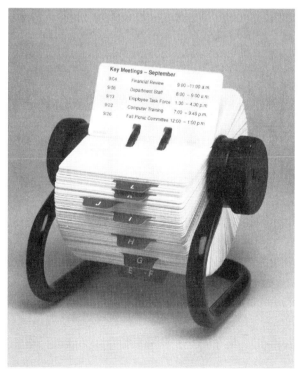

FIGURE 3-4 A Card File Holder. (Courtesy of Newell Office Products Company.)

er, often called a rotary card file holder. You can keep the business cards that you receive in a similar type of holder. In addition, there are computer software programs that create address books and even dial a telephone number automatically.

Long-Distance Services

Long-distance telephone charges can be a major expense for a business. Businesses in the United States can select from several alternate long-distance phone companies and calling plans to reduce their long-distance phone charges.

A business selects a long-distance provider and the local telephone company automatically sends the long-distance calls to the company selected. All the long-distance companies use the same phone numbers and area codes. The user simply dials "1," the area code, and the phone number without ever thinking of the particular long-distance company being used.

Most of the major long-distance companies provide the same basic services, including long-distance telephone calls to foreign nations. However, if you are to use another long-distance company, it is important to know the special prefix code to access the specific system.

A business should select the long-distance service *that meets its needs at the lowest cost.* Businesses that are heavy users of long-distance telephone services can seek specialized services tailored to their needs.

WATS (wide area telephone service) provides a business with dedicated lines for outgoing long-distance service at a flat hourly rate. Also, many businesses provide their customers with a toll-free telephone service using an "800" area code. As the 800 area code has filled with more users, the phone system has added 888 and 877 as other toll-free area codes. As the 888 and 877 area codes fill, the phone system will add additional area codes for toll-free calling.

Some businesses use nationwide phone numbers that start with the "900" area code. Businesses that use a 900 area code are selling information or providing a service, and phone calls to the 900 area code are not free. The caller usually must pay a charge that can range from a dollar to several dollars per minute. The per minute charge is supposed to be disclosed at the beginning of the phone call and typical charges for a call are sometimes disclosed in written material about the phone service. The 900 phone services should be used with care, since the per minute cost is charged even if the caller is on hold; therefore, the calls can quickly become expensive.

Often, a company needs quick communications between offices in distant cities. The company may use a dedicated *private-line* service that links the offices. The employee accesses the private line by dialing a simple code, perhaps the number "8," and then dials the office in another city. Large companies with many offices can install their own phone system and rent lines from a long-distance carrier. The federal government, for example, has its own phone system, FTS (Federal Telephone Service). Some companies have established their own private telephone systems by using satellite communications at different office sites. In these situations, the company can call offices in different cities without using the regular telephone system.

In Canada, a business would obtain its long-distance service through the local telephone company, which would provide long-distance service through the Stentor Alliance or other long-distance providers. The primary provider of international long-distance service in Canada is Teleglobe Canada, although other providers are also entering the international long-distance market to originate calls from Canada.

Calling Long Distance

Most long-distance calls are made by dialing the phone number directly. Dial "1," then the area code and the telephone number. This is a total of 10 digits (e.g., 1-605-555-1212) In the United States if you do not know the number, you can obtain phone numbers by dialing "1," the area code, and 555-1212. You will be asked for the city and name of the party you are calling. Most local telephone directories contain a list of selected cities and their area codes. Many telephone companies now charge a nominal fee (e.g., 50 cents) for locating a telephone number for you.

If you would like the party you are calling to pay for your long-distance call, you place a *collect* call or a *reverse the charges* call. This type of call can be made by dialing "0," the area code, and the telephone number. After dialing, an operator will ask for your name. Then the operator will ask the party called if they will accept the charges from the caller.

Another type of call made through the operator is a *person-to-person* call. This type of call will allow you to speak only with the specific person requested. If that person is not available, there will be no charge for the call. This type of call is very expensive, so many offices do not use it.

Changes in Area Codes

As more people and offices add phone lines for computers, fax machines, and cellular phones, area codes are running out of phone numbers. As a result, many new area codes are being added each year. Sometimes a city will get a new area code or be split between two area codes. Occasionally, an area will have two area codes, with all new phone numbers assigned to the new area code. This may mean that two people on the same street would have different area codes. You should always be aware that an organization can have a new area code even if it does not move. Sometimes the first notice of an area code change is when you try to complete a phone call and receive a message that the area code has changed or the phone is not in service. Call information at the old area code by dialing the old area code + 555-1212 and verifying the area code and phone number. If you find that an area code has changed, be sure to make the change in all phone lists as well as any programmed fax machines, computer dialers, or phone dialers.

Time Zones

Before making any long-distance calls, determine the time of the place you are calling. The mainland United States is divided into four time zones: Eastern, Central, Mountain, and Pacific. Alaska is 1 hour earlier than the Pacific time zone and Hawaii is 2 hours earlier than the Pacific time zone. Canada includes the same four time zones as the mainland United States, plus the Atlantic time zone for the Maritime provinces, which is an hour later than

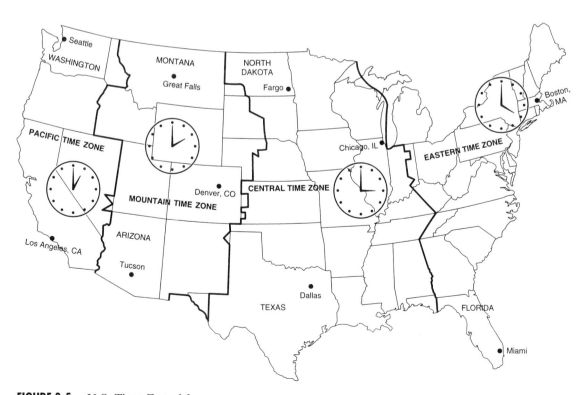

FIGURE 3-5 U.S. Time Zone Map.

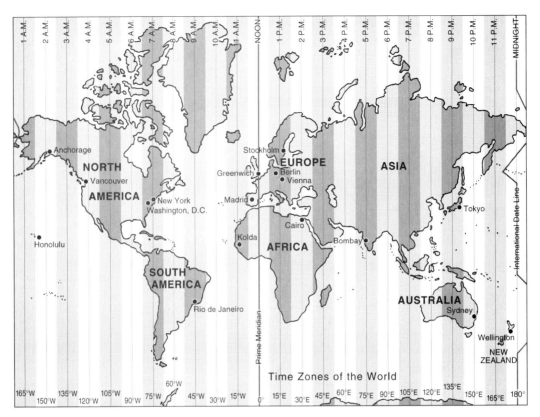

FIGURE 3-6   Worldwide Time Zone Map.

the Eastern time zone. The time of the island of Nova Scotia is 1/2 hour later than the Atlantic time zone. Most telephone books include a map of the time zones in the United States and Canada.

The section of your local telephone book dealing with foreign telephone calls often includes information about the time difference between a foreign country and *standard time.* Standard time is usually the time zone for the area represented by the telephone book. In a New York City telephone book, for example, France is indicated as "+6 hours" from Eastern Standard Time (9 A.M. in New York City is 3 P.M. in Paris). Japan is "+14 hours," so when it is 9 A.M. in New York City, it is 11 P.M. in Tokyo. Many countries move their clocks an hour forward in the summer for Daylight Saving Time. If a time difference of an hour or two is critical for reaching your party and you are unsure of the time in a foreign country, dial the telephone operator and ask for the time in the city you are calling.

Calling Foreign Long Distance

Making a call to some foreign countries can be as easy as making a domestic long-distance call. Long-distance calls among the United States (including Hawaii and Alaska), Canada, and many islands of the Caribbean are dialed the same as domestic long-distance calls, "1" + area code + phone number.

Many foreign countries can be dialed directly. Foreign long distance is usually accessed by first dialing "011" (instead of "1" for domestic long distance). Then a two- or three-digit International Access Code, called a *country code,* must be dialed. Some countries then use a *city code* (one, two, or three digits) before the local phone number. For example, calls to Mexico City must use a country code of "52" and a city code of "5" before the local telephone number is dialed. Local phone numbers will vary in different countries. In the United States and Canada all phone numbers are in the format 555-1212.

Lists of country and city codes of foreign nations that can be directly dialed are often included in the front sections of telephone books. Most frequently called foreign countries can be dialed directly. If an International Access Code for a country is not listed in the front

```
┌────────────────────────────────────────────────────────┐
│                                                        │
│   Date of Call _____ │
│                                                        │
│   Telephone Number Called _____ │
│                                                        │
│   Person Called _____ │
│                                                        │
│   Name of Company _____ │
│                                                        │
│   Reason for Call _____ │
│                                                        │
│   Name of Caller _____ │
│                                                        │
│   Telephone Number of Caller _____ │
│                                                        │
│                                                        │
└────────────────────────────────────────────────────────┘
```

FIGURE 3-7   A Long-Distance Record.

of your city's telephone directory, contact the operator and ask if the nation can be dialed directly. If the country cannot be dialed directly, the operator must place the call. A long-distance operated-assisted foreign call may involve your local operator contacting several international operators to establish a circuit to the country you are calling. Completing an operator-assisted foreign call to a country without direct dialing access can be time consuming, so you should plan extra time to complete a telephone call of this type.

Long-distance calls to each foreign country are a little different since the local phone systems are so different. It will be helpful for you to keep a file of foreign long-distance calls made, which includes the local telephone number, a complete set of the access codes required, the time difference from your city, and any special problems encountered in making the call. Because of the time zone differences or the amount of time required to make some international calls, fax and E-mail are often used to send international messages.

Some offices request that a record be made of all long-distance calls. This record is used to verify phone charges that appear on the company phone bill.

Credit Card and Phone Card Calls

Most long-distance services allow their subscribers to make long-distance telephone calls from locations other than the office, including pay telephones. By first calling the long-distance company, then entering a personalized code number, a person can make a long-distance call and the charge will be included on the regular monthly phone bill. Some long-distance companies provide plastic credit cards with magnetic strips that can be used in specialized telephones. The caller places the credit card in the telephone, then dials the long-distance call, and the credit card charges the phone call automatically. In addition, calls made from pay telephones may be charged to a MasterCard or Visa account. Prepaid *phone cards* contain a magnetic strip on which funds are "deposited." The user inserts the card into a telephone and makes a call and the charge for each call is deducted from the funds recorded on the phone card. To avoid problems, prepaid telephone cards should be purchased from reputable telephone companies.

Specialized Telephone Services

In addition to the standard telephone service, many specialized services have been developed to provide efficient voice communications for the office.

- *Automatic callback.* This feature can be used when a call is made to a phone that is in use. When the phone is free, the system redials the number automatically and notifies the caller.

- *Call block.* This feature sends incoming telephone calls to a recorded message indicating that the call will not be accepted.
- *Call forwarding.* This feature allows calls to be forwarded from one telephone to another. All calls from an unattended telephone can be forwarded to a telephone that is attended.
- *Call return.* The number of the last *incoming* call is dialed automatically.
- *Call waiting.* This feature allows a single-line telephone to handle two telephone calls when the phone is in use. A beep signals that an incoming call is waiting. This feature allows the first call to be interrupted while the second call is answered. It is then possible to return to the first caller.
- *Caller ID.* The caller's telephone number is displayed.
- *Different rings.* Internal calls (calls from within the same company) and external calls (calls from outside the company) can be distinguished by the type of ring heard.
- *Holding.* To place a call on hold, depress the hold button. Calls may be placed on hold while another call is being answered or while information is being found. Telephone receivers should not simply be left open and placed on the desk, because the caller can hear office background noises and conversations.
- *Multiline telephones.* One telephone can have more than one telephone line. If a line is being used, a constant light on the telephone line is lit. A flashing light indicates that a line is ringing.
- *Preferred call forwarding.* This feature permits calls from specific telephone numbers to be forwarded.
- *Repeat number.* Repeating the last number dialed can be done by depressing one key on the telephone.
- *Speed dialing.* Numbers that are frequently called can be coded so that they can be dialed quickly using one or two digits.
- *Transferring.* It is possible to transfer a call from one extension to another extension within the same company by dialing the last four digits of the number.

Most large offices have established internal telephone systems that provide direct telephone numbers for each extension and include many of the specialized services noted above. *PBX* systems are purchased from private vendors that place the switching equipment on the company premises. *Centrex* systems, on the other hand, place switching equipment in the telephone company's facility.

Specialized Telephone Equipment

Cellular Telephones

Cellular phones are small, wireless phones that permit a person to be called while they are out of the office. Cellular phones weigh less than a pound and can fit into a pocket or purse. Most metropolitan areas and many rural areas of North America are served by cellular services. Cellular service is also available in many areas of Europe, Asia, and South America. A cellular phone operates like a traditional telephone with its own telephone number and can be dialed like any other telephone. Cellular telephones come with many features, including the ability to connect to a fax machine or computer. Special services such as caller ID and voice mail can also be used with some cellular telephones.

Satellite Telephones

There are two principal limitations to traditional cellular telephones. Although they are very convenient, there are large areas of the country where cellular service is unavailable. Persons traveling to regions of any country outside major cities may find that they are outside the service area of their local cellular phone service. When they have the greatest need for telephone communications, such as in remote areas or for emergencies, cellular phone service may not be available. Persons traveling outside North America, or even within the United States and Canada, may also find that their cellular phone does not work with the local cellular service because of incompatible technology. There are literally dozens of different cellular telephone standards used around the world, and a cellular phone that works in Athens, Georgia, may not work in Athens, Greece, or in the country of Georgia in eastern Europe.

Satellite telephones have been developed to provide a single telephone service from anywhere in the world to anywhere else in the world. A satellite telephone is very similar to a cellular phone, except that it uses communication satellites overhead as part of the phone system. A satellite phone is portable and can be placed in a briefcase or carried in a pocket. Placing or receiving a call on a satellite phone is the same as using a cellular phone. Some satellite phones also work as cellular phones and will try to use the local cellular service before accessing the satellite service. Satellite phone service is more expensive than cellular service but is a way for a busy executive to stay in touch when regular phone or cellular service does not exist or is unreliable.

Paging Equipment

A *beeper*, a paging device, is a small receiver that can be carried and "beeps" to indicate that a message has been received. Beepers or pagers can also notify receipt of a message by lighting up or by vibrating. A telephone number or short message is displayed and then the person paged makes contact with the caller by using a regular telephone. Some paging equipment can record a voice message. Paging service costs much less than cellular services and are usually used where people have relatively easy access to a telephone to contact the person placing the page.

Airline Telephones

Airline telephone service is available while flying in commercial airplanes over the United States and Canada. Calls can be made from airplanes to anywhere in the continental United States, Canada, U.S. Virgin Islands, Alaska, Hawaii, and Puerto Rico. Many airlines offer this customer service on both transcontinental flights and on short shuttle service between major cities. In some airplanes the telephones are located at the individual seats; other airlines have several phones located in the passenger cabins. The service is operated by the use of a major credit card. To operate the phone, insert the credit card and remove the handset and place a call. When the handset is returned, the call is charged to the credit card and the credit card is then released. Use of airline telephones is expensive and should be used only when the cost is justified.

Satellite communications permit phone calls to be made from specially equipped airplanes flying over the oceans. Voice calls and faxes and even computer connections to the Internet can be made to anywhere around the world. Calling from midocean is very expensive and is not available on all airplanes that fly across the ocean.

Telephone Ethics

Personal telephone calls should not be made from an office telephone. However, it is difficult to avoid all personal telephone calls during office hours. Essential personal calls should be kept short and be limited to an absolute minimum. Some offices have stated policies regarding making and receiving personal telephone calls on business phones. Ask what the company policy is and adhere to it without exception.

Office telephones should not be used for personal long-distance calls. Occasionally, companies will make their long-distance service available to employees for personal use. Be sure of company policy before using the company's long-distance service. Do not simply assume that the company allows employees to use the long-distance service because co-workers make personal long-distance calls from the office.

Speakerphones

A *speakerphone* is a telephone with an audio speaker and microphone so that several people can participate in a conversation. Many desktop phones have speakerphones built in, and separate speakerphone attachments can be used so that the microphone can be placed in the middle of a table during a group meeting. For private conversations, the speakerphone can also be used as a regular telephone without the speakerphone feature activated. A call from a speakerphone is placed in the usual manner, then the speakerphone attachment is turned on. Using a speakerphone is a simple method of bringing two groups of people together for a meeting.

Speakerphones are also used by one person when holding a telephone handset may be inconvenient or tiring. Speakerphones are often used during audio conference calls, which may last an hour or more. Speakerphones are also useful if you need to get out of your chair or use both hands for other activities during the call. If you do not have a private office, your end of the conversation can be overheard by another person in the room; therefore, you should be considerate of other people in your office when using a speakerphone. You should not interfere with the privacy of others in your office by using a speakerphone and also recognize that your phone conversation will not be private. It is therefore common courtesy to ask your caller if you may put them on a speakerphone so they are aware that their call is not private.

Conference Calls: Audioconferencing

Travel is expensive in both time and money, so executives frequently use conference calls that allow persons at several locations to converse at the same time. A conference call is usually set up with an operator in advance of making the call. At the time the arrangements are made, the employee notifies an operator of the time of the call, as well as names, locations, and telephone numbers of persons included. The operator then makes the several telephone calls on the same line so that all callers can participate. Internal telephone systems in many businesses are equipped with conference-call capabilities that allow employees to place their own conference calls. Directions for using these systems are usually found in an office telephone manual.

Tips for conference calls

- It may be difficult to distinguish voices in a teleconference with several participants, so identify yourself the first few times you begin speaking.
- When you speak, face the microphone.
- Remember that the person listening cannot see you. Your words should convey your message, as you cannot use verbal cues or gestures to support your statements.
- Do not interrupt another speaker.
- Do not make a private comment to another person in the room; it could be overheard.
- When the telephone conference is over, thank the person who arranged the call.

Video Teleconferencing

Video teleconferencing is usually more expensive than audio teleconferencing but allows the participants to see each other. Often, one-way video teleconferencing is used where the main speaker is seen by the participants and the participants can respond to the speaker via telephone. Video teleconferencing is often used for staff training and requires video cameras, camera operators, and expensive video channels or satellite communications. It is usually expensive to set up a video teleconference and arrangements must be made for both sending and receiving the video signal. Some large companies have established their own full-time video teleconferencing facilities. In many large cities, businesses that provide video teleconferencing services have been established for the occasional user of this service.

By using special equipment, video signals can be sent over telephone lines. This equipment is referred to as *codec* (code/decode) equipment and compresses the video signal at the sender's end for transmission. The recipient must have compatible decoding equipment to expand the video signal. Using codec equipment, videoconferencing can be used by businesses on a routine basis. Videoconferencing is now being used to answer customer questions and solve technical problems. If there is a problem, all the customer does is call the technician who has the expertise to solve it.

With advances in computer technology, videoconferencing is also available on a desktop computer connected to the Internet. Using a small camera clipped to a computer monitor and inexpensive software, the costs of establishing a videoconference between several sites is now within reach of many offices. The quality of the video picture, however, will vary with the sophistication of equipment/software used and the speed of Internet access—and can range from still pictures (*freeze frame*) occupying a part of the computer screen, *slow scan* (a slow-motion picture), to a *full-motion video* picture that fills the monitor screen. If several sites are involved in the videoconference, they may each be seen in a box occupying a portion of the screen. By using videoconferencing over the Internet, small businesses can conduct meetings across the country while saving the time and cost of staff travel.

▼ SPEAKING BEFORE A GROUP ▼

As you advance up the career ladder, you may be asked to speak in front of a group. At the conclusion of a project, oral presentations are often given to other members of the department, supervisors, or members of the board of directors. Community groups may call on you to address their organizations. Being comfortable speaking in front of a group is an asset to your career advancement. Each speech should be designed to meet the specific needs of the listeners. The research techniques used when collecting data for a written report are also used when writing an oral report or speech. When developing the speech, review the goals and interests of the audience and prepare your thoughts to meet audience needs. Never allow personal biases or prejudices to be expressed, and do not use an ethnic joke that may offend someone.

Hints to giving a successful speech

1. Determine your objectives and know your topic well.
2. Organize your thoughts with an outline.
3. Remember that the audience is interested in themselves. Explain how your ideas will benefit them.
4. Include the fundamental points in your speech, but do not overwhelm the audience with too many facts. A handout sheet with additional facts can be distributed.
5. Do not memorize your speech. Prepare notes on 3 x 5 in. or 4 x 6 in. cards or prepare a sheet of keyboarded notes. List specific words or phrases that you want to use. If you know your topic well, your notes should be a guide to keep your thoughts organized.
6. Under some circumstances, the complete speech may be written. It is easier to read a keyboarded double- or triple-spaced speech than a handwritten speech.
7. Practice delivering the speech to your family or in front of a mirror.
8. Since you do not want people to look at your clothing instead of listening to you, wear conservative clothing. A traditional suit for a man can be enhanced by an attractive tie, and a woman can enliven a conservative outfit with a scarf or jewelry.
9. When the occasion requires you to thank the organization for inviting you, begin your speech by expressing your pleasure at receiving the invitation.
10. Begin each speech with an attention-getter, which can be a joke, anecdote, question, or quotation.

11. Do not talk to your audience in a condescending manner. The audience may tune you out if they feel you are patronizing them.

12. During the speech:
   - Stand so that you can be seen and heard.
   - Be enthusiastic.
   - Smile.
   - Appear interested in your audience and in the topic of your speech.
   - Pause between major divisions of the speech. This will allow the audience to understand your topic better.
   - Speak clearly and distinctly.
   - Move your head so that you view the entire audience.
   - Appear to look people in the eye. If gazing directly at people disturbs you, appear to look at them but look directly over their heads.
   - Use charts or large transparencies to illustrate the speech. Transparencies that are copies of a keyboarded page are too small to be read by the audience. Using a word-processing package with a variety of point sizes makes enlarging the type size easy. Also, many photocopiers have the ability to enlarge text.
   - Do not turn off all the lights in the room. People need some light to take notes. A dark room encourages people to daydream or doze, especially after eating.

13. Distribute handouts after the speech. If they are distributed before the speech, people may read them and not listen to you; or people may leave before the speech is completed.

14. Always ask for questions at the end of the speech. If no one has questions and you must fill the time, have a list of additional thoughts to discuss or questions you can ask the audience.

Visual Aids for a Presentation

Visual aids enhance a presentation in several ways. People remember more from a picture than they do when they listen to a speech. Visual aids reinforce the oral message, create a mental image that is easy to remember, and create additional interest in the oral presentation. Pictures, displays, and charts add variety and therefore simulate the listener's involvement in the presentation. To enhance the effectiveness of your speech, use some of the visual aids listed below.

Easels and Flipcharts

Easels and flipcharts hold large sheets of paper. Visuals on the pages can be prepared before the meeting or can be written on during the presentation.

Transparencies

Transparencies are sheets of clear plastic that can be prepared prior to a presentation or written on during it. Transparencies must be used with an overhead projector. Prepared transparencies with letters and images in a variety of colors can be produced by photocopiers. Transparency sheets are available in many colors and add visual variety to the presentation. Transparency markers, which allow the speaker to write directly on the transparency, are available in a range of colors. Transparencies can be mounted in hinged Vugraph frames to permit the overlay of several transparencies in a sequence to create a complex visual.

Slides

Slides can include photographs or other graphic material and must be prepared well before the meeting. Slides cannot be altered during the presentation and must be shown by using a slide projector.

Computer Presentations

There are many computerized presentation packages that add graphics and designs to augment a presentation. These computer programs can produce graphs, charts, or text and often include prepared artwork. Computer presentation software is discussed further in Chapter 5.

CHAPTER REVIEW

1. Explain voice mail.
2. Explain E-mail.
3. Explain fax.
4. Describe the appropriate voice techniques to be used when answering the telephone.
5. What information should be included in telephone messages?
6. Explain how a speakerphone is used.
7. Describe six of the specialized telephone services explained in this chapter.
8. Explain how paging equipment is used.
9. List two hints for a teleconference.
10. List three hints for a successful speech.
11. Describe visual aids that can be used when speaking to a group.

ACTIVITIES

1. Find a telephone partner for role playing. One person will be the caller and the other will be the administrative assistant answering the telephone. In the first role-playing activity, the administrative assistant will be pleasant when the caller requests an appointment. In the second role-playing activity, the administrative assistant will be rude and bored. Notice how the rude administrative assistant causes the caller to become angry and upset. After the two role-playing activities, reverse the caller and administrative assistant roles and do the calls again.

2. Prepare a personal telephone directory listing all friends and businesses that you call frequently.

3. Visit an office supply store and write a description of three types of telephone directories.

4. Visit an office supply store and look at the types of message pads available. Write a paragraph describing each pad and noting the differences. Be sure to note the prices of pads available.

5. Using telephone directories (available at libraries) for various cities, obtain the telephone numbers of three of your friends or relatives who live in other states. Include the area code.

6. Consult an 800 directory. List the names and phone numbers of three companies that you might want to call.

7. Keep a record for two days of all the telephone calls that are received in your home. Indicate which calls are personal and which are business.

8. Prepare a message form for all the telephone calls received at your home for a five-hour period.

9. Ask an administrative assistant to describe three difficult types of telephone calls that are often received. Explain how the calls were handled.

10. Using a tape recorder, prepare a recording of your voice. Speak in a conversational tone. Listen to the tape and analyze your voice. Is it too high pitched? Does it sound whinny?

Is it difficult to understand? Do you speak in an enthusiastic and friendly manner? What changes should you make in your voice?

11. Using the Internet, find two telephone numbers of businesses.

PROJECTS

Project 5

Key in the letter to Ms. Mollie C. Hayes, 818 Oakmont Drive, Seattle, WA 98028. Use a modified block letter style and provide any additional information needed to complete the letter. The letter is from J. C. Murray.

Dear Mollie:

I do not know if you have heard the news. At last month's board of directors meeting, I announced my intention to retire in about a year. The Board appeared surprised about my announcement, but I have been thinking of retiring for a long time. As you know, I would like to spend more time with my family.

You have several potential candidates for my position in your department, and I hope that you will encourage them to apply for the job. When we met at the Houston convention, we discussed possible employment opportunities with my company.

I hope you and your family are well. Please give them my regards. We should plan another party again soon.

Project 6

Send this memo to the staff. It is from Nicole J. Nelson.

Please join me in welcoming Ms. Laura Berkeley as our new Communications Director. Ms. Berkeley will be arriving next week, and she is very excited about the opportunities and challenges facing her at our company.

Ms. Berkeley, who received both her undergraduate and graduate degrees in communications from Michigan State University, comes to us from Northeast Communications, Inc. Ms. Berkeley is highly respected in the communications field and will be a fine addition to our company.

A reception will be held in her honor on Friday from 2 to 4 P.M. in the Board of Directors Conference Room.

I look forward to seeing you at the reception. Ms. Berkeley is anxious to begin her work here, so take this opportunity to welcome her and offer her your support.

HUMAN RELATIONS SKILL DEVELOPMENT

Praise

Most people enjoy receiving praise for a job completed satisfactorily. Unfortunately, some managers do not praise often enough and some do not give praise at all. Praise increases job satisfaction and demonstrates that the company knows how valuable the employee is.

- What do you say to an employer who praises you for a job well done?
- How can you encourage your employer to reward the staff with positive comments when a job has been completed?
- In your role as supervisor, what would you say to an employee who stayed late to complete an important last-minute report?
- What would you say to praise your employer?

Prejudice

Do not allow your personal prejudice to influence your work in the office. Here are some examples of unfounded prejudices: Have you always thought that people with a certain color of hair are rude? Do you think that people who wear unusual or flashy clothing are not professional? Do you think that people who are heavy (or slender) are not as smart as others? Do you have a dislike for people who have unusual accents? Do you dislike persons who have a particular personality trait? Everyone with whom you work should receive your respect and courtesy. Treat every colleague as a professional, and expect to receive the same treatment in return.

- What are your personal biases?
- How are you going to control (or overcome) your biases?
- Have you demonstrated a negative reaction to a person because of a personality trait? What was the trait?

SITUATIONS

How would you handle each of the following situations?

- At 2 P.M. today Robert Murray arrived for his appointment with your employer. Unfortunately, you scheduled the appointment with Mr. Murray and your employer for *tomorrow* at 2 P.M.
- This is the third time that you have not received a telephone message. What are you going to say to your assistant?
- You made airline reservations with a travel agent for two members of your department. The reservations were on flight 270 with a connection in Dallas to flight 89. When you received the tickets, you noticed that both persons have reservations on flight 270, but one connected with flight 83 and the other person connected with flight 89.

PUNCTUATION REVIEW

Punctuate each of the following sentences.

1. Due to a recent increase in the cost of materials we must adjust our prices by 3 percent for each unit
2. Mollie who is the manager frequently took the train because it was more convenient
3. Katie also registered for the lecture
4. I need the following items audiotapes videotapes and transparency markers
5. Through a new computerized reservation system that was shown yesterday by Travelers Incorporated business travelers will be able to get information from their travel agents about hotel chains such as Hyatt Marriott and Sheraton
6. For office managers this certificate can serve as a valuable tool for performance evaluations which are the keys to advancement
7. Janie the computer was moved to the new building

8. However Nelson Wagner Jr noted that the action signaled new confidence in the industry

9. Jack asked did interest rates rise

10. Under the new legislation a tax credit was given to the students under the age of 25 and those earning less than the minimum poverty level wage

11. The stock market had a net gain of 29.34 points but my stock price declined

12. The planned merger of ATEX and METRA which should occur in January is the brainstorm of three people Janice Helfstein Olga Rocher and Phillip Francis

13. Since office rents are high in the East they moved the company headquarters to the Midwest

14. Most people prefer to be close to their offices but housing downtown is very expensive

15. Alicia changed the filing system therefore the efficiency of the office was increased

▼4▼
Processing the Mail

OBJECTIVES

After studying this chapter, you should be able to:

1. Process and sort the incoming mail.
2. Prepare a mail register of incoming mail.
3. Prepare a chronological register of incoming mail for a traveling executive.
4. List the services offered by the U.S. Postal Service (USPS).
5. Explain the classes of mail offered by the U.S. Postal Service.
6. Explain franked and penalty mail.
7. Evaluate express mail services.
8. Recognize the two-letter abbreviations for states and Canadian provinces.
9. Explain the use of ZIP codes.

▼ PROCESSING INCOMING MAIL ▼

Mail Delivery

One of the responsibilities of an administrative assistant is to process incoming mail. In a small company, the mail is delivered once a day by a postal carrier. In a large business, the mail may be taken to a company's central mailroom, where it will be sorted by building, department, or floor before it is delivered to the individual offices. Depending on the volume of mail and the size of the company, deliveries may be made more than once a day. While the central mailroom relieves the administrative assistant of some of the routine duties of processing the mail, the presence of a central mailroom also means that an additional step has been added to the mail-sorting process. This extra step may mean delays of half a day or more in both receiving and dispatching the mail.

When the mail is received, it is opened and stamped with the date of receipt. The stamping can be done by hand with a rubber stamp or by a machine, which may indicate the time and date of receipt. Documenting the date of receipt is critical for many businesses. Although most mail is opened by the administrative assistant, company policy may permit mail addressed to specific people or mail designated "personal" to be distributed unopened.

Sorting and Distributing the Mail

Depending on the size and layout of the office, the mail should first be sorted according to department, floor, section, office, or similar division. The mail should then be sorted for each person within an office. It is usually the administrative assistant's responsibility to sort general mail addressed to the office so that it is forwarded to the proper employee. In many offices, mail is often addressed to the office head although actually intended for other office staff. The administrative assistant must know how to distribute the mail efficiently so that the proper person receives it quickly. All payments may be forwarded to one person, all invoices to another, and correspondence regarding a specific project may be directed to the person responsible for that project. You should keep a list at your desk of how projects are assigned in your office to aid in the sorting of mail.

Often, action is taken on the mail by the administrative assistant before the mail is distributed to other employees. Receipt of the item might be entered into a computer log, a tracking number may be assigned, or data entry may be made of the action requested or to whom the mail is directed.

Regular mail is usually placed in individual mailboxes, often stacked trays, which are in a central location. Express mail and mail for top executives may be taken directly to the addressee.

Depending on the volume of mail and the procedures of the office, individual mail may also be sorted according to urgency of the item.

Individual mail should be sorted in the following categories:

- Express mail, certified, and registered mail
- First-class and personal mail
- Newspapers, magazines, advertising materials, and catalogs
- Packages

In some offices if the supervisor is out of town, a chronological list of all mail received may be prepared. This list enables the returning executive to review quickly all mail received.

Coding the Mail

After receiving the mail, some executives *code* or write notes in the margins indicating what is to be done with the letter. Examples of notes are "file," "find file folder," "answer this letter," "talk with (another person) about the letter," and "what do you think of this suggestion." Color coding can be used to indicate the processing procedure. For example, a blue check mark may mean "file," a red check mark may mean "hold for response," and a yellow check mark may mean "handle for me."

Mail Roster
Clifton Lamb
April 3–7, XXXX

Date	Item	What Was Done with Item	By Whom
4/3/XXXX	Letter P & M Company	Sent to Terri	Julie
4/4/XXXX	Letter B. G. Corporation	Waiting	Maria
4/5/XXXX	Report Zev Co.	Sent to Ted	Maria
4/7/XXXX	Insurance policy	Sent to Terri	Julie

FIGURE 4-1 A Mail Roster for a Traveling Executive.

May 17, XXXX

Ms. Susan Churchill
8934 Jefferson Blvd.
Indianapolis, IN 46260

Dear Ms. Churchill:

I have carefully read the report of your last trip to the South Pacific, and I am impressed with your findings.

I do need clarification of a few points.

check the file   1.   What is the projected cost to refurbish the lobby of the Island Hotel?

2.   How long do you anticipate the renovation will take?   *3 months*

3.   Would you recommend Polynesian Construction, Inc., or R. N. Woo Construction Company?

4.   Do you recommend refurbishing the entire hotel at one time or refurbishing over a period of years?

As we discussed at our last teleconference, I am eager to begin this project. I would appreciate receiving your responses as soon as possible.

Sincerely,

Write a response for my signature

J. B. Samson

rty

FIGURE 4-2   A Coded Letter.

Rubber stamps can also be used to speed the coding process. Stamps would imprint the mail with the codes used most often, permitting an executive to check the code appropriate for the item. To speed the processing of the mail even more, a single stamp with the date of receipt and coding may be used.

After a manager codes the mail, an administrative assistant completes the action required. In some offices, an administrative assistant opens the letter, reads it, and completes the necessary action. The letter is then filed in the appropriate file. A copy of the letter with a note indicating the action taken is given to the manager so that the manager can monitor the action or make revisions before the letter is mailed.

▼ INTERNAL DISTRIBUTION OF MAIL ▼

Mail can be forwarded to people within an office through the use of a routing slip. This procedure allows the same mail to be sent to one or more employees and indicates what

```
    Sent to _____

    Sent by _____

    Date _____

    Procedures

        Read _____

        File _____

        Forward to _____

        Discuss with _____

        Handle _____

        Other _____
```

FIGURE 4-3   A Routing Slip.

employees should do after receiving the mail. An administrative assistant should develop and reproduce a routing slip that is appropriate for their office.

Interoffice envelopes are used to send items within the same company. Interoffice envelopes are not sealed and are often large enough to contain several pieces of 8 1/2 x 11 in. paper without folding. The envelopes can be used several times, each user crossing out the name of the previous user and writing the name of the new addressee on the next available line. A supply of interoffice envelopes should be made available to employees who send interoffice mail.

```
                        FOR YOUR INFORMATION


        Sent By         _____

        Date            _____


                        Date            Comments

        Woo Chang       _____      _____

        Rhonda Chapel   _____      _____

        Brad Dunigan    _____      _____

        Leroy Fessmeyer _____      _____

        Barbara Gladden _____      _____

        Rodney Healy    _____      _____

        Elaine Johnson  _____      _____
```

FIGURE 4-4   A Routing Slip for Mail Circulated among the Office Staff.

INTER-DEPARTMENTAL MAIL

Name _____   Name _____
Dept. _____   Dept. _____

Name _____   Name _____
Dept. _____   Dept. _____

Name _____   Name _____
Dept. _____   Dept. _____

Name _____   Name _____
Dept. _____   Dept. _____

Name _____   Name _____
Dept. _____   Dept. _____

Name _____   Name _____
Dept. _____   Dept. _____

Name _____   Name _____
Dept. _____   Dept. _____

FIGURE 4-5   An Interoffice Envelope.

▼ PREPARING MAIL TO LEAVE THE OFFICE ▼

Folding the Letter

Most letters prepared on regular-size stationery, which is 8 1/2 x 11 in., can be folded in thirds and mailed in standard business-size No. 10 envelopes. To fold a letter so that it is placed in the envelope properly, start with the letter facing you as you would read it. Pick up the bottom of the letter and fold it about one-third of the way up. Then fold the top of the letter down so that it is about 1/4 in. short of the first fold. This 1/4-in. gap will assist the reader in unfolding the letter. Place the letter in the envelope with the 1/4-in. gap facing you and toward the top of the envelope. Documents of more than about five pages are usually too thick to fold and place in a No. 10 envelope. These thicker documents should be mailed in large manila envelopes.

Two-Letter State Abbreviations

All mail leaving the office must contain a properly addressed envelope. From a mail processing perspective, the two most important parts of the address are the two-letter state abbreviation and the ZIP code. When the U.S. Postal Service (USPS) began using scanning equipment to sort the mail, it requested that two-letter state abbreviations be used to expedite the mail. The following two-letter abbreviations for the U.S. states and Canadian provinces are always capitalized.

State Abbreviations

Alabama	AL	Arkansas	AR
Alaska	AK	California	CA
Arizona	AZ	Colorado	CO

Connecticut	CT	New Hampshire	NH
Delaware	DE	New Jersey	NJ
Florida	FL	New Mexico	NM
Georgia	GA	New York	NY
Hawaii	HI	North Carolina	NC
Idaho	ID	North Dakota	ND
Illinois	IL	Ohio	OH
Indiana	IN	Oklahoma	OK
Iowa	IA	Oregon	OR
Kansas	KS	Pennsylvania	PA
Kentucky	KY	Rhode Island	RI
Louisiana	LA	South Carolina	SC
Maine	ME	South Dakota	SD
Maryland	MD	Tennessee	TN
Massachusetts	MA	Texas	TX
Michigan	MI	Utah	UT
Minnesota	MN	Vermont	VT
Mississippi	MS	Virginia	VA
Missouri	MO	Washington	WA
Montana	MT	West Virginia	WV
Nebraska	NE	Wisconsin	WI
Nevada	NV	Wyoming	WY

Other Abbreviations

American Samoa	AS	N. Marianas Islands	MP
District of Columbia	DC	Puerto Rico	PR
Guam	GU	Virgin Islands	VI

Canadian Province Abbreviations

Alberta	AB	Nova Scotia	NS
British Columbia	BC	Ontario	ON
Manitoba	MB	Prince Edward Island	PE
New Brunswick	NB	Quebec	QC
Newfoundland	NF	Saskatchewan	SK
Northwest Territories	NT	Yukon Territory	YT

Addressing Envelopes

The USPS uses computer scanners called *optical character readers* (OCRs) to read the mail so that it can be processed efficiently. To enable the computer to read the envelope, follow the suggestions listed below.

- Use a block style for the address.
- Capitalize every letter and omit the punctuation.
- Use the two-letter state abbreviation. (If the state name is spelled in full, it is too long for the computer to read.)
- The city, state, and ZIP code must be in the last line of the address.
  The city name must not contain more than 13 characters. If the city name is too long, use the *approved* abbreviation for that city. Approved abbreviations are in the abbreviation

section of the *National Five-Digit ZIP Code and Post Office Directory*, which is discussed later in the chapter.

- Leave two to five spaces between the two-letter state abbreviation and the ZIP code.
- A notation—PERSONAL, CONFIDENTIAL, HOLD FOR ARRIVAL, or GENERAL DELIVERY—is keyboarded in all capital letters two lines below the return address and 1/4 in. from the left edge of the envelope.
- A mailing notation—REGISTERED MAIL or CERTIFIED MAIL—is keyboarded nine lines from the top right side of the envelope and is directly below the location of the stamp or postage meter. The notation must end at least 1/2 in. from the right edge of the envelope.
- Keyboard the ATTENTION line as the second line of the address.

The following is an example of an address prepared according to the U.S. Postal Service guidelines.

```
COOPER AND SONS
ATTENTION MR THEODORE COOPER
1902 BRANCH DRIVE
DAVENPORT IA 67992
```

The U.S. Postal Service suggests that addresses placed on letter-size mail be located within an imaginary rectangle (the OCR read area) on the front of the letter formed by the boundaries shown in Figure 4-6.

Minimum and Nonstandard-Size Mail

Minimum Size Standards

The USPS will accept mail less than 1/4 in. thick only if the item is rectangular and is:

- At least 3 in. high, and
- At least 5 in. long (items to foreign countries must be 5 1/2 in. long), and
- At least 0.0007 in. thick (about the thickness of a postcard)

Mail not meeting these standards will be returned.

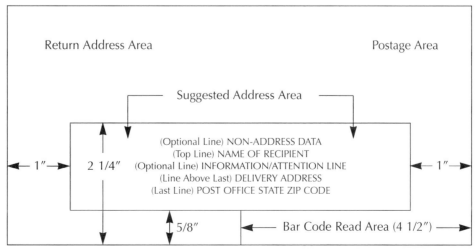

FIGURE 4-6 How to Address Envelopes.

Nonstandard-Size Mail

A fee for mailing nonstandard-size mail will be charged if first class, single-piece standard A, or international mail weighs 1 ounce or less and exceeds any of these size limits:

- Height exceeds 6 1/8 in. or
- Length exceeds 11 1/2 in. or
- Thickness exceeds 1/4 in.

ZIP Code and ZIP + Four

The ZIP code is also used to expedite mail delivery. The original ZIP code was five digits. In 1983, the USPS expanded the ZIP code to nine digits to refine the sorting of mail. The nine-digit ZIP code includes the original five digits plus a hyphen and four additional digits (for example, 28050-4327). The *National Five-Digit ZIP Code and Post Office Directory* (Publication 65) can be purchased from the U.S. Postal Service or from private publishers. If your office does not have a *National Five-Digit ZIP Code Directory*, you can call a local post office to obtain the ZIP code of a specific location. ZIP code directories are also available as computer software packages. In addition, the USPS Internet site can be used to find the ZIP code of any address in the United States (Internet address: www.usps.gov).

Another innovation to assist in the sorting of mail is the use of bar codes on envelopes. Mailers may use a ZIP code plus a bar code. The information content of the bar code is indicated by the height of the bars. The bars represent the nine digits of the ZIP Code Plus Four and an extra digit for error correction. Word-processing software can be used to print the proper bar codes on envelopes automatically.

Canadian and Foreign Postal Codes

The Canadian government and other governments have their own versions of ZIP codes used to speed mail delivery. The forms of these codes differ from those used in the United States and may combine letters and numbers in varying combinations. For example, the postal code for a location in Canada will be in the following form: letter, number, letter, space, number, letter, number, for example, L8E 4Y2.

▼ PROCESSING OUTGOING MAIL ▼

For an administrative assistant, the processing of outgoing mail is a much more complex task than the processing of incoming mail. You will have to prepare the mail for delivery across your city or across the world. Mail must comply with regulations or standards established by the USPS or other carriers. In preparing outgoing mail, you should select the fastest, safest, and most economical method for delivery. The decision is based on the requirements of the document contained in the envelope.

To process outgoing mail, you must first understand the services and regulations of the U.S. Postal Service, which handles most of the mail delivered in the United States. Other carriers provide specialized services that supplement the services of the USPS.

United States Postal Service (USPS)

The USPS provides a wide variety of services to deliver mail anywhere in the world. Fees are charged depending on the *class* of mail and any *special mailing services* required for the item mailed.

Classes of Mail

Express Mail. USPS offers express mail delivery service 365 days a year. Mail and packages sent using express mail next-day service can be taken to over 40,000 designated express mail post offices, generally by 5 P.M. or deposited in one of 26,000 express mail collection boxes across the country. USPS letter carriers will accept express mail and by calling 1-800-222-1811, USPS will even pick up express mail at your office. Local post offices can provide specific express mail pick-up times for the local area.

Items sent by express mail are automatically insured up to $500 against loss or damage, and additional insurance can be purchased up to $5000.

Depending on where the mail is sent, express mail will be delivered to the address on the package by noon or by 3 P.M. the next day. In some areas of the country, USPS may not be able to deliver express mail overnight but guarantees a second-day delivery service.

USPS also provides express mail international service to nearly 200 countries and territories around the world. Express mail military service can be sent to select U.S. military addresses (APO and FPO addresses) at domestic prices.

First-Class Mail.　First-class mail is the standard method for sending letters, business correspondence, and checks, as well as personal letters and cards.

If first-class mail is not letter-size, make sure to mark it "First-Class." The USPS also recommends that nonstandard-size first class mail be placed in a large green diamond-bordered envelope. First-class mail is generally delivered overnight to nearby cities and within 2 days to nearby states. Delivery by the third day can be expected for remaining outlying areas. You can check with the local post office to determine delivery times from your area.

First-class mail can be insured and can also be combined with special mailing services, which are discussed later in this section. These special services include certified mail, registered mail, and COD. A certificate of mailing and restricted delivery can be also be purchased for first-class mail.

First-class items weighing more than 11 ounces should be sent using priority mail.

Priority Mail.　Priority mail consists of packages up to 70 pounds. Letters over 11 ounces can also be sent via priority mail for preferential treatment at a lower cost than express mail. A special 2-pound envelope is available where the rate of postage is the rate charged for a 2-pound piece of priority mail, no matter how much the material in the envelope weighs. Priority mail can be insured, registered, certified, or sent COD for an additional charge.

Periodicals.　The USPS has a special rate of postage that can be used by publishers and registered news agents for mailing periodicals such as magazines.

Standard Mail A.　Standard mail A is used for bulk mailings of advertising, catalogs, and so on. Special reduced rates are available to churches and other charitable organizations. To use standard mail A rates or the nonprofit standard mail rates, an organization must send at least 200 items or 50 pounds of material for each mailing.

Standard Mail B (Parcels).　Standard mail B service is used for parcels weighing 1 pound or more and up to 70 pounds. The parcel's total dimensions (length, width, and depth) can measure up to 108 in. The USPS goal for parcel delivery is 2 to 9 days, depending on distance. Parcels may be sent more quickly by priority mail.

Special Mailing Services

Certificate of Mailing.　The USPS provides several alternatives for documenting that a letter was mailed. The simplest is the certificate of mailing. A certificate of mailing is a stamped receipt that can only be purchased at the time of mailing. It is an inexpensive way of obtaining proof that mail was received by a USPS employee. The certificate of mailing does not provide proof that the mail was delivered to the addressee nor does it provide insurance coverage for loss or damage to the item. This method is often used when mailing tax returns.

Certified Mail. Certified mail is used when a mailing receipt and a record of delivery to the addressee's post office is needed. For an additional fee, a return receipt signed by the addressee may be obtained. Certified mail does not provide additional security, and it does not travel faster than first-class mail. Certified mail is only available for first-class or priority mail.

COD. COD means "collect on delivery." This service is used to deliver merchandise ordered by the addressee. When the item is delivered, the addressee pays the cost of the item plus postage and a money order fee. COD service can be used for merchandise sent by first-class mail, express mail, priority mail, or standard mail A or B. This service is not available for international mail or for mail addressed to APO and FPO addresses.

Insurance. Insurance coverage up to $5,000 can be purchased for standard mail A or B, as well as standard mail matter mailed at the priority mail or first-class mail rate. Insurance up to $25,000 can be purchased for registered mail.

Registered Mail. This is the safest way to send valuables through the mail. Movement of the mail is recorded by a series of signed receipts at each stage of delivery from the sender to the addressee. When the item is mailed, its full value must be declared. Insurance protection for the item up to a total value of $25,000 can be purchased for domestic delivery. Registered mail to Canada is subject to a $1,000 indemnity limit. For all other foreign countries, the indemnity limit is currently $42.30. First-class or priority mail postage is required on domestic registered mail. A receipt of delivery is available at an additional cost. The return receipt will show to whom, when, and where the item was delivered. Registered mail must be taken to a clerk at a post office for mailing and cannot be placed in a mail box or a slot at the post office.

Restricted Delivery. By using a restricted delivery, the sender specifies that the mail can only be delivered to a specific addressee or to someone authorized in writing to receive mail for the addressee. However, restricted delivery mail addressed to federal and local government agencies and officials will be delivered without the addressee's written authorization. Restricted delivery can be used only for registered mail, certified mail, COD mail, and mail insured for more than $50.

Return Receipt. A return receipt documents proof of delivery and can be purchased for mail sent COD, express mail, insured for more than $50, registered, or certified. A return receipt shows who signed for the item and the date it was delivered.

Special Delivery. Effective June 8, 1997, USPS eliminated domestic special delivery service. Suggested alternatives for expedited delivery service are express mail or priority mail.

Special Handling. Special handling service is required for parcels whose unusual contents require special care in transit and handling except those sent by first-class mail. Examples of such contents include live poultry or bees. Special handling is available for standard mail A or B only, including insured and COD mail. This service provides preferential handling to the extent practical in dispatch and transportation. Special handling service is not necessary for sending ordinary parcels even when they contain fragile items. Breakable items will receive adequate protection if they are packed with sufficient cushioning and clearly marked FRAGILE. Use insured or registered mail for valuable or irreplaceable items.

Government Mail (Penalty Mail/Franked Mail)

The federal government sends business letters and checks by *penalty mail*. Special envelopes for penalty mail sent by the federal government are usually imprinted "Official Business, Penalty for Private Use" and the name of the federal agency. Members of Congress and other government officials are permitted to send mail by *franked mail*. Franked mail uses the original signature or a printed signature of the sender instead of a stamp. Envelopes using penalty or franked mail are available only in offices authorized to use that type of mail.

International Mail

The postal rates for international mail varies with the weight of the envelope and the specific destination. Most international mail is now sent using air mail service. However, packages may be sent by surface mail, which may take several weeks or even months to arrive at its destination. Information about international mail rates is included in a postage chart available from the U.S. Postal Service and is available on the USPS Internet site.

Post Office Boxes

Post office boxes and drawers may be rented from many post offices. Boxes and drawers are located in the post office and mail is placed directly in them after it is sorted by postal clerks. Whenever the lobby of the post office is open, the mail may be retrieved.

Non-USPS Services

Like most countries of the world, the United States and Canada give government agencies such as the USPS and Canadian Post the exclusive right to deliver first-class mail. Delivery of other mail or packages, however, may be left open to competition from private companies. Delivery of packages and express mail are two areas where competition among providers has developed.

Package Delivery

There are several companies that provide delivery of packages in competition with the USPS. One of the largest of these companies is UPS (United Parcel Service). If a business has an account with UPS, it pays a weekly charge to have a driver pick up packages. However, if the business does not have a UPS account, packages can be picked up for a fee, or the business can take the package to a UPS office. The package will be delivered to the addressee and UPS will obtain a signature verifying delivery. If the addressee is not at home, UPS will attempt delivery three times. UPS rates are very competitive with those of the USPS. Package delivery is also available from many of the companies that provide express mail service. Mailing establishments such as Mail Boxes, Etc. provide letter and package mailing services and office supplies.

Express Mail

Express mail is a specialized service that provides quick delivery of small packages and documents. Express mail is used when time-sensitive documents must be sent to another party. While the express mail service business was founded to provide guaranteed overnight delivery within the United States, in some areas of the country express mail service is available only on a two-night (second day) basis. Several companies in addition to the USPS provide express mail services.

Providers of express mail services

- U.S. Postal Service
- FedEx (Federal Express)
- United Parcel Service
- Airborne Express
- DHL

Express mail companies have expanded and specialized their services to meet different needs. The express mail carriers may deliver mail early in the morning at one price and offer a lower price if delivery can wait until the afternoon. The following are examples of services available from two express mail carriers.

The U.S. Postal Service provides the following services:

- Express mail custom design service
- Express mail next-day service
- Express mail second-day service
- Express Mail Military Service

Federal Express provides the following services:

- FedEx Same Day Service
- FedEx Priority Overnight
- FedEx Standard Overnight
- FedEx 2Day
- FedEx First Overnight
- FedEx International Services
- Saturday and Sunday delivery

If you need to use an express mail service, first determine if your company has a contract with an express mail company. A contract will enable the express mail company to bill your office directly for the delivery. If your office does not have a contract or if you wish to evaluate the cost and efficiency of your present express mail service, you should consider the following:

- Pickup charges
- Location of mail-drop-off boxes
- Whether the customer must deliver the package to the carrier
- Delivery to the community of the addressee
- Delivery by a specific time

FIGURE 4-7 Sample Waybill.

- Weekend pickup and delivery
- Mailing cost
- Insurance availability and cost

Courier and Air Courier Services

Many large metropolitan areas are served by courier services that will pick up and deliver a package or document in a matter of hours. A phone call is placed to a courier service, and a messenger will pick up the package for immediate delivery. In downtown areas, couriers often use bicycles to speed documents through congested city streets.

There are sometimes circumstances when documents or packages must be sent to another city and even a next-day delivery service would miss the deadline. Airlines and specialized delivery services can place a letter or small package on the next flight to the destination city. Airline services may only deliver the item to the airport and require pickup of the item at the airport by the receiving party. Specialized delivery services may complete the delivery to the recipient's address.

Postage Meters

Instead of placing individual stamps on letters, most businesses use a postage meter to print the postage on an envelope. Mail sent using postage meters can be delivered quicker than mail with stamps since metered mail requires less processing by the USPS. To use a postage meter, the meter must be registered with the U.S. Postal Service and a set amount of postage is prepaid and set in the meter. Modern postage meters have a built-in computer modem,

FIGURE 4-8 Mail Room Using Postage Equipment. (Courtesy Pitney Bowes Inc.)

FIGURE 4-9 Desktop Postage Equipment. (Courtesy Pitney Bowes Inc.)

and postage can be purchased electronically over the phone. With older meters, a part of the meter called the *meter head* is taken to the post office with a check for the amount of postage to be purchased. The post office then breaks the seal on the meter head, adjusts internal counters to equal the additional postage being purchased and reseals the meter head. The amount of the postage purchased and the new meter reading is then entered on the meter *log book* or *control book*. The meter log book or control book is used by the business to record the postage used and by the post office to verify proper use of the meter.

The operator of a postage meter can set the proper amount of postage to be printed for each letter or package for different weights and classes of mail. The postage meter cannot print directly on large envelopes and packages. The postage for these items is printed on a gummed tape, which is then placed on the oversize envelope or package.

Many postage meters moisten the envelope flap and seal the envelope as the postage is printed. The operator needs to check the water reservoir frequently to determine if there is sufficient water.

Postal Scale, Postage Rate, Fees, and Information Chart

A business using a postage meter has the responsibility of calculating the correct postage required on each piece of mail. Most businesses use a postal scale, which is a sensitive scale that weighs envelopes accurately to the half ounce. Use of a postal scale can save up to 20 percent of postage costs since the correct postal charge can easily be determined rather than simply placing an extra stamp on an envelope "just in case" the envelope is too heavy. A scale is especially useful for businesses that mail large envelopes (reports, catalogs, etc.) which vary in weight. Many postal scales display the postage required for an item automatically, while older scales may have built-in charts that must be consulted to determine the amount of postage required for each class and weight of mail.

Postage charts that list the postage required for all classes and services of mail are available from the U.S. Postal Service. These charts also list postage required for foreign countries. The information on the postal charts is revised when postage rates change.

Collecting Outgoing Mail

Outgoing mail is deposited in a collection box for pickup by the post office. Office buildings usually have mail-drop boxes or mail slots on each floor, in the lobby of the building, or in close proximity to the building. It is often the administrative assistant's responsibility to deposit the outgoing mail in the collection box. If you are depositing mail, check the collection time posted on the box to determine if the mail will be picked up later that day. Collection times vary from box to box. Locate a box where the pickup is after 5:30 P.M. so that last-minute documents can be deposited quickly for pickup.

In a large office, outgoing mail may be collected for processing by the mailroom employees before the mail is sent to the post office. Outgoing mail is often collected by the mailroom staff when incoming mail is being delivered. Outgoing mail can also be taken directly to the mailroom for processing. The office may require that outgoing mail be sorted by the first three ZIP code digits in order to qualify for discounts on postage. Some offices require that each piece of mail be coded so that postage can be charged to the office originating the mail. It is important to learn the requirements for sending outgoing mail so that the mail can be processed quickly and postal costs charged to the correct office.

CHAPTER REVIEW

1. Explain how a letter is coded.
2. Explain the use of a routing slip.
3. What is the purpose of a mail register?
4. Explain the purposes of registered and certified mail.
5. Explain priority mail.
6. Define franked and penalty mail.
7. What criteria should be considered when using express mail?

ACTIVITIES

1. How would you send each of the following?
   a. A letter to Paris, France
   b. A gift package to a client in Albany, NY
   c. A letter that must be received by tomorrow
   d. A package that must be received by tomorrow
   e. A stock certificate
   f. A letter to someone in Guam
   g. A package from Boston to Seattle that must be received tomorrow

2. Go to the post office and locate the private boxes available for rent. Check the lobby hours, and ask the price to rent a box.

3. Verify the current rates for first-class letters and postcards.

4. Call three express mail carriers and compare their rates for mailing a five-page letter. Is the location for mail drop-off convenient for you? Do they have an office pickup service? By what time do they guarantee delivery? What is the cost for the service?

5. What is the cost to mail a letter to Mexico, to Italy, and to England?

6. Describe the proper materials used when mailing a package. Where in your area would you purchase the materials, and which company would you use to send the package?

7. Ask an assistant how much time is devoted daily to sorting and processing mail.

8. For one week keep a mail register of all of the mail received in your home.

9. Prepare a routing slip to send a newspaper or magazine article to four members of your class.

10. What is the closest post office to your school? What is the last time that mail is picked up there? If you miss the last pickup there, what is the next-closest location, and what is the time of the last pickup there?

11. Where is the main post office in your area? During what hours are the lobby windows open?

12. Address an envelope to each of the following people.
    - Marilyn Horan, Acting Director, Watkins Industries, 3409 Research Lane, Detroit, Michigan 48875
    - Shu Tau, Administrative Assistant, Brandywine Inc., 4877 Garden Avenue, Chicago, Illinois 60067
    - Reynolds Manufacturing, 19 Wood Drive, Columbus, Ohio 43227, Attention of Lucy Wagner
    - Personal letter to Stanley R. Wells, Boyer and Sons, 404 Vine Street, Columbia, Maryland 21045
    - Certified letter to Paula T. Huffman, Managing Director, Birch Systems, Ft Wayne, Indiana 46815

PROJECTS

Project 7

Create the form below, and write a memo to Peter Bahrami, Ralph Harris, Sarah Rothman, and Pepe Gomez asking them to complete this form ASAP. The memo is from you and your title is Director.

Activity	Percentage of Daily Time Spent
Using E-mail	
Faxing	
Sorting mail	
Filing	
Answering telephone	
Writing reports	
Writing letters	
Making travel arrangements	

Project 8

Create the following table and calculate mailing costs for each month.

Mailing Costs in Dollars

DEPT.	JAN.	FEB.	MARCH	APRIL	MAY	JUNE
101	2500	1875	900	800	2500	2500
102	1600	2200	800	900	2300	1500
103	1800	2500	750	700	2600	2200
104	2250	1300	500	600	1800	2700
105	3600	1500	900	750	1700	2000
106	1500	2400	500	900	2000	2500

HUMAN RELATIONS SKILL DEVELOPMENT

Office Friendships

Remember that the office is the place where you work, not the place where you play. Do not tell office friends all the details of your personal life. These people may later supervise you, and the details of your personal life may have a negative impact on their evaluation of your work. It is also possible that an office friend, with whom you later have a disagreement, might tell others the details of your personal problems. Be friendly with everyone in your office, but do not divulge all the secrets of your life.

- Have you ever told someone about an event in your life and later wished you had never mentioned it?
- What would you do if your supervisor began telling you personal information you did not want to know?
- Describe the types of information about yourself that you would like to share with your co-workers.

Working with Disorganized People

It can be discouraging to work with disorganized people, particularly when their behavior affects you. Postponing the beginning of meetings because a person is always late, waiting for materials to be found, and delaying projects because a person has not completed a portion of the project can be very frustrating. Depending on the person, there may be little you can do to remedy the situation. You can diplomatically encourage the person to become organized, discuss the importance of being prompt, and tactfully express your frustration about the situation.

- Are you a disorganized person?
- What can you do to become more organized?
- What can you do if your supervisor is disorganized?
- How would you encourage a co-worker who is disorganized to become more organized?
- Do you arrive on time for events?
- Do you have friends who are habitually late for events?
- How can you encourage a person to be prompt?

SITUATIONS

How would you handle each of the following situations?

- You arrive on time at your office, but you cannot find your office keys.
- Your supervisor would like you to do personal errands when the supervisor is too busy to do them. You are told that the errands can be done on company time.
- Two weeks ago you mailed a business deposit to the bank. Since you did not receive a return receipt, you called the bank. The bank told you that they did not receive the check.

PUNCTUATION REVIEW

Punctuate each of the following sentences.

1. Edward K Bowman our president has meetings in Virginia Pennsylvania and New Jersey
2. Bill the executive director joined the company in June of this year
3. The most effective manager Ms Engle is well organized
4. Yesterdays price report while representing only a single month gave no indication that inflation is a growing concern to the economic future of the nation
5. Of course we missed the train and were late for the meeting
6. Since fall is here we must reevaluate the project

7. Food prices after increasing 3.6 percent in January declined 2.4 percent last month which is further evidence that the effects of the drought may be less than originally feared by economists

8. The west coast office assistant I understand is the employee of the month

9. No the salary was not the issue

10. Her next interview is in Chicago Illinois on Friday April 17 at 10 AM

11. The presentation was a success and we received the contract

12. You will I think benefit from the Friday seminar

13. Several economists cautioned against expecting such price increases to continue Ms Woo for example said that the high costs of raw materials are expected to decline shortly

14. Wendy who will be on a business trip the month of October is the new director

15. The bank was closed yesterday and I wanted to cash a check so I would have sufficient cash for my next business trip

▼5▼
Computers in the Office

OBJECTIVES

After studying this chapter, you should be able to:

1. Understand the terms associated with computers.
2. Understand the terms associated with printers.
3. Understand the use of a variety of computer software programs for the office, including word processing, databases, and spreadsheets.

▼ INTRODUCTION TO COMPUTERS ▼

Computers have become an integral part of the everyday life of the office employee. In addition to word processing, computers are used in the office for record keeping, budgeting, retrieval and analysis of data, daily calendars, messages, and many other tasks. It is almost impossible to function in today's modern offices without the ability to operate computer equipment. Proficiency in computers requires hands-on experience with specific equipment. In this chapter we present general computer terminology and concepts and introduce some computer programs commonly used in the office. Many schools offer courses in specific computer programs where students acquire in-depth information and learn procedures about these and other programs.

The terms *hardware* and *software* are often used when discussing computers. Computer *hardware* is the physical equipment that makes up a computer system. The computer hardware, however, will not operate unless the equipment is used with *software*. The software consists of various *programs* (the instructions) that tell the computer equipment what to do. Different software programs permit the same hardware to perform numerous functions, such as word processing, database management, and accounting.

▼ HARDWARE ▼

Hardware is the physical part of a computer system and consists of several parts. While each computer system is different, a typical computer system may include a central processing unit (CPU), keyboard, monitor, disk drives, CD drive, modem, and printer. The CPU, disk drives, CD, and modem are usually contained within a single computer case. The monitor, keyboard, and printer are usually each separate items which are connected to the computer by a cable. Many computers are also connected to *peripheral* devices such as scanners and audio speakers.

CPU

The *central processing unit* (CPU) is the part of the computer that interprets the software, performs calculations, and sends instructions to the other hardware in the system. The CPU

FIGURE 5-1   Computers in an Office Setting. (Courtesy of International Business Machines Corporation. Unauthorized use not permitted.)

is actually a small silicon *computer chip*. The type of computer chip used determines the capabilities and speed of a computer. The speed of a computer is based on the number of calculations it can do each second. A computer rated at 200 MHz will perform about twice as many calculations per second as one rated at 100 MHz. (*MHz* stands for *megahertz* and is used to indicate the speed of the computer processor.) Next to the CPU in the computer case are other computer chips, which serve as the computer's memory. These chips are called *RAM*, for *random access memory*. A typical computer has 16 MB, 32 MB, or 64 MB of memory. *MB* refers to *megabyte*, which is the unit of measure for computer memory. The computer can store 1 million characters, such as letters or digits, in each MB of memory.

Keyboard

A *keyboard* is the primary input device of the computer system and is used to enter (or keyboard) information into the computer. Computer keyboards are similar to those on a typewriter, with extra keys to assist in operating computer programs. Most computer keyboards have a *number keypad* to the right of the alphabetic keys. This keypad is similar to the keypad on a calculator and speeds the entry of numbers. Special *function keys* may be placed either to the left of or above the alphabetic keys or in both locations. These function keys, usually consisting of 10 or 12 keys, are often simply labeled F1, F2, and so on, and can execute an instruction automatically with a single keystroke. Computer keyboards also have special keys labeled *Alt* and *Control*. The use of the Function, Alt, and Control keys change with each software program. These keys are also used in combination with other keys (such as simultaneously pressing Alt and the letter P) to increase the flexibility of the computer program.

Keyboards are usually not built into the computer case but are connected to it by a long cord. The keyboard can then be placed where it is most comfortable for the operator. Unfortunately, computer keyboards are not fully standardized and may contain from 84 to 103 keys. While the placement of letters and numbers corresponds to the standard typewriter layout, placement of other function and control keys varies widely. Check the placement of all the keys before using a new computer keyboard since manufacturers vary the placement of the specialized keys.

Monitors and Displays

The video screen on the computer is called a *monitor* or *CRT (cathode ray tube)*. This display is similar to a television set and brings text and graphic images to the screen. Most monitors on full-size and portable computers have color displays that generate over 254 colors. Some computer companies build the monitors as part of the computer console, while others permit the selection of a variety of different monitors that are connected to the console by a cable. The minimum useful size for a monitor on a regular computer is about 12 in., and monitors of 15 in. and 17 in. (or even 19 in.) are useful when detailed graphics are required.

Smaller computers such as notebooks or personal digital assistants contain flat panel displays in place of monitors. These displays can range to 14 in. in size and are often in color on the larger notebook computers. On the smaller hand-held computers and personal digital assistants, the displays may show only a few lines of text in monochrome. Some of these flat panel displays are *backlit* to improve the legibility of the display.

Disks and Disk Drives

Computer programs and information can be saved on magnetic disks, tapes, or cassettes. The most common way to store computer programs or information is on magnetic disks, either using *diskettes* or *hard disks*. Diskettes are thin, portable disks and are manufactured in several sizes, the most common being 3 1/2 in. Disks are inserted into a disk drive, and the information on the disk is "read" by the computer. The first floppy disks were 8 in. and 5 1/4 in. and were easily bent, and were, therefore, called *floppy disks*. The common diskette, 3 1/2 in. size, is enclosed in a hard plastic case to give the disk a greater degree of protection.

The size of the disk, the density, and the number of sides used determine the amount of information that can be stored on a floppy disk. Most diskettes now are *double sided*, which permits information storage on both sides. The density, which increases the amount of information that can be stored on a disk, can also vary from *double density* (which records on both sides of a disk) to *high density* (which records twice as much information on each side as a double-density disk). Manufacturers continually develop new systems to increase the storage capacity of computer systems. For example, while the standard 3-1/2 in. diskette can store 1.4 MB of information, there are systems that can store more than 100 MB of information on a single 3-1/2 in.diskette or on a tape cartridge. The type of disk drive or tape cartridge system connected to the computer determines the size and type of disks or cartridges that can be used with that system.

Diskettes record information *magnetically*, and the information on the disk is read by tiny *heads* in the disk drive. All diskettes are *very* fragile, even the 3-1/2 in. diskettes, which are encased in plastic. They can easily be damaged and the information stored on them will be destroyed. It is much easier to take care of a diskette than to try to recreate all the information it contains! If a diskette is partially damaged, it may be possible to retrieve some lost information using special programs. However, retrieving "lost" information is always difficult and often impossible.

Proper care of diskettes

1. Keep dirt, dust, and oil away from a diskette.
2. Coffee or soft drinks spilled on a diskette may damage the disk so that it cannot be read by the disk drive.
3. Keep diskettes away from magnets, which can destroy the information recorded.
4. Disk drives have a small light to indicate when the drive is in use. Do not remove a diskette from the disk drive when the light is on.
5. Make backup copies of all material stored on diskettes.
6. Store diskettes at room temperature, keeping them away from extremes of hot and cold.
7. When mailing computer diskettes, place them in specially designed disk mailers.

The storage capacity of any diskette is limited and modern computer programs are too large to fit on a single diskette. When working with a computer, it is very inconvenient to change or *swap disks* constantly. Diskettes are therefore used for small files. Diskettes are convenient for transferring small files from one computer to another, or for storing backup copies of data for safekeeping.

Hard Drives, Tapes, and Cartridges

The main memory storage devices on computers are *hard disks*. A hard disk is a magnetic storage device with a much greater storage capacity than that of a floppy disk. A hard disk can store many programs and hundreds of pages of text, and it is usually built into the computer. The computer can quickly retrieve information from any part of the hard disk. As the size of computer programs have expanded, the amount of hard disk storage found on computers has greatly increased. A hard disk commonly contains hundreds of MB of memory, and larger hard disks can store several billion characters of memory. (A billion characters of memory is referred to as a *gigabyte, GB*.)

Tapes and cartridges are also used to store data. Accessing information on a tape or cartridge drive is slow compared with hard disk drives. Tapes and cartridges are usually used on external disk drives to copy and store all the data from a hard disk as a *backup* in case the hard disk is damaged.

CD Drives

Diskettes and hard disks are *magnetic* disks that can easily record information from a keyboard or other input device. A *CD (compact disk)* is a storage system that saves information *optically*. CD computer disks are similar to CD audio disks, and it is possible to play a standard audio CD on a computer CD drive. However, the benefit of a computer CD is that instead of just recording music, they can record sound, video, and thousand of pieces of computer information. A computer CD disk can store an encyclopedia's worth of information on a single disk. Many computer programs are now distributed on CDs because of the large amount of information contained in the program. A CD that contains programs or large reference databases and is meant only to be read is called a *CD-ROM* (compact disk—read only memory). It is also possible to create a computer CD in the office for storage of large amounts of information. Using a *recordable CD* (CD-R) permits the storage of as much as 450 diskettes on a single CD. A CD-R can only be recorded once. Once the information is written on a CD-R, it is used as a CD-ROM and the information is protected from changes. Another type of CD that can be created in the office is a *rewritable CD* (CD-RW), which can be rewritten many times like a regular computer diskette.

Modems

Modems permit a computer to interconnect to other computers over regular phone lines or to the Internet. A modem is a small device, usually inside the computer console, although it can be a separate box connected to the computer by cable, which allows a computer to talk to other computers. Modems are available in different speeds, from 14.4 to 56 *kbps* [*kbps* stands for *kilobits per second* (1 kilobit is 1,000 bits of information)]. The faster the modem, the quicker information is transferred from one computer to another. High-speed connections are possible using other technologies, such as cable modems, ISDN or DSL telephone lines, and T-1 fiber communications.

Audio Speakers

Computers that are used for *multimedia* are often connected to external audio speakers. While full-size computers may have small built-in speakers, external audio systems are often used to provide the volume and sound quality required in systems where audio and video are important parts of the computer experience. External speakers can range from small inexpensive speaker boxes to full stereo systems.

Scanners

A scanner is an input device that reads printed or graphic material, including photographs, prepared art, and business logos and converts the material into a computer file. The file can then be stored and processed. Using a scanner, a photograph can be *scanned* into a computer and then inserted in a document or report. A page of text can be scanned into a computer rather than having to be entered by the keyboard. If the computer has *optical character recognition* (OCR) software, the text can then be inserted into a word-processing package for editing. Some electronic scanners are so small that they can be held in one hand.

Printers

A *printer* is a primary *output* device of the computer. A printer provides the hard copy—a single-page letter or a multipage report—that can be distributed throughout an office or around the world. These printed copies can be in English or in many foreign languages. Printers can also create transparencies for overhead projectors, detailed graphs, and complex engineering drawings. Printers with a variety of capabilities are available in many price ranges to serve a variety of needs. Printers can use different widths and types of paper. Printers that use *single-sheet-feed* paper can use special paper such as letterheads and can change paper size or color quickly.

Listed below are two types of printers commonly used in offices.

- A *laser printer* uses a beam of light to form images on paper. Laser printers are high-quality printers, but they are expensive. Laser printers can reproduce high-quality graphics and letter-quality documents. Since a laser printer is not limited by a typing element or a specific number of dots, it can produce a wide variety of images. A laser printer can easily print different typefaces and different sizes of print. A laser printer can print letters sideways on paper, called *landscape printing*, in addition to regular printing, which is called *portrait printing*. Laser printers can print detailed graphics and are used to print documents created with desktop publishing programs. Some laser printers can print in color as well as black and white.

- An *ink-jet printer* sprays the ink onto paper to form letters and characters. Ink-jet printers have many of the same capabilities as laser printers but are lower in cost, although the quality of the printing is not as exact as that of laser printers. Ink-jet printers are often used for color printing since the cost per page is so much less than that for laser color printers.

Hardware Operating Systems

The parts of the computer—the monitor, CPU, and disk drives—are no smarter than a toaster unless there is an *operating system* that connects them and allows them to work. The operating system is a specialized type of software that directs information between each of the pieces of hardware and the CPU. The operating system is a piece of software placed on a computer by the manufacturer, and the operating system on a hard disk drive is usually automatically *run (booted)* when the computer is turned on. Different computers use different operating systems. Most standard home computers and many office computers use an operating system that is compatible with the IBM PC system. The IBM PC system originally used the Microsoft DOS (disk operating system) program as its operating system. This operating system has evolved into Windows 95, Windows 98, and Windows NT. Other operating systems in use include IBM's Operating System/2 (OS/2), which is found on Microsoft-compatible computers, and Unix, which is used on more powerful workstations. The Apple MacIntosh series of computers uses an operating system referred to as OS, such as OS 8. While programs written for one computer operating system often cannot be used with another computer system, software is available that can be used with several types of computer operating systems. Many programs now available on CD can run on both PC and Apple systems.

As electronics become smaller and cheaper, a wide variety of specialized computer and computerlike devices have been developed to serve the needs and wants of the public. A computer no longer needs to sit on a desk top with a monitor, CPU, and hard and/or floppy disks. There are now a whole range of computers, many designed to perform a specific function or to attract the user by being smaller than comparable units. Some companies build computers when they have received an order with the specific requirements of the individual purchaser.

In addition to the "standard" desktop computer, there are several categories that are commonly used to distinguish the varieties of computers available. Unfortunately, what one person may call a laptop computer may be referred to by another person as a notebook computer. The distinction between computer types has blurred and many features usually found on larger computers are often found on smaller models, especially as electronics become smaller each year.

Network PCs

Network PCs are computers that are designed to connect to a network and use the network for memory, disk storage, and processor power. Network computers may be designed to work with a local area network (LAN), which links computers within an office, or to access the Internet. With a network computer, many users are connected to the network and depend on the power of the network instead of using the power of their own computer. These computers receive most of their data from the network and may not have diskettes or a hard disk drive. The amount of memory may be limited since most of the data processing is done via the network. The main advantage of network PCs is that they are cheaper to purchase and maintain than a full desktop computer for each employee. Since they are more limited in function than a full computer, they may also be easier to operate than a full computer.

Notebook Computers

Notebook computers combine the CPU, monitor, and disk drive into a single, small, portable unit. The miniaturization made possible by modern electronics provides a full computer system in a single case the size of a briefcase. Notebook computers may weigh

FIGURE 5-2   A Notebook Computer. (Courtesy of International Business Machines Corporation. Unauthorized use not permitted.)

less than 10 pounds and include a battery so that the computer can be operated anywhere. Although notebook computers cost more than a comparable full-size computer and may not be as powerful as the latest office computer, their portability has made notebook computers very popular. Notebook computers can operate the same software as full-size computers, although some notebooks use special disk drives or software, due to size and weight limitations.

Today, many business travelers carry a notebook or laptop computer when they travel. The computer's battery should always be charged before leaving on a trip. It is always wise to take an extra battery, an extra telephone cord, an electrical adapter to convert a three-hole to a two-hole plug, a good-quality cushioned carrying case, and an extra electrical extension cord. Also, always carry extra diskettes and an emergency startup disk when traveling with the notebook. Unfortunately, these extra items add considerable weight to the computer system.

While on the trip, the traveler can check E-mail and complete job assignments. Most hotels that are frequented by the business traveler have updated their wiring systems to accommodate computers. Business hotels also have access for their guests to send and receive faxes. If the traveler does not have a computer to check E-mail, there are companies that for a fee will allow the client to send and receive E-mail.

Hand-held Computers and Personal Digital Assistants

As electronics become smaller each year, notebook computers have shrunk and are now small enough to fit in the palm of a hand. These computers are about 6 x 4 x 1 in. in size. The size of the computer is limited by the size of the keys. The keyboard on these computers are small and barely usable for touch typing. Palm-top computers usually have no floppy drives or hard disk, but store their information in built-in memory. Some of these small computers have a limited operating system such as Windows CE, which permits them to run smaller versions of regular computer programs and to share information with full-size computers. Some of these electronic devices, sometimes called *personal digital assistants* (PDAs), have no keyboards at all but receive data from keypads or touch screens. Some PDAs are optimized for receiving E-mail, either from a phone connection or by wireless modem.

Electronic Organizers

Electronic organizers are so small and light they often fit into a coat pocket or purse and can be carried throughout the day. Because they are so small, they can only store a limited

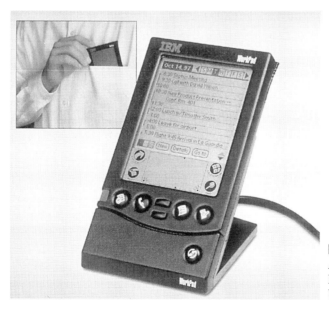

FIGURE 5-3 A Personal Digital Assistant. (Courtesy of International Business Machines Corporation. Unauthorized use not permitted.)

amount of information but are useful to keep schedules, mailing lists, or notes. Their main strength is replacing a pocket calendar or scheduler since information can be organized, searched alphabetically, searched by date, and so on. The screens on electronic organizers display only a few lines of text and the keyboards are so small that it is often difficult to keyboard quickly on them. Some electronic organizers have no keyboards at all and use a touch-sensitive screen. There is no standard type of electronic organizer or operating system. Some electronic organizers are designed to perform specific functions such as taking orders.

Some electronic organizers have the ability to exchange information with regular computers. This is especially useful so that information can be easily downloaded from a regular computer to the organizer. You may be asked to keep your executive's schedule on a computer program, which can be transferred to the organizer so that the executive can have an updated schedule when going to a meeting or on a trip.

▼ SOFTWARE ▼

Computer Programs for the Office

There are variety of programs available to organize and run an office efficiently. Commercial programs can be purchased from a computer store and programs can be written by a computer programmer to meet the unique needs of a particular office. The needs of an office will determine the computer programs used. For example, a travel office will use a reservation program to book airline flights, an auto-parts store will use an inventory program to aid in the reorder of sold parts, or a doctor's office will use a scheduling program to schedule patient appointments.

There are, however, several types of computer programs that are commonly used to support the basic functions of the office. These programs include: word processing, desktop publishing, database management, spreadsheets, graphics, electronic calendars, scanning software, and Internet browsers.

Word Processing in a Modern Office

The marriage between information and electronic technology has had a significant impact on the procedures of the modern office. The major activity of most offices is the processing of information: ideas, data, and policies expressed in words or numbers. Modern offices have invested in a wide variety of electronic technology designed to speed the processing of words so that information can be prepared, analyzed, distributed, and stored rapidly and efficiently.

Perhaps the most common computer program used in offices is word-processing software. Today's word-processing software does more than just assist the office worker in the preparation of reports and letters. Word processing includes many features that increase the productiveness of the office worker and enhance the quality of the finished product. These features include spelling checkers, thesauruses, graphic packages, and clip art. Many word-processing packages also have the ability to send faxes or E-mail, provide access to the Internet, and create Internet Web pages.

Word-processing application packages contain templates, which are a set of predefined styles for word-processing projects. Most packages have templates for letters, reports, memos, newsletters, calendars, faxes, envelopes, and many additional styles.

Desktop Publishing

Word-processing programs provide the office with the ability to design and produce its own newsletters, brochures, forms, and manuals. The software can be used by people who possess little artistic ability or design background to produce a professional-quality product. Many word-processing software programs permit the operator to perform basic desktop publishing without the need for specialized software. Popular word-processing programs such as Microsoft Word and WordPerfect provide for the use of numerous type styles and type sizes. Charts, graphs, drawings, and pictures can be included in documents. Text can be printed in columns or around illustrations. A picture can be inserted and placed anywhere on a page with the same ease as moving a paragraph. These features are programmed into the software. The use of a mouse is required to take full advantage of desktop publishing programs.

Additional desktop publishing programs are available with advanced or specialized features. Some programs are available for designing office forms, while others concentrate on designing banners or cards. More complex software programs are used for designing newsletters and brochures. The printing of brochures, forms, or other material developed with desktop publishing programs usually requires the use of laser jet printers, which can reproduce the full graphics capability of the program. Two commonly used desktop publishing packages are Adobe PageMaker and Microsoft Publisher.

Integrated Software

Word-processing software often forms the core of a group of integrated software packages, which becomes a single *suite*. For example, a word-processing program may be linked with a spreadsheet, database, scheduler, presentation program, and communications program. Data from the database can be moved to the spreadsheet easily, and then it can be included in a document written on the word processor. Although many programs permit data to be incorporated from other programs, it can be done more easily in an integrated program. Integrated software uses common keystroke commands in all parts of the program, thus making the programs easier to learn. Examples of integrated suites are Microsoft Office, Corel PerfectOffice, and Lotus Suite.

Database Management

Before computers came into the modern office, employees kept handwritten records for each customer, employee, project, or inventory. All of the records for students in a college, for example, contained the same type of data: name, address, student ID number, department, and major. Separate folders were kept with specific information about each student. The folders were organized either by student name or student ID number so that the staff could update the information after a student registered for a class, paid tuition, and received a grade.

In today's office, a computerized file using a database management program would be used instead of handwritten records. In addition to student records, databases can be used for a wide variety of functions where consistent information is required for a large number of items, including personnel, inventory, and sales records.

The value of database management programs is their ability to *store* and *organize* large amounts of data. A handwritten file folder can be organized in only one way. The data in a database management system, however, can be organized and sorted in many different ways. The computer can print the data into reports or process the data for individual client records.

The data in a database program are collected into *fields*, each field containing one piece of information. Different fields about a college student could contain information such as last name, first name, college identification number, number of credit hours earned, date of enrollment in school, and so on. The collection of fields for each student would be called a *record*. All of the student records would be considered a *file*.

Entering information into the records can be done at any time using a *data-entry screen*. These screens are written to ask for the specific information required for the file and they can be designed to minimize operator errors. For example, the attempted entry of the date of February 30 would not be accepted if the data-entry screen were programmed to accept only valid calendar dates in the format 02/20/2001.

After data entry, the information in the file can be sorted by several fields, selected, analyzed, summarized, and printed into reports. A variety of reports can be programmed in advance and printed whenever required. A college, for example, can use the database to review the progress of all students who entered school in a specific year by retrieving such information as which department students are enrolled in, how many are still enrolled, and how many credit hours they have earned toward graduation. A report of this nature can be prepared in a matter of minutes using a computer, while the same report prepared from handwritten records could take days to prepare.

One of the most powerful aspects of database management systems is the ability to link the data from more than one file. If two databases have a field with identical information, such as a student identification number, they can be linked and new databases can be created. Reports can be created from the new database without having to reenter information into the computer.

Access, dBASE, and FoxPro are examples of database management programs. Some widely used database programs have the ability to create custom menus, screens, and reports for use by operators who do not have a knowledge of the database program itself. Many employees will use a *personnel system* or an *inventory system* on a computer when they are actually using a *database management system* where the screens have been customized for use by a specific office.

Spreadsheets

Computer spreadsheet programs are useful to persons working with numbers. Spreadsheets are constructed of grids consisting of horizontal *rows* and vertical *columns*. A single spreadsheet can consist of hundreds of rows and columns. A number can be inserted at the intersection of the row and column, this location is called a *cell*. Numbers in any cell can be added, subtracted, multiplied, or divided by any other number, or cell, on the spreadsheet. Each cell can also represent a complex mathematical formula.

Companies use spreadsheets to analyze financial data. The main advantage of a spreadsheet is the ability to change any number and have that change reflected automatically in all of the other numbers or formulas on the spreadsheet. This feature of spreadsheets is used to consider "what if," and it is very useful in making projections. In seconds, an operator can see the affect of changing a single number or of changing a series of numbers. Then a decision can be made to accept the "what if" or not to accept it. Spreadsheets are, therefore, very useful in preparing budgets and sales projections.

Spreadsheets are usually printed with columns of text and numbers, but many spreadsheets can display the data in the form of graphs as well. Some spreadsheets can exchange information with word-processing software so that the information can be incorporated in the text of another document, such as an annual report or in a presentation. Spreadsheets can be formatted to accept changes in fonts, point size, row height, and column widths. Clip art may be inserted and borders and shading may be added to enhance the appearance of a presentation. Excel and Lotus 1-2-3 are two examples of the many spreadsheets available.

Graphics

The expanding graphics capabilities of computers can be used in many ways. Many word-processing programs can insert graphics into text; and of course, desktop publishing can make use of a wide variety of graphic images. There are also programs available that produce only graphic material rather than dealing with text. The imaginative use of graphics can make reports and other printed materials more interesting.

Clip Art

Some graphics or desktop publishing packages come with clip art. Clip art consists of drawings or graphic symbols that have been placed in a computer file on a disk. Specific items of art can be "clipped" from the disk and inserted into a project. Clip art can usually be changed in size or modified by the user.

Drawing and Charting Software

There are many software programs available that can aid people with little artistic ability to prepare attractive graphic material. With the appropriate software, anyone can draw perfect circles, squares, and straight lines. Charting software automatically prepares professional-looking charts in a matter of minutes.

Computer-Aided Design

Computer-aided design (CAD) allows a designer to see a design on the screen in three dimensions before it is produced. CAD is a quick way to fully visualize a design and often reduces the need to build test products.

Presentation Software

Speakers at conferences or meetings often use presentation software to prepare visuals to highlight the main points of their speech. With presentation software, graphics, text, and artwork can be combined for display to large groups using slides and overhead transparencies. By linking a notebook computer to a projection system, a presentation can be displayed directly from the computer. Sound and moving video can be added to the text and graphic material to enhance the presentation. Computer software can create a powerful presentation that an audience will remember after the meeting is long over.

Scanning Software

Specialized software is required to use *scanning hardware*. This software allows the particular items to be scanned. Scanning software may permit each image scanned to be given a name so that it may be filed and easily retrieved. A page scanned into a computer will usually be stored as a single image. For text, however, it is often more useful if the resulting computer file can be edited. By using *optical character recognition* (OCR) software, the computer will be able to recognize each letter in a document so that it can be edited by word-processing software. OCR software is not perfect and the document must be checked by an operator before being accepted for further editing.

Project Management

Project management software is used to develop timetables for completing projects. With project management software, a project is broken down into many steps. Each step is assigned an amount of time to be completed. Using project management software, time lines can be created for a project. It then is easy to determine the effect of a delay in any of the steps of the project on the overall completion of the project. Project management software is often used to plan complex projects which require the efforts of many people to complete.

The Internet and Internet Browsers

The Internet is one of the most significant developments in computers in recent years. The Internet links millions of computers around the world and permits easy exchange of information. This information can include graphics, pictures, sound recording, voice, and video as well as simple text. Most people use a part of the Internet referred to as the *World Wide Web* (or more simply, the *Web*). The Web uses a special computer language called *HTML (HyperText Markup Language)* for display of graphics and text. Internet browser software is used to connect to the Internet, search for information in HTML on the network, and download the results to the user's computer. The two most common Internet browser software are Microsoft Explorer and Netscape Navigator.

Web Development Software

Many people and offices can develop their own Web pages using software designed to write easily in HTML. Although special development software is available, many word processing and presentation programs are available that will automatically convert a file into HTML for posting on the Web. With this software, literally everyone can become a worldwide publisher by posting their own information on the Web.

Calendars, Reminders, and Scratchpads

Computerized calendars and appointment and reminder systems can be used on one computer or several computers connected to a network. Many of these programs are *memory resident*, in that they are always available in memory and can be placed in a window over another program by executing two keystrokes. These programs may also serve as an electronic scratchpad, and they may include a calculator. All information entered into these systems can be saved in computer files for later use. These programs can be purchased as separate computer packages and are included as features in integrated suites of software. Information in calendar and reminder programs can often be transferred to notebook computers, palm-top computers, and PDAs so that they are available while the employee is outside the office.

Antivirus Programs

A *virus* is an extremely dangerous computer program designed to damage your computer files. Viruses can destroy computer data or even erase all data on a hard disk. Viruses can be received from an E-mail message, a shared diskette, or can be downloaded from a World Wide Web site. It is important to use an *antivirus program* to safeguard your computer. An antivirus program should be used to check a diskette and hard drive to determine if it contains a virus. If a virus is detected, the antivirus program will remove the virus from the computer before it causes damage.

Computerized Payroll

Computer software packages maintain payroll records. Each employee's data—hourly rate, number of hours worked, tax deductions, medical deductions, and other payroll deductions—are inputted into the computer so that the payroll can be processed. Using computer software decreases the amount of time required to complete the payroll and increases its accuracy.

▼ ADDITIONAL COMPUTER TERMS ▼

It is essential for you to understand the following terms if you are going to work with computers.

- *Artificial intelligence.* Technologies that try to achieve humanlike attributes of intelligence such as reasoning.
- *Backup.* A duplicate of information or a program that is saved on storage media in case the original is damaged. Backups may be placed on diskettes for storage away from the computer. A backup may also be made on a hard disk to save the original data before making changes in a document. Since copying all files for all employees to floppy disks takes time and could become a storage nightmare, companies use a tape backup system. A tape backup system is an efficient and reasonably priced method to backup files on the hard drive. There are three types of backups: *total, modified files only,* and *selective files.* A *total backup* backs up the entire hard drive to a tape. A *modified files only backup* backs up only those files that have been changed since the last backup was done. A *selective backup* backs up only those files that are selected. Some systems make backup copies automatically in the middle of the night, while others do the backup at the end of the day.
- *Bar code.* A series of spaces and lines that the computer translates into a number. Bar codes are often used for inventory control.
- *BBS.* An electronic *bulletin board system* that maintains a centralized collection of information as electronic messages. Your office may maintain a BBS to share information with customers.
- *Bit.* A single binary digit. Computers store all information as the binary digits "0" or "1." Eight *bits* of memory are called a *byte.*

FIGURE 5-4 Scanning a Bar Code. (Courtesy of International Business Machines Corporation. Unauthorized use not permitted.)

- *Boot.* To start a computer and load a program. A "cold" or "hard" boot is performed by turning the computer on. A "warm" or "soft" boot, which restarts the operating system after the computer is on, is accomplished by pressing several keys, such as Control, Alt, and Delete, at the same time.
- *Byte.* Eight bits of memory are necessary to represent a single letter, number, or other computer character. Bytes are used as a measurement of memory storage. A *kilobyte* is 1,024 bytes, a *megabyte* is 1 million bytes, and a *gigabyte* is 1 billion bytes.
- *Cache memory.* Consists of high-speed memory chips that hold the most frequently used data and instructions. By having this information on hand, the computer saves the time required to access the data on a hard disk.
- *Communications satellite.* A satellite that acts as a relay station for an earth station by receiving data, amplifying it, and retransmitting it to another earth station. Using communications satellites, computer networks can reach locations unserved by regular phone lines or cables.
- *Copy protect.* A term that can refer to a program or a diskette. Some computer *programs* are copy protected, which means that they cannot be copied to another disk. A diskette can also be copy protected to prevent someone from writing information on it. Diskettes usually have a series of notches in their corners. To write information on a diskette, a standard diskette usually has an open notch near its bottom, right corner, and a closed notch at the lower left corner. These diskettes can be copy protected to guard against accidental overwriting by sliding a tab down on the left notch of the diskette to open the notch. (The other notch will not have a sliding tab.) You cannot copy information to a disk with both notches open. Program diskettes often do not have any notches on the bottom, which protects them from being accidentally overwritten.
- *Cursor.* A highlighted area on the monitor that marks the place where data entry will begin.

Additional Computer Terms   **91**

- *Digital camera.* A camera that uses silicon chips, not traditional film, to record images. A digital camera, with appropriate software, allows the user to display a photograph on the computer screen, edit it, and print it on a color printer.
- *Documentation.* An instruction manual explaining computer hardware or software.
- *Downtime.* Time when the computer is not working. It can be scheduled (for example, for maintenance) or unscheduled (computer problems).
- *Fiber optic cable.* A transmission medium that transmits data as pulses of light. A LAN or Internet connection using a fiber optic cable can exchange data much faster than one using phone lines or coaxial cable.
- *File server.* A computer that manages a LAN. Files servers have enough memory and speed to store programs for quick access by many computer users.
- *Gateway.* An item of computer hardware that connects a LAN to outside computer systems.
- *Graphical user interface (GUI).* Uses *icons,* which are small stamp-size pictures, to represent programs, files, or operations. Icons are used in many Windows and Apple computer programs.
- *Groupware.* Software that helps several users to work together on projects and share information.
- *Home page.* The screen that welcomes a user to a Web site and often has text and/or graphics.
- *HTML (HyperText Markup Language).* A specialized method of creating Web pages that allows a Web document to be read by any computer that has HTML software.
- *Image processing system.* Uses scanners to capture and electronically file an exact copy of a document. In addition to recording the document, these systems can record pertinent information about the document—for example, date of processing or handwritten notations attached to the document.
- *Integrated services digital network (ISDN).* A technology that allows images, voice, and data to be transmitted simultaneously as digital signals over regular telephone lines.
- *Internet.* The worldwide group of connected networks that allows public access to information on thousands of subjects. The user may view, print, or save the information. Business research may be conducted quickly and efficiently without leaving the office.
- *Internet relay chat (IRC).* Chatting or holding a live conversation on the Internet by keyboarding messages while reading responses on the screen. This service allows the user to have a real-time written conversation on the Internet. Persons in different locations converse with each other by the use of an Internet relay chat program. One advantage of an internet relay chat is immediate feedback.
- *Intranet.* An internal network that uses Internet and Web technologies.
- *Java.* A new object-oriented programming language designed specifically for use on the World Wide Web.
- *License.* There are regulations concerning the use of computer software. When someone purchases commercial computer software, the purchaser is only authorized, or *licensed*, to use that software. The purchaser cannot change the software or copy the software without permission from the copyright owner. Software *piracy*, which is the illegal copying of software, is a concern in the office. Most software packages provide a license for one station only. Instead of purchasing an individual package for each user, offices may purchase a *site license*, which allows a specified number of computers to use the same software package.
- *Local area network (LAN).* A communications network that connects two or more computers in a limited geographic area. LAN's are usually contained within a single building but can connect computers in different buildings if they are close together. The LAN allows each computer on the network to share hardware, software, and

information resources. For example, a client file may be stored on the *file server* and everyone in the office may access the file. See also *MAN* and *WAN*.

- *Mapping software.* Consists of computer software that uses graphics, database management, and spreadsheet features to display data geographically. Information can be presented in a map to display differences in income, education, or accident levels by using mapping software.
- *Metropolitan area networks (MANs).* Exchanges that are located in large metropolitan areas that carry Internet communications traffic. A MAN is used to transfer data from one provider to another. See also *Local area network* and *Wide area network*.
- *Modem.* A device that changes the computer's digital pulses (0's and 1's) into analog signals so computer information can be sent over telephone lines. A modem can be used as both an input and an output device.
- *Mouse.* A pointing device that allows the operator to move the cursor and input commands without using the keyboard. A small box about 2 x 3 in. is rolled on a tabletop to move the cursor around the computer monitor.
- *Multimedia.* The combining of text, graphics, sound, and video into one project.
- *Network.* A group of computers that are connected electronically so that they can communicate with each other.
- *Network printer.* A printer that is connected to a local area network and has many users printing on it.
- *Online service.* A business that provides people and businesses with a connection to the Internet. Some of the companies providing this service to paying subscribers are the Microsoft Network, America Online, Prodigy, Dow Jones News Retrieval, and CompuServe. Other online services provide free business news, travel information, daily news, weather, and information on a multitude of topics. These services can provide valuable information to the office employee.
- *PC fax.* A computer that has the capabilities of a fax machine. The computer must be turned on to receive a fax.
- *Personal information management software (PIM).* Helps to keep track of personal information such as messages, appointments, calendars, note pads, and so on.
- *Plotter.* A printing device used to produce graphics using a moving pen.
- *Presentation monitors.* Monitors 25 to 36 in. in size, used when making presentations to midsize groups.
- *Random access memory (RAM).* The *working memory* of a computer that is used to store programs temporarily. When the computer is turned off, the information in RAM is lost.
- *Read-only memory (ROM).* *Internal memory* that is built into the hardware and cannot be changed by the operator. When the computer is turned off, the information in ROM is not lost.
- *Search engines.* Computer programs on the Web that help users search for information. After the user enters a word or phrase, a search engine will review thousands of computer sites to find sites that may contain the type of information requested. If the user is too general when requesting information from a search engine, the results may be thousands of possible sites that may contain the requested information.
- *Shareware.* Software programs that are distributed at little or no charge, often by user groups. The programs can be distributed online, on diskette, and by bulletin board systems. The user is frequently asked to pay for a shareware program after receiving the program. Shareware programs often mimic features of popular commercial software, but the quality of the program is generally unknown.
- *Trackball.* A pointing device that performs the same function as a computer mouse. Since notebook computers are not used on a desktop, there is often no surface on which to place a mouse to move the cursor. A trackball is a like a large marble located near the notebook computer's keyboard. The top of the ball is rotated by a finger, which moves the cursor on the screen.

SITE NAME	TYPE OF INFORMATION	ADDRESS
Congressional Quarterly	Congressional information	www.cq.com
C-SPAN	C-SPAN	www.c-span.org
Federal Statistics	Federal statistics	www.fedstats.gov
Hewlett-Packard	Information about Hewlett-Packard	www.hp.com/
Internet Travel Network	Assistance in buying airline tickets	www.itn.net/itn
Library of Congress	Library of Congress	www.loc.gov
Long Business and Economic Library, U.C. Berkeley	Long Business and Economic Library, U.C. Berkeley	http://library.berkeley.edu:80/BUSI
The Wall Street Journal	*The Wall Street Journal*	www.wsj.com
The New York Times	Electronic version of each day's edition of *The New York Times*	http://nytimes.com
TravelWeb	Assistance with hotel reservations	www.travelweb.com
United States Postal Service	ZIP code information	www.usps.gov/ncsc/lookups/ lookup_zip+4.html
World Wide Web Consortium	Information about the World Wide Web	www.w3.org/pub/www/

FIGURE 5-5 Typical World Wide Web Sites.

- *Touch screen monitors.* Permit data or requests to be entered into the computer by touching the screen instead of using the keyboard. Touch screens, which are often found in public places such as shopping malls and airports, allow the user to obtain information easily. Some personal digital assistants use touch screens to enable the input of data since they are too small to have keyboards.

- *Virtual reality.* A computer-created environment that places the user in the middle of a computer-generated image. A three-dimensional electronic game is an example of virtual reality. In this type of game, the user wears special glasses to see the computer-generated environment. Sensors in the game machine record the user's body gestures, and the view of scene changes as the viewer moves. Virtual reality software creates a three-dimensional site that the user can view. Looking at the proposed results of a remodeling or construction project is an example of virtual reality.

- *Voice recognition software.* Provides a way to enter information into a computer directly from spoken words. Using a small microphone, the computer converts spoken words into digital information that can be entered into a word-processing package or other office software.

- *Web addresses.* Each computer on the World Wide Web has a unique address so that it can be accessed by other computers. Many addresses begin with www and the parts of the address are separated by periods. Web addresses typically end with designators that indicate the type of organization sponsoring the computer site. Typical designators are

.com for commercial organizations, *.edu* for educational institutions, *.org* for nonprofit organizations, *.gov* for governmental agencies, and *.net* for networks.

- *Wide area network (WAN).* A communications network that covers a large geographical area. These networks use satellites, microwaves, and fiber-optic cables to interconnect computers across the country or around the world.

- *World Wide Web (WWW).* The World Wide Web (often simply call the *Web*) is a part of the Internet that uses computers, which are Web servers, to store files called Web pages. A person seeking information locates an appropriate Web page. Each Web page has a special code, a *uniform resource locator* (URL), which gives the address or location of the Web site or page. Some typical Web addresses are listed in Figure 5-5.

▼ THE PAPERLESS OFFICE ▼

Imagine an office where everyone in the office is linked via a computer network. All information is received electronically directly into a computer and work is done on documents in the computer. Computers are used to rearrange information using word processing, spreadsheets, database, presentation, scheduling, graphic design, and a variety of other programs into required reports. These documents are edited on the computer and sent directly to users over the office local area network. People read documents on their computer screen and respond via E-mail. Documents are stored in computer files. The use of computers, in this vision, results in the "paperless office."

Unfortunately, although computers have become universal in offices and the power of computer programs has multiplied, the result has not been the paperless office. Indeed, the ability of computers to churn out documents has in many respects resulted in more paper, not less. The ability to revise documents easily with word-processing software often results in more time and paper spent in editing documents. The usefulness of databases to sort data into a report often results in more requests to sort the data a little differently than before. Printing a report on a computer laser printer is no more difficult for 10 copies than for 5 copies and takes just a few more minutes. While many offices have made great strides in using computers, the paperless office has not arrived.

CHAPTER REVIEW

1. Define hardware and software.
2. Explain the differences between a hard drive and a diskette.
3. Describe printers.
4. Define the following computer terms:
   a. *Boot*
   b. *Copy protect*
   c. *Modem*
   d. *Mouse*
   e. *RAM*
   f. *ROM*
5. Explain the advantages of desktop publishing.
6. What is the purpose of a database management program?
7. Explain the "what if" feature of a spreadsheet.
8. List six types of computer software used in an office.
9. What is an antivirus program?
10. Explain six computer terms listed in the text.

1. Read an article about the features of the newest version of any popular word-processing program. Prepare an oral and written summary of the article.

2. Survey several computer magazines and list the names of database management programs, word-processing programs, and spreadsheets advertised or discussed.

3. Read the advertisements in three computer magazines and compare the price of three word-processing packages.

4. Ask a friend who works in an office which word processing, spreadsheet, and database management packages are used in the office. Write a report describing the features they like and the features they dislike.

5. Go to a computer store and see what electronic calendar programs they carry. Write a short report about the features of the various programs.

PROJECTS

Project 9

Keyboard the following letter and make all decisions concerning the letter style. Supply any additional information necessary. The letter is from Van Quieret, President of Russell Corporation. Send this letter to Phyllis Maller with a copy to Daniel Kinsley, Meeting Coordinator. Ms. Maller's address is 324 Dixie Street, Moscow, ID 83843; and Mr. Kinsley's address is 8912 Columbia Blvd., Tucson, AZ 85701.

There will be a stockholders' meeting on Monday, June 4, in my office, which is in the Dalton Building, 2004 K Street, NW, Washington, DC.

We would like all stockholders to be present as there will be a discussion of changes in the bylaws. After the discussion, a vote will be taken on the proposed new bylaws. If you cannot be present, please send your proxy to me prior to the meeting.

In addition to the discussion of the bylaws, we will review the Meadman Report and make a final decision on it. I am enclosing a summary of that report.

I hope to see you on June 4.

Project 10

Keyboard the following letter and make all decisions concerning the letter style. Supply any additional information necessary. Send this letter to the attention of Raymond A. Barron, Truax Corporation, 3859 Plains Drive, Chicago, IL 60627-1057. Include a subject line. The letter is from Denise D. Berlin, Purchasing Manager.

Thank you for the demonstration of your desktop publishing software. Also, I appreciated the specification sheets and computer documents you left with us. They have been helpful in reviewing your product.

If you have any additional information to add to your proposal, please fax it to me immediately.

As I mentioned, we are evaluating several packages. We have a committee already studying the proposals. As soon as a decision is made, I will call you.

HUMAN RELATIONS SKILL DEVELOPMENT

Social Behavior in the Office

Social etiquette is important for your success in the business world. Congratulating supervisors or co-workers on happy occasions and expressing sympathy on sad occasions are part of daily life in the office. Your colleagues will expect you to be able to express your feelings appropriately. Business events may occur outside the office building. You may meet colleagues at a company dinner, at a co-worker's wedding, or at a funeral for a member of a co-worker's family. Away from the office environment, a hug may be a better expression of your feelings than a handshake. However, before you make an outward gesture, always think about how the recipient of the gesture is likely to react.

- Are you knowledgeable about current rules of business and social etiquette?
- At a business dinner, would you know which piece of silverware to use, which plate is your butter plate, and which glass is yours?
- What would you say when you are introduced to your supervisor's spouse at a company dinner?
- How would you express your joy when your manager becomes engaged?
- How would you express your sorrow at the death of a co-worker's mother?

Dealing with an Angry Client

You may need to calm an angry client on the telephone or in person. Identify why the client is angry but do not to react to the anger personally. When you become angry you lose your ability to handle the situation objectively. Once you have determined the reason for the client's anger, encourage the client to discuss the problem even if the client needs to shout to do it. The anger should dissipate as the client discusses the problem. Once the client calms down, a solution to the problem can be discussed.

- Discuss the last instance when you were an irate client or customer.
- What types of business situations make you angry? Why?
- How would you handle an agitated client who had spoken to you in an angry way several times in the past?
- What tone of voice would you use with an irate client?

SITUATIONS

How would you handle each of the following situations?

- You made a mistake and scheduled two appointments at the same time on the same day. Both clients are now waiting to see your supervisor.
- As a supervisor, you must deal with the problem of personal use of the company copy machine. Company regulations prohibit personal use of the photocopier, but employees have been using the machine. While walking past the copy room, you notice Jennifer copying a cookbook. What would you do?
- The refrigerator and coffeepot in the lunchroom have become dirty and no one wants to clean them. As a supervisor, what should you do?

PUNCTUATION REVIEW

Punctuate each of the following sentences.

1. Sue asked when is the PSI meeting
2. Yes I have an account at that bank

3. Ralph asked if we joined the Wellness Program

4. Marcie Ross who prepared the communications has been with the company since March 17 1996

5. I transcribed the affidavit replied Martin

6. The mail which is electronically transferred is available every morning at 6 A.M.

7. Whether you are expanding your computer network system creating new databases or developing new application packages you most continually update your skills

8. We service the geographic areas of U.S. Virgin Islands Puerto Rico and Hawaii

9. On his way to the New York shuttle he shouted call my office for me

10. In managing this project Ms Wingate demonstrated considerable skill and professionalism

11. As you mentioned the duties were not explained

12. Our director Mr Wood attended the University of Rochester

13. Max said I cannot locate the executive director

14. Charlton Corporation is located at 289 West Field Drive Sarasota Florida

15. We offer a flexible reporting service which allows the customer many options

▾6▾
Management of Records: Filing

OBJECTIVES

After studying this chapter, you should be able to:

1. Set up a file drawer and prepare file folders.
2. Understand the concepts of subject and geographic filing.
3. Understand the concepts of electronic filing.
4. Apply alphabetic filing rules to a filing system.

▼ WHY FILE? ▼

Every office receives information, letters, reports, applications, or orders that relate to the business. After these documents are processed, they must be stored in an organized way so that they can be retrieved quickly and easily when they are required. The ability to locate these documents is vital to the efficiency and success of an office. Documents or files that cannot be found when required cause many problems:

- Valuable office time is wasted looking for lost files.
- It is embarrassing to tell clients that their files cannot be found.
- A file that cannot be located may contain valuable information that will require considerable time and expense to reassemble.

▼ FILE CABINETS ▼

File storage facilities have evolved from wood to metal cabinets, and then to a variety of efficient storage units. Two of the most commonly used file storage units in the modern office are vertical file cabinets and lateral file cabinets.

- *Vertical file cabinets* are available in two-, three-, four-, and five-drawer models, with one drawer stacked on top of the other. Each drawer is approximately 28 in. deep and can be pulled forward to its entire length. Vertical cabinets, therefore, must be placed where room is available for a person to work when a drawer is fully extended. Vertical files may be purchased in legal-size widths, for papers 8 1/2 x 14 in. or in letter-size widths, for papers 8 1/2 x 11 in.
- *Lateral file cabinets* are approximately 15 in. deep and from 36 to 42 in. wide. Opening a drawer exposes all files in the drawer at once. Lateral cabinets take up more wall space than vertical files, but they can be used along walkways because of their design. Lateral files are available in models that contain two, three, four, five, or six drawers, and they are available for storage of legal- or letter-size paper.

FIGURE 6-1 A Built-in Movable Filing System.

There are many other styles of file storage units that meet specific needs, such as cabinets for storing microfiche, microfilm, computer paper, and computer disks and tapes. In addition, file storage units can be built into a wall. These storage units include large electrically operated filing systems that move files from top to bottom and manual floor-to-ceiling sliding filing shelves. Small pigeonhole units can also be built into a wall for placement of working files. The styles of filing storage units have changed to meet the requirements of user needs and the new technology.

▼ SETTING UP FILES ▼

File Folders

Before a document can be placed in a file cabinet, a file folder with a label should be prepared. There are a large variety of file folders, labels, and accessories available, each designed for a specific purpose and all intended to simplify the filing process. The most common file folder is made of heavy manila paper and comes with a tab on which to place a label. The tab may extend across the entire top of the folder *(full cut)*, across a third of the folder *(third cut)*, or across a fifth of the folder *(fifth cut)*. The use of third- or fifth-cut folders enables filing personnel to stagger the labels for easy reading or to designate subdivisions of a project. File folders are creased on the bottom so that the folder can expand to hold more paper without blocking the folder label.

Some offices use hanging folders which are suspended from tracks along the sides of the file drawer. Several folders can be placed in the same hanging folder thus aiding in the

FIGURE 6-2 A Pigeonhole Filing System.

grouping of related folders. Other types of folders include plastic file folders, which are good for heavy files, and expanding folders, which are designed with expansion folds at the bottom to accommodate several inches of documents. Also, file folders may contain fasteners to secure papers. Some folders have a fastener in the front for a limited number of pages, while others fasten all the papers in the folder. File folders with internal panels are available so that papers can be grouped together for easy reference.

Folders are available in a multitude of colors, which can aid in the design of the filing system. The use of colored folders can reduce errors and save time when filing or retrieving documents.

Folder Labels

When purchased, adhesive folder labels are attached to a backing sheet. The label should be keyed while it is *still attached to the backing sheet*. Labels are also available which can be printed from a computer. After the label is keyed or printed, it is removed from the backing sheet and quickly placed on the file folder. If a label has a *line of color*, the label should be prepared so that the color is at the top of the label. Color-coded labels are often used as a method of organizing a filing system and are found in a variety of colors, sizes, and shapes.

When keying a folder label for the name of a person, key the last name, then a comma, space, then the first name, space, and then the middle name or initial. Labels for company names are keyed according to the indexing units discussed later in this chapter.

Organizing the File Drawer

An efficient filing system should contain *guides* that organize the contents of the file drawer. The guides direct the eye to the desired file. Guides are made of heavy cardboard or other substantial material. The guides contain captions, which are the filing divisions—that may be chronological, alphabetical, geographical, numerical, or subject. The labeled file folders are then placed in the drawer using the guides and divisions.

File Folder Label	_____
Date Borrowed	_____
Borrower	_____
Department	_____ Telephone Ext. _____
Date Returned	_____

FIGURE 6-3 A Folder Checkout Slip.

A well-organized filing system goes beyond the preparation of file folders and takes into account how the files are used in the office. In some offices, files may be borrowed by employees and not returned. To solve this problem, a *checkout system* should be established for files. When files are borrowed, only *complete folders* should be taken. Individual items *should not be removed* from file folders. A designated employee may be in charge of a file checkout system, or each person who borrows a file may be responsible for completing a checkout slip. A sample checkout slip is shown in Figure 6-3. The checkout slip may be a 3 x 5 in. card kept in a box or a large cardboard sheet placed in the file where the folder was kept. Regardless of the system used, an established procedure should be followed to encourage prompt return of file folders.

Because filing space is usually limited and expensive, inactive or old files should be moved to an *inactive storage area* so that active files are accessible. Files can be moved at a specific time or whenever the file drawers are full. In some offices during the month of January, all files before a specific date are removed to inactive storage so that there is ample room for the new files. Inactive files can be placed in corrugated or plastic storage boxes which are purchased from office supply stores. These boxes are available in legal and letter size.

▼ STORAGE OF DOCUMENT IMAGES ▼

Although most offices store original documents in large filing cabinets, modern office technology can be used to store the image of documents in electronic or photographic form. Storing documents electronically or photographically saves significant space and a copy of a document can be printed easily when a paper copy is required.

Microfilm

Microfilm photographs documents on high-resolution film and stores the information in miniature form. Thousands of pages of documents can be easily photographed on a single piece of microfilm. This process greatly reduces the requirements for storage space. A room full of paper documents can be contained in a single microfilm drawer.

Microfilm is available in several forms:

- *Microfiche* is a 3 x 5 in. sheet of film on which pages are photographed in columns and rows. Each page can be located easily without having to go through all the previous pages.
- *Cassettes, cartridges,* or *reels* of microfilm contain as many as 5,000 pages of copy which are photographed consecutively.
- *Aperture cards* are keypunch cards that have an opening in which a frame of microfilm is mounted.

- *Microfilm jackets* contain clear material sealed together on at least two sides. Inside the jacket are channels where the microfilm can be placed. Individual frames can be inserted easily; consequently, updating of files is a simple task.

Microfilm must be placed in a microfilm reader, which enlarges the image so that it can be read. Many microfilm readers can also print a page from the microfilm.

Computer Storage

Computers are used to store files electronically. As discussed in Chapter 5, documents can be entered into a computer using a scanner. Each page of the document is stored as an image. Computer software treats the documents as through they were stored in a filing cabinet. Documents can be organized in folders, drawers, and cabinets. Electronic notes can be attached to the documents, just as handwritten notes are attached to paper documents.

Electronic storage of document images requires considerable memory and would overwhelm the hard drives of most computers. Copies of documents generated by computers are stored in several ways.

- *CD*—either a CD-ROM or writable CD. Documents can be stored on a CD, read on the computer, and a paper copy printed.
- An *optical disk* stores a large amount of text on a rigid plastic disk about the size of a record. More information can be stored in a smaller area on an optical disk than can be stored on microfilm. Since information stored on an optical disk can be retrieved randomly, it is an efficient method of storing and retrieving.
- *Computer output microfilm* (COM) allows the computer to process data and store it on magnetic tape or on a microfilm recorder. The microfilm recorder converts the data to images and stores it on film. After the film is developed, it is viewed at a microfilm reader.

▼ FILING SYSTEMS ▼

There are five types of filing systems that are commonly used to organize documents for easy retrieval. They are the chronological, subject, geographical, numerical, and alphabetical filing systems. The chronological filing system was discussed in Chapter 1. Rules for consistent filing have been developed by many organizations, but some offices use their own filing procedures instead of standardized rules. Therefore, whenever you are working with a new filing system, review the system carefully before filing or retrieving documents.

Subject Filing

Subject filing is a system where files are arranged by the *topic of the document* rather than the name of a person or company. An example of subject filing is a letter concerning the purchase of the Webster Building. This letter would be filed under the topic, Webster Building. Topics in subject files are arranged alphabetically and filing requires an understanding of how the files are organized. To facilitate locating files, a *cross-referencing system* using an index of subjects is often established.

Geographical Filing

Geographical filing is a system where files are arranged according to geographical location. Businesses that are organized by geographical locations, such as sales districts, often use geographical filing. Files are arranged alphabetically within the geographic divisions.

File drawers are usually established with the main geographical categories as the primary guides. Secondary guides are used for subdivisions. For example, this system would use the state as the primary guide and the city as the secondary guide. The file folder would first list a city name and then a specific client in that city.

Numerical Filing

Numerical filing assigns a number to each company, person, or project. The numerical code is placed on each document to be filed. Numerical files are often used in banking, credit card accounts, and accounts receivable, where each client has a separate account number. The account numbers are a quick way to identify persons who may have similar names. To assist in locating files, a cross-referencing system using a card-file index or computer list of clients and their numeric codes is established.

Alphabetical Filing

Although *alphabetical filing* is the most commonly used filing system, there is no single set of alphabetical rules used by all offices. While some offices use filing rules developed by the Association of Records Managers and Administrators (ARMA), alphabetical rules vary from office to office. As an employee, you should study the filing system used in your office prior to filing documents.

An understanding of the alphabetical system is also required to establish and use subject and geographical filing systems. In this chapter we provide common alphabetical filing rules used in many offices, examples of the filing rules, practice exercises for each rule, and a continuous review of rules learned previously.

The first step when filing is to *index* the name. Indexing means dividing the name of a person, company, or title into separate units.

Filing rules follow alphabetical order. Since "a" comes before "b," "apple" would be filed before "banana."

When filing two names, look at the first letter of each name to determine which would be filed first. If the two first letters of each name are the same, look at the second letters and follow the alphabetical order of the second letters. If the second letters are the same, look at the third letters, and so on. This procedure will determine which name should be filed first.

▼ ALPHABETIC FILING RULES ▼

Rule 1 Simple Personal Names

- When filing personal names, divide the name into the following indexing units.

    Unit 1   last name
    Unit 2   first name
    Unit 3   middle name or initial

Name	Unit 1	Unit 2	Unit 3
Lillian Kay Martin	Martin	Lillian	Kay
Edward Fairfax	Fairfax	Edward	
Stacy Ann Moore	Moore	Stacy	Ann
Kenneth Ted Hardy	Hardy	Kenneth	Ted

- After determining the indexing units, alphabetize the names according to unit 1. The group of names above would be filed in the following order:

Unit 1	Unit 2	Unit 3
Fairfax	Edward	
Hardy	Kenneth	Ted
Martin	Lillian	Kay
Moore	Stacy	Ann

- If you have two unit 1's that are exactly alike, unit 2 will determine which name will be filed first. If units 1 and 2 are exactly alike, alphabetize according to unit 3.

Name	Unit 1	Unit 2	Unit 3
Patricia Dunlap	Dunlap	Patricia	
Roger Dunlap	Dunlap	Roger	

Patricia Dunlap would be filed before *Roger Dunlap*.

- Individual letters are considered as indexing units. The period following the initial is ignored.

Name	Unit 1	Unit 2	Unit 3
Emma B. Ball	Ball	Emma	B
Doyle R. Beyer	Beyer	Doyle	R

Rule 2   File "Nothing before Something"

- Consider the following names. Since *Orlans* is the last name for both persons, look at the first name—*L.* and *Libby*. The initial *L* has nothing following it, so *L* would be filed before *Libby*.

Name	Unit 1	Unit 2	Unit 3
L. Orlans	Orlans	L	
Libby Orlans	Orlans	Libby	

- Consider the following two similar names.

Name	Unit 1	Unit 2	Unit 3
Robert France	France	Robert	
F. Frances	Frances	F	

France is filed before *Frances*.

France_	[File the blank space (nothing) before the *s*.]
Frances	

PRACTICE 6-1

Divide each name into its indexing units and enter them in the following table. Use the Order column to indicate the order in which the names would be filed. For example, write 1 beside the first item to be filed, write 2 beside the second item, and so on.

1. Holly Arnold
2. Amos J. Homer
3. Norma Joan Pendell
4. Anne Elizabeth Anderson
5. Donna Emily Parker
6. Louis K. Yeager
7. Donna Emilyann Parker
8. Louis Kenneth Yeager
9. Greg Snyder

10. Randy Ray Tuckwillar
11. Martha R. Norris
12. Norma Jean Pendell
13. Lillian Phyllis Martin
14. Henry R. Feliciano
15. Cyrus Martine
16. Argelio F. Fellows

No.	Unit 1	Unit 2	Unit 3	Unit 4	Order
1					
2					
3					
4					
5					
6					
7					
8					
9					
10					
11					
12					
13					
14					
15					
16					

Rule 3   Identical Names

• If people have identical last, first, and middle names, then the city, then state, then street name, and then street address are used to determine the filing order. Consider the following two similar names.

Guerrero Leven
890 Butler Road
Ft. Wayne, Indiana

Guerrero Leven
712 Grazing Drive
Chicago, Illinois

Mr. Leven of *Chicago* would be filed before *Mr. Leven* of *Ft. Wayne.*

Unit 1	Unit 2	City
Leven	Guerrero	Chicago
Leven	Guerrero	Ft. Wayne

Rule 4 Seniority Titles

- Seniority titles are used as the last indexing unit in a name. Seniority titles include *Junior, Senior, Jr., Sr., II,* and *III.* Spell in full *Jr.* and *Sr.*

Name	Unit 1	Unit 2	Unit 3	Unit 4
Richard B. Davis	Davis	Richard	B	
Richard Davis, Jr.	Davis	Richard	Junior	
Richard Davis, Sr.	Davis	Richard	Senior	
Donald R. Miller, Jr.	Miller	Donald	R	Junior

Rule 5 Company Names

- Index names of companies according to how the names are written on the letterhead.
- However, if the company name contains a person's first and last names, some organizations use the person's last name as the first unit and the first name as the second unit.
- The rules in your office may vary when indexing company names containing first and last names. Review your company's procedures before filing materials.

Name	Unit 1	Unit 2	Unit 3
Broad Equipment	Broad	Equipment	
Sunny Day Deli	Sunny	Day	Deli
Ronald Watson Jewelers	Ronald	Watson	Jewelers
(alternate method)	Watson	Ronald	Jewelers

Rule 6 Abbreviations

- Abbreviations in business names should be spelled in full. Examples of abbreviations in business names include Incorporated *(Inc.),* Company *(Co.),* Limited *(Ltd.),* and Manufacturing *(Mfg.).*
- The terms *Mr., Mrs.,* and *Ms.* preceding personal names are not considered abbreviations and are not used as an indexing unit. They may, however, be placed in parentheses at the end if necessary for clarification.

Name	Unit 1	Unit 2	Unit 3
Champagne Interiors Inc.	Champagne	Interiors	Incorporated
Mrs. Sally Rogers	Rogers	Sally (Mrs.)	
Mr. William Rogers	Rogers	William	

Rule 7 Possessives

- If a name is possessive, ignore the apostrophe.

Name	Unit 1	Unit 2	Unit 3
Chuck's Garage	Chucks	Garage	
Frances' Gift Shop	Frances	Gift	Shop
Royce's Fruit Market	Royces	Fruit	Market

PRACTICE 6-2

Divide each name into its indexing units and enter them in the following table. Use the Order column to indicate the order in which the names would be filed. For example, write 1 beside the first item to be filed, write 2 beside the second item, and so on.

1. Martin J. Davis III
2. Elmer I. Elliott, 900 Pear Drive, Austin, TX
3. Dennis K. Watson, Senior
4. Paul R. Bates, Senior
5. Lottie Russell, 8934 Crown Avenue, Tacoma, WA
6. Phil W. Morgan, 5810 Earlston Drive, Seattle, WA
7. Floyd Haque
8. Phil W. Morgan, 3478 Albia Road, Portland, MA
9. Cecil's Department Store
10. Horn's Antiques, Ltd.
11. C. Jay Istar, Junior
12. Kelly's Leather Shop
13. Jerry's Garage
14. Elmer I. Elliott, 1723 Eagle Court, Atlanta, GA
15. Martin J. Davis II
16. Lottie Russell, 700 Fordham Drive, Salem, OR
17. Paul R. Bates, Junior
18. Ronald Freeman, Jr.
19. Eugene Frederick, Jr.
20. J. Elmer Elliott, 3078 Veirs Road, Bethesda, MD
21. Dennis K. Watson, Jr.
22. S. Hanson
23. Shamsul Hanst
24. Floyd D. Haque
25. Phil S. Morgan, 2309 Diamond Avenue, Portland, OR
26. M. Shamsul Hanst
27. Samuel Hanson
28. C. Jay Istar, Senior
29. Krammar's Grocery
30. Randy's Bakery

No.	Unit 1	Unit 2	Unit 3	Unit 4	Order
1					
2					
3					
4					
5					
6					
7					
8					
9					
10					

No.	Unit 1	Unit 2	Unit 3	Unit 4	Order
11					
12					
13					
14					
15					
16					
17					
18					
19					
20					
21					
22					
23					
24					
25					
26					
27					
28					
29					
30					

Rule 8 Personal Titles

- If a name contains a title, disregard the title if it is used with a complete name. Place the title in parentheses at the end.

Name	Unit 1	Unit 2
Dr. George Quade	Quade	George (Dr.)
President Harold Roselli	Roselli	Harold (President)
Sylvia Walters, Ph.D.	Walters	Sylvia (Ph.D.)

- If a title is used with an incomplete name, the title is the first indexing unit.

Name	Unit 1	Unit 2
Father Malone	Father	Malone
Rabbi Wise	Rabbi	Wise

Rule 9 Married Women's Names

- A married woman's name is indexed according to her name.

Name	Unit 1	Unit 2	Unit 3
Joyce M. Davis	Davis	Joyce	M
Brenda Sue Morell	Morell	Brenda	Sue
Mrs. Fred Sikes (Linda)	Sikes	Linda	

- Some companies place the husband's name in parentheses.

Name	Unit 1	Unit 2
Kate Mullens (Mrs. Harry Mullens)	Mullens	Kate (Mrs. Harry)

- *Ms.* or *Mrs.* may be placed in parentheses at the end.

Name	Unit 1	Unit 2	Unit 3
Ms. Helen C. Harvey	Harvey	Helen	C (Ms.)

- If only the husband's name is given, index as follows:

Name	Unit 1	Unit 2	Unit 3
Mrs. Harry Mullens	Mullens	Harry (Mrs.)	

Rule 10   Hyphenated Names

- A hyphenated name is considered as one indexing unit, and the hyphen is ignored.

Name	Unit 1	Unit 2	Unit 3
After-School Plaza	AfterSchool	Plaza	
Jane Bailey-Starr	BaileyStarr	Jane	
Mason-Todd Garage	MasonTodd	Garage	
Peck-Boyd Shop	PeckBoyd	Shop	
Kay Stone-Albert	StoneAlbert	Kay	

Rule 11   Directions

- If a business names contains a directional word that may be written as one or two words, index it as one word.

Name	Unit 1	Unit 2	Unit 3
Northwest Business	Northwest	Business	
North West Foods	NorthWest	Foods	
Southwest Service Center	Southwest	Service	Center

PRACTICE 6-3

Divide each name into its indexing units and enter them in the following table. Use the Order column to indicate the order in which the names would be filed. For example, write 1 beside the first item to be filed, write 2 beside the second item, and so on.

1. Judge Richards
2. Adkins-Anderson Clothiers
3. Leslie Pratt-Wallace
4. Senator Robert C. Byrd

5. Mrs. Sharon Salamon, Mrs. John
6. Sister Melissa
7. Judge Raymond Rebuck
8. Mini-Mart Stores
9. Louise Abbott-Lawford
10. Mary-Rose Foods
11. Congresswoman Barbara Jordan
12. W. Richard-Hardkins
13. Ms. Hanna Haye
14. South East Movies
15. Dr. Mary Salcetti
16. Reverend Iverson
17. Edward Recht, Senior
18. North West Cleaners
19. Judge S. Rebuck
20. Reverend Daniel P. Villegas

No.	Unit 1	Unit 2	Unit 3	Unit 4	Order
1					
2					
3					
4					
5					
6					
7					
8					
9					
10					
11					
12					
13					
14					
15					
16					
17					
18					
19					
20					

Rule 12   Minor Words

- Do not consider minor words as indexing units. These words are placed in parentheses at the end of the indexing unit. Examples of minor words are *the, and, for,* and *&*.

Name	Unit 1	Unit 2
The Clays	Clays (The)	
Kids on the Move	Kids (on the)	Move
Young & Bates	Young (&)	Bates

Rule 13   Prefixes

- If a name begins with a prefix, consider the prefix and the word that follows as one unit. Examples of prefixes are *l', el, la, las, mac, mc,* and *o'*.

Name	Unit 1	Unit 2	Unit 3
Jose DeSardo	DeSardo	Jose	
El Grande Hotel	ElGrande	Hotel	
Pierre La Piana	LaPiana	Pierre	
Belle LaPlante	LaPlante	Belle	
Richard N. LeVan	LeVan	Richard	N

Rule 14   Numbers

- Business names with numbers are divided into indexing units as written. If the number is spelled out, index it spelled out in alphabetical order. Numbers in digit form are considered one unit and written in digit form. Business names in digit form are filed in numerical order before alphabetical names are filed.

Name	Unit 1	Unit 2	Unit 3
24 Hour Shop	24	Hour	Shop
500 Lounge	500	Lounge	
Big Ten Shop	Big	Ten	Shop
Biglerville 2000 C1ub	Biglerville	2000	Club
One Beacon Place	One	Beacon	Place

PRACTICE 6-4

Divide each name into its indexing units and enter them in the following table. Use the Order column to indicate the order in which the names would be filed. For example, write 1 beside the first item to be filed, write 2 beside the second item, and so on.

1. The Ladder Store
2. Peter W. LeBrun
3. P & R Incorporated
4. 52 Week Travel
5. The Big Men
6. Nancy McDonald
7. Hartz & Porter
8. T. M. LeBlanc
9. Martha Sue O'Connor
10. Luigi Ira LeBow
11. Amy McCabe, D.D.S.
12. U. S. Construction
13. Atkins and Jackson Associates

14. Women for Success Inc.
15. Rollins Shoes
16. Young at Heart Golf
17. Clay's Bed and Bedding
18. 300 Sovern
19. Come and Go Cleaners
20. Jose's Books
21. J. W. Rollins Shoes
22. Romeo Design Interiors
23. Cooking 24 Hours
24. Dr. Amy Sanford
25. Books on Travel

No.	Unit 1	Unit 2	Unit 3	Unit 4	Order
1					
2					
3					
4					
5					
6					
7					
8					
9					
10					
11					
12					
13					
14					
15					
16					
17					
18					
19					
20					
21					
22					
23					
24					
25					

Rule 15   Banks

- Index banks according to the most important word.

Name	Unit 1	Unit 2	Unit 3
Maine Federal Bank	Maine	Federal	Bank
Reid Thrift Bank	Reid	Thrift	Bank
Saving Bank of Roanoke	Roanoke	Savings	Bank (of)

- If the bank names are exactly alike, use the city, state, street, and building number in that order to determine the filing order. Consider the following three branches of the Chain Savings Bank:

Chain Savings Bank
200 Williams Drive
Boston, MA

Chain Savings Bank
500 Colonial Drive
Boston, MA

Chain Savings Bank
3200 Hampton Lane
Braintree, MA

Unit 1	Unit 2	Unit 3	Address
Chain	Savings	Bank	Boston, MA Colonial Drive
Chain	Savings	Bank	Boston, MA Williams Drive
Chain	Savings	Bank	Braintree, MA

Rule 16   Radio and Television Stations

- Radio and television stations are indexed as though the call letters were a word. When *AM*, *FM*, or *TV* are included with the call letters, they are Unit 2.

Name	Unit 1	Unit 2
KANG	KANG	
KONG-FM	KONG	FM
KONG-TV	KONG	TV
WZTF(FM)	WZTF	FM

- Some companies use the words *Radio Station* or *Television Station* as the first two units.

Name	Unit 1	Unit 2	Unit 3
KANG	Radio	Station	KANG

Rule 17   School Names

- A school name is indexed in the order written unless it contains a person's first name and last name. In that case the last name is the first indexing unit. The words *College*, *University*, and *School* are never used as the first indexing unit.

Name	Unit 1	Unit 2	Unit 3	Unit 4
Arnold Junior High School	Arnold	Junior	High	School
The John Dewey School	Dewey	John	School (The)	
University of Maine	Maine	University (of)		

- If there are schools with identical names, arrange them by city first and then by state.

Green Elementary School, Dayton, Ohio
Green Elementary School, Fairmont, West Virginia

Unit 1	Unit 2	Unit 3	City
Green	Elementary	School	Dayton
Green	Elementary	School	Fairmont

PRACTICE 6-5

Divide each name into its indexing units and enter them in the following table. Use the Order column to indicate the order in which the names would be filed. For example, write 1 beside the first item to be filed, write 2 beside the second item, and so on.

1. McArthur Federal Savings, 2200 Lake Street, Dayton, OH
2. Berkeley Springs Country Inn
3. College of William and Mary
4. Washington Federal, 702 Russell Avenue, Seattle, WA
5. Valley Bank, 307 Jefferson St., Rockville, MD
6. McArthur Federal Savings, 300 Wilkins Blvd., Cincinnati, OH
7. WETA-FM
8. Oaklands High School, 3789 Spring Drive, Norfolk, VA
9. WKZA-TV
10. Captain Standish Motor Lodge
11. Kensington Elementary School
12. University of Rochester
13. San Diego High School
14. Oaklands High School, 3200 Luck Road, Houston, TX
15. Valley Bank, 3000 River Rd., Bethesda, MD
16. Oahu High School
17. William Howard Taft Elementary
18. WCHS
19. The Bank of Cincinnati, 1775 Hughes Drive, Cincinnati, OH
20. WWVA-TV

No.	Unit 1	Unit 2	Unit 3	Unit 4	Order
1					
2					
3					
4					

No.	Unit 1	Unit 2	Unit 3	Unit 4	Order
5					
6					
7					
8					
9					
10					
11					
12					
13					
14					
15					
16					
17					
18					
19					
20					

Rule 18   Churches and Synagogues

- When indexing churches and synagogues, the first unit is the word that identifies the organization. Do not use *church* or *temple* as the first word. When in doubt about how to file a church or synagogue, cross-reference the file.

Name	Unit 1	Unit 2	Unit 3
B'nai Israel Temple	B'nai	Israel	Temple
Church of Hope	Hope	Church (of)	
St. John's Church	Saint	Johns	Church

- Some companies will not spell out *Saint* and will file the name as written.

Rule 19   Organizations

- When indexing organizations, use the most distinctive word as the first unit.

Name	Unit 1	Unit 2	Unit 3
United Guild of Barbers	Barbers	United	Guild (of)
The Pharmacy Association	Pharmacy	Association (The)	
Retired Teacher's Club	Teachers	Retired	Club

- Most telephone directories do not index using this rule. Telephone directories usually list organizations in the order the name is written. For example, American Teacher's Association would be listed in the telephone directory in that order. Also, common abbreviations and acronyms are usually listed in the telephone directory without spelling out the name.

Rule 20 Newspapers and Magazines

- In most instances, magazines are indexed in the order in which the names appear. Newspapers should be filed with the name of the city as the first indexing unit. If the name of the newspaper does not begin with the city name, place the city name first, followed by the name of the newspaper.

Name	Unit 1	Unit 2	Unit 3
Journal of Accountancy	Journal (of)	Accountancy	
Kirby Post Dispatch	Kirby	Post	Dispatch
Time Magazine	Time	Magazine	
Daily News (Tilden)	Tilden	Daily	News
The Washington Post	Washington	Post (The)	

Rule 21 United States Government Agencies

- United States government agencies are indexed as

Unit 1 United
Unit 2 States
Unit 3 Government
Unit 4 Main word in the name of the division

United States Government will be units 1, 2, and 3 in all of the following examples.

United States Government Department of Labor, Bureau of Labor Statistics

Unit 4	Unit 5	Unit 6
Labor	Statistics	Bureau (of)

United States Government Department of Commerce, Patent & Trademark Office

Unit 4	Unit 5	Unit 6
Patent (&)	Trademark	Office

Rule 22 Political Subdivisions

- Index political divisions by name of the state, county, or city. Then index by the name of the department or division, using the most important word first. If needed for clarity, include the state name.

Name	Unit 1	Unit 2	Unit 3
Board of Education, Houston	Houston	Education	Board (of)
Idaho Department of Parks	Idaho	Parks	Department (of)

PRACTICE 6-6

Divide each name into its indexing units and enter them in the following table. Use the Order column to indicate the order in which the names would be filed. For example, write 1 beside the first item to be filed, write 2 beside the second item, and so on.

1. First Baptist Church
2. Association of Retired Judges
3. Department of Water and Sewer, Knoxville, TN
4. St. Mark's Church

5. Mapping Agency, U.S. Department of Defense
6. American Association for Counseling
7. U. S. Department of Commerce, Bureau of Economic Analysis
8. Anaheim Examiner
9. First Montrose Church
10. Institute of Cardiology
11. Department of Recreation, Nashville, TN
12. Church of Christ of Danville
13. Dallas Daily Reporter
14. American Psychology Association
15. Department of Travel, Chattanooga, TN
16. Housing and Community Development, KY
17. The New York Times
18. Temple Shalom
19. Maryland Boating Association
20. The Pasta Depot

No.	Unit 1	Unit 2	Unit 3	Unit 4	Order
1					
2					
3					
4					
5					
6					
7					
8					
9					
10					
11					
12					
13					
14					
15					
16					
17					
18					
19					
20					

▼ FILING HINTS ▼

1. Develop a master index of the filing system and make it easily accessible to everyone who uses the files. The master index should include the divisions of the filing system. Also a list of all folders in subject and geographical files is particularly useful.
2. Repair torn pages before filing them.
3. Remove all paper clips before filing and staple the pages of multipage documents together. (Paper clips can attach pages together that should be in *separate files*.)
4. Code documents before filing to simplify the filing process. The code is the name or number of the file where the document should be filed. Use the master index to assign the code and write the code in the top right corner of the paper. For example, on an incoming letter, you might simply underscore the name of the company in the letterhead with a red pen. On a copy of an outgoing letter, you might underscore the name of the company in the inside address.
5. Establish a specific time each day to file, because a large stack of unfiled documents may become so large that it becomes a major project. In addition, a seemingly lost document may actually be in the *to be filed* pile.
6. Prior to filing, arrange all papers in the order in which they will be placed in the file cabinet.
7. If a file folder is too full, divide the contents into two folders.
8. Use a *miscellaneous folder* for each file subdivision until there are sufficient documents to establish a separate folder. The minimum number of documents to start a new folder is usually five.
9. Allow about 4 in. of free space in each file drawer for working room.
10. Stagger the heading tabs on file folders to make it easier to find materials.
11. To locate missing papers:
    - Carefully check the folder where the paper is supposed to be.
    - Check the folders in front of and behind where the lost item should be.
    - Consider alternative ways that the item could have been filed and look in those folders. For example, it could have been filed under the first name instead of the last name.
    - Ask other employees if they have the folder.

CHAPTER REVIEW

1. Explain subject filing.
2. Explain geographical filing.
3. Explain numerical filing.
4. Explain the nothing-before-something rule.
5. Explain the rule for filing of a hyphenated name.
6. Explain the rule for filing of a United States government agency.

ACTIVITIES

1. Visit an office supply store and look at the variety of file folders, labels, and filing storage units available. Prepare a written report describing your findings. Be prepared to give an oral summary of your report in class.
2. Ask three business people:
   a. What type of filing systems they use.
   b. What type of filing storage units they use.
   c. If they use a cross-reference system.

   Prepare both an oral and a written report describing the comments you receive.

Project 11

Create the following memo from Michelle Kaplan, Managing Director, to Theodore Nash, Executive Director, concerning file cabinets.

This memorandum is being prepared in response to your request for reorganization of the filing system.

As we discussed, the reasons to reorganize are:

1. The need to archive files that are crowding the office environment.

2. The need for additional filing cabinets.

The staff appreciates the opportunity to provide input in meeting this challenge. We are well aware of the unsightly conditions that exist in the file cabinet space adjacent to the offices. The current conditions are not only very inefficient in locating files, but also reflect poorly on the staff in the eyes of those in industry who visit us. The following recommendations, if adopted, will increase the efficiency of the files, will reflect a proper image of the department, and will provide a more pleasant office environment for the staff.

The current files are retained in the individual offices. All other files are kept in the outer offices entered through the reception area. Currently, this room has 26 file cabinets, varying in type, size, and color. These cabinets are used to store the following:

- Files for approximately 1,000 projects.

- Approximately 300 new proposals.

- Approximately 200 projects that were not reactivated from the preceding year.

- Records of the 20 years of the department.

- Stock of forms.

- Stock of miscellaneous publications that are distributed to other departments.

There is an increasing need for space to contain the files for these projects.

1. More projects are entering the department than are leaving.

2. The size of the files have increased dramatically from the original projects.

With the increased requirements of recent years, the size of the folder of the average completed current project that enters the system is twice the size of those projects processed in the 1990s which are being removed from the cabinets as they leave the department.

As a result of these factors, there is simply not enough room in the existing 26 file cabinets for files, storage of forms, and historical or processing information on the most recent projects. Files of every nature are placed on the top of cabinets and in boxes or in stacks on the floor.

Information in these files must be readily accessible to the staff. These files are used to monitor the current projects. During the processing of projects, the files are consulted to review prior support of the applicant and provide background material useful to the staff in their evaluation of proposals.

Recommendations for the reception room

The following recommendation provides for more efficient use of the space in the reception room to ensure that sufficient file space is available for the files, forms, and information.

- Obtain 20 uniform lateral files, five drawers high, for placement in the outer offices. To accommodate the available space, 11 of these lateral files should be the 42-in. size, while the nine others should be the 36-in. size.

- Relocate three cabinets that do not have pull-out drawers and are six shelves high, to Building 800. These cabinets will be used as storage of forms and will not interfere with the use of this area as a miniconference room and office for visiting associates.

- Relocate the five lateral files in this room to employee offices to create additional storage in those locations.

The 20 lateral file cabinets will be a much more efficient use of space and will actually provide 46 percent more shelf space than currently occupied by the 26 file cabinets in this room. Additional storage space will be created in the staff offices and in the reception room.

As a result, file space will be available for both the current folders and those files that are projected to enter the system in the next several years. Also, the appearance of the room would be greatly improved.

Project 12

Send this memo to the staff. It is from Mary C. Putnam, Director.

We are happy to announce the opening of our employee day-care center.

January 6 our new $2 million 200-child day-care center will open. Children 3 months and older will be accepted into the all-day program. In addition, there will also be a program to meet the needs of children in school. Bus service from the elementary schools in the community will be provided, thus eliminating a transportation problem for parents.

Registration will begin October 1, and forms may be obtained from the benefits department in Suite 205.

Costs for the program will be shared by the employee and our company. Therefore, the employee cost will be very reasonable.

At 9 A.M. on September 1, there will be a meeting in the auditorium to explain the details of this service. We hope all employees with children will be able to attend this discussion.

HUMAN RELATIONS SKILL DEVELOPMENT

Standing up for Your Rights

Being agreeable in the office is important, but being agreeable should not interfere with your principles. You should not allow a colleague to take advantage of you. Assertive behavior (standing up for your rights) is acceptable; aggressive behavior (influencing others by physical or emotional force) is not acceptable.

- When was the last time someone took advantage of you?
- Describe the personality traits of the last person who took advantage of you.
- When was the last time you asserted yourself?
- How did you feel when you asserted yourself?
- Describe the last time you used aggressive behavior.

Accepting and Rejecting Advice from Co-workers

During your business career, it is possible that you may work with someone who freely gives advice about all situations. Unsolicited suggestions can be annoying. Dealing with this advice in a diplomatic manner can be the difference between a comfortable working relationship and an antagonistic one. It is not essential for you to *accept* the advice, but it may be wise for you to *listen* to it. First of all, the suggestion may be beneficial to you. If you choose not to follow the recommendation, that is your decision. Consider the reason the counsel is given. Perhaps, the giver's objective is to get attention and recognition. If that is the case, just listening should solve the problem.

- Describe the personality traits of the people from whom you accept advice.
- Describe the last time you were wise to accept someone's advice.
- Describe the last time you advised someone. Were your recommendations followed?
- Describe how you would handle an overbearing person who is attempting to counsel you although you did not seek the guidance.

SITUATIONS

How would you handle each of the following situations?

- Your supervisor, Ms. Canton, is with Ms. Taylor and has asked you to bring Ms. Taylor's file to her office. Although you saw the file yesterday, you cannot find the file now.
- Although you left your office in plenty of time to pick up your supervisor at the airport, there was an accident on the interstate and traffic was delayed. When you finally arrived at the airport, your supervisor was furious at you for being late.
- You were invited to your supervisor's house for dinner, and you spilled coffee on the new oriental rug in the living room.

PUNCTUATION REVIEW

Punctuate each of the following sentences.

1. Economic expansion is often accompanied by rising costs but the consumer continues to purchase goods and services
2. Jack asked did interest rates rise
3. Have you planned the convention Sara asked
4. My attorney Laura Reston is well known in the community
5. Web City for example is a large retail discount store located near Interstate 15
6. The director Phil Joseph moved from Houston to San Diego
7. The new employee Patricia Wilson was late for work
8. We are sorry that you did not receive your supply order by your due date therefore we will credit your account for $100
9. The office supply store which is on Route 28 is open after work
10. Doug said the computer paper arrived damaged
11. No the package was not delivered
12. The meeting is scheduled for Monday August 6 XXXX
13. Her office was in an old dingy building
14. Jane Kipper Ph.D. will address the next session at the conference
15. John Tasky II was my roommate in college

Levine Research and Management
324 Research Drive
Suite 600
East Meadow, NY 11557

At 2 P.M. on May 19, XXXX the Research Committee will meet in Room 620 of our offices.

AGENDA

1. Minutes of last meeting

2. Review of Ms. O'Leary's proposal

3. Plant specifications

4. Review of computer purchase

5. Set date of next meeting

6. Adjournment

shr

FIGURE 7-2   An Agenda.

Agenda

Each person attending the meeting should have a copy of the *agenda*, which is a list of items to be discussed at a meeting. Prior to the meeting, it is best to send a copy of the agenda to all participants so that they will have an opportunity to prepare for the items to be discussed. If the agenda is not sent in advance, it should be distributed at the beginning of the meeting. Even if they are sent in advance, additional copies of the agenda should be available at the meeting for those who did not bring one. The agenda will be determined by the supervisor, but the administrative assistant will be responsible for keyboarding, duplication, and distribution of the agenda.

▼ ATTENDING A MEETING ▼

Suggestions for the presider

*   Do not schedule meetings the day before a holiday or on Friday afternoons when people are anxious to leave for the weekend.
*   Distribute the agenda well in advance. Your associates might like to read and think about the agenda.
*   In advance, decide how long to wait for late participants.
*   Be aware of the nonverbal communications in the meeting room.
*   Be aware of any tension between participants.
*   Do not allow discussion to ramble on.
*   Do not allow the meeting to divert from the agenda.
*   If one person monopolizes the conversation, encourage others to speak.

Suggestions for the attendee

- Prepare yourself for the meeting by reading background material about the agenda items.
- Bring key documents such as the agenda and pertinent reports to the meeting, but do not overburden yourself with background material.
- Make notes during the meeting. You will not remember everything.
- Meet new business associates at the meeting. Do not talk only with co-workers you know.
- Thank the meeting organizer.

▼ PLANNING A MEETING ▼

Meetings require careful preparation, but having sufficient time to plan a meeting is frequently a luxury. Therefore, you should establish a basic plan for meetings and keep it in your files. Whenever you are asked to arrange a meeting, your plan will be available. Before you make any definite decisions about a meeting, review your company's meeting policy and bring any questions you have to your supervisor's attention.

Your plan should include a checklist so you are sure that every detail is covered. You should not assume that any aspect of the meeting will be taken care of by someone else. Do not leave any question unanswered. If you omit important details, any resulting mistakes will reflect on you and your supervisor.

Factors to be considered when planning a meeting

1. What is the purpose of the meeting? What are the goals?
2. When will the meeting be held? Before a final date and time are selected for the meeting, important people who will attend the meeting should be contacted to verify that they are available.
3. Where will the meeting be held? The number of participants, the facilities available, the length of the meeting, and your office budget will help determine the location for the meeting.
4. How many participants will attend, and who are they? If a similar meeting has been held in the past, how many people have attended? What does the follow-up report for that meeting indicate?
5. What is the planned length of the meeting? Will the meeting be scheduled for an hour, several hours, one day, or several days?
6. How many meeting sessions will be planned? If this is a large meeting with concurrent sessions, how many meeting rooms are required?
7. When will the meeting begin, and when will it end? To keep a meeting short, schedule it before lunch or at the close of the business day. People are usually eager to leave for lunch or to go home.
8. Will food be served? If food is served, money must be included in the budget to cover its cost. You will also need to determine whether a meal or a snack will be served. An early morning meeting often begins with coffee, donuts, pastries, bagels, and so on.
9. Is special equipment required for the meetings? If so, what equipment is necessary—an overhead or slide projector? Are any other items needed? How will the equipment be obtained? Who will operate the equipment? During what sessions will the equipment be needed?
10. Will the meetings be recorded in audio or video format?
11. What is the budget for the meeting?
12. Will there be exhibits or displays?
13. Will there be out-of-town guests for the meeting? If so, will hotel accommodations be required? Will transportation costs need to be built into the budget?
14. Will RSVP notes be sent out?
15. How will the meeting be evaluated?

After the preceding factors have been considered, you are ready to begin implementing the meeting plan. If the meeting will be held at a location other than your office, arrange a visit of the facility. The visit will provide information regarding the site as well as a sense of the site management's responsiveness to your needs.

Where to Have the Meeting

Meetings can be held at hotels, motels, restaurants, private clubs, resorts, state parks, and similar locations. Past experience and recommendations from friends and business associates will help you select a good facility for your meeting. If your company has held a similar meeting in the past, pay particular attention to what the evaluations of those meetings indicated about the meeting facilities.

Factors to be considered when selecting a location for your meeting

1. Is the location convenient for those attending? Is it close to main roads or interstate highways? If attendees are flying in, is the facility conveniently close to an airport?
2. Are there a sufficient number of meeting rooms?
3. Are the chairs in the room comfortable? Are tables available if necessary?
4. Will the meeting room accommodate the anticipated number of participants?
5. Are meeting rooms comfortably climate controlled? (This can be a major factor in making a meeting a success.)
6. Is there sufficient lighting?
7. Are there shades or drapes to block the sun if necessary?
8. If equipment such as overhead projectors, slide projectors, or screens are needed, will the facility supply them? What is the cost of supplying this equipment?
9. Is there a sound system available? Are microphones hand-held, lavaliere style, or on a podium?
10. Are there sufficient electrical outlets in the meeting rooms for the equipment?
11. Is there a technician available if there is a problem with the equipment?
12. Are the employees pleasant? Do they seem to be efficient and interested in servicing your meeting?
13. What is the quality of the food? Is the food served quickly? What is the cost for food service?
14. Is the site clean and attractive?
15. Is parking available? Is it adequate for the size of the meeting? Is there a parking fee?
16. If a loading dock is necessary, is it available and convenient?
17. Is a lobby or registration area available? Is the area large enough, and is it convenient to the meeting rooms?
18. Is there an area for displays or exhibits?
19. For longer meetings, will the meeting room be available for 24 hours, or will someone else use it for a portion of the day? What security is available to protect equipment and other important items?
20. Are the facilities accessible to disabled persons?
21. Is there a satellite hookup?

When evaluating potential meeting sites, it is a good idea to complete a site evaluation form (see Figure 7-3).

Food Service

When planning a meeting, decide if food will be served. The time of day and length of the meeting will determine whether or not food will be served, and your food budget will often dictate the menu. In addition to meals (breakfast, lunch, or dinner), food can be served as snacks during breaks or before and after the meetings.

SITE EVALUATION FORM

Date of Visit _____

Facility _____

Address _____

City _____ State _____ Zip _____

Telephone Number _____

Contact Person _____ Title _____

Date(s) Facilities Available _____

Overall Appearance of Facility _____

Atmosphere of Facility _____

Desirable Features _____

Description of Meeting Rooms _____

Number of Meeting Rooms _____

   Per Day Cost _____

Number of Sleeping Rooms _____ Quality _____

   Per Night Cost _____

Quality of Food _____

Quality of Food Service _____

   Cost of Food Service _____

Special Equipment/Services/Available (i.e., lectern, audiovisual, etc.) _____

Handicapped Access? _____

Additional Comments _____

FIGURE 7-3   A Site Evaluation Form.

If food is going to be served, the availability and cost of food should be considered before making a decision on the location of the meeting. The cost of the food may be based on the number of meals served. Sometimes the more meals served, the lower the cost per person. Ask for sample menus and prices for each menu. When selecting menus, do not limit your choices to your favorite foods; select foods that appeal to everyone.

If a meal is served, there may not be a charge for use of the meeting room. A free meeting room usually requires that a certain number of persons purchase a meal. Ask in advance if there is a separate charge for the room. Also, decide if each participant will pay for the meal or if the company will pay for the meal. If each participant is supposed to pay for the meal, will separate checks be provided? Decide whether the meal is to be ordered from the menu or whether a menu will be selected prior to the meeting.

Today many people are on special diets: for example, low-sodium, low-fat, or vegetarian diets. It is important to consider these preferences when selecting a menu. Be sure to ask if it is possible to prepare a vegetarian meal or if the meeting facility can accommodate people on special diets. Since many convention or meeting facilities will not allow you to bring in any food, confirm their policy regarding outside food if you intend to provide your own.

Hotel/Motel Rooms

Reservations should be made for the meeting participants who plan to stay overnight. Most hotels or motels have a variety of rooms; for example, a single, double, twin, or suite. When making reservations, determine the type of room desired before making the reservation. If you are making several reservations, a block of rooms can be reserved. One of the advantages of reserving a block of rooms is that hotels usually reduce the price of rooms when they are reserved in quantity. Also, if meeting participants are paying for their own hotel rooms, you will need to decide whether the participant or the company will make hotel reservations. If the company makes the reservations, you may need to get credit card numbers (with expiration dates) from the participants so that you can guarantee the reservations when you make them. Meeting participants usually are encouraged to make their own hotel reservations and are instructed to tell the hotel that they are attending your meeting in order to obtain special room rates.

When selecting a hotel or motel, ask about the facilities available for guests. For example, does the hotel or motel have a coffee shop, room service, free continental breakfast, free local telephone calls, swimming pool, or health club?

Additional information regarding hotels is provided in Chapter 8.

Contracts for Meeting Rooms

When a decision is made concerning a meeting location, a contract should be signed. Although you may not be the person who signs the contract, read it carefully to verify that everything you discussed is included. Nothing should be omitted. For example, if a reception table is promised, it should be written into the contract. Your contact person at the hotel or restaurant may have changed jobs by the time you have the meeting, and the new employee may be unaware of an oral promise.

Audio and Video Conferencing

As discussed in Chapter 3, audio- and videoconferencing are often cheaper alternatives than bringing participants together at a meeting. These technologies are also used within a traditional meeting setting to bring in participants who could otherwise not be present. Experts or high-level government or business officials may be able to participate in your meeting for an hour via videoconferencing when they would otherwise be unable to attend. Many meetings are held for the purpose of being able to hear from people via teleconferences when it would be impossible to schedule a personal visit of that person. If audio or video teleconferences are included on the agenda of your meeting, the availability of equipment required to support these teleconferences will be a major requirement in the selection of a meeting site.

Very Important People

If *VIPs* (very important people) will be attending your meeting, they may be given special treatment. VIPs may include company officials, honored guests, or invited speakers. Discuss with your supervisor whether any people should be given VIP treatment. You should consider the following in dealing with VIPs:

- Who are the VIPs?
- Will the VIPs be met at the airport or train station? Who will meet them?

- Will there be baskets of candy, fruit, nuts, or flowers in their hotel rooms?
- Will you need a car and/or driver for the VIPs?
- Tell the bell captain and meeting services manager who the VIPs are.
- As an extra gesture, you might want to gather information about the likes and dislikes of the VIPs.

Identification Badges

To help remember names and meet new business associates, people attending meetings often wear name or identification badges. For those participants preregistered for the meeting, name tags can be prepared in advance; but pens and extra name tags should be available for persons who register at the meeting. Wearing the tag on the right shoulder allows another person to see your name easily while shaking your hand.

The use of a name tag is not limited to a large meeting or conference. Identification badges can be helpful for a small group where the participants are not acquainted.

Additional Thoughts

As they occur, inform the facility of all changes in the meeting plans. A last-minute increase in the number of participants may be difficult for the facility to accommodate, or removing several unoccupied luncheon tables may be impossible at the last moment.

Will a packet of meeting materials be given to each participant? What will be in it? Who will prepare and distribute the packet? Will paper and pens be provided for note taking?

Decide in advance who will pay the bill for the meeting and decide how it will be paid—cash, check, credit card, or direct billing.

Consider transportation needs. Must someone be picked up at the airport? If the guest and the driver do not know each other, identification will be necessary. Prepare a sign for the driver with the name of your organization.

Send a map and information about ground transportation to out-of-town participants.

▼ MEETING DAY AND FOLLOW-UP ▼

The Day of the Meeting

Arrive early and verify that everything is completed to your satisfaction. Have available extra copies of the agenda, pens, meeting packets, maps of the area, and anything else that would be helpful to attendees. If flowers, candy, nuts, or similar items have been ordered, verify that they have been delivered and that they are placed where you want them.

When the meeting begins, adhere to the time schedule you have set. Deviating from the schedule could cause problems for the service staff. If lunch is scheduled for 12 noon and the meeting runs late, the restaurant may have difficulty serving the lunch at 1 P.M. Also, take breaks when they are scheduled because during the breaks the service staff may straighten the meeting room.

After the Meeting

As you plan the meeting, keep notes of the names of everyone who was helpful. After the meeting, write thank you letters to everyone who helped you. In some instances, a gift or tip should be given to those who assisted you.

Meeting Follow-up

A working meeting where the participants are asked to complete specific projects or research particular ideas needs a *follow-up*. If the work assignments or decisions arrived at during the meeting are not implemented, the meeting has not accomplished its objectives.

It may be the administrative assistant's responsibility to follow up and contact the participants to determine if they have the materials they agreed to prepare, if they have talked to the people with whom they were to communicate, or if they have reached the goals that were established.

After the meeting, the person who sponsored the meeting should have a summary prepared. Notes may have been taken by the assistant or by one of the meeting's participants. It is often the administrative assistant's duty to prepare a written report of the meeting and send a copy to all the participants.

CHAPTER REVIEW

1. Describe the desirable features of a meeting room.
2. List five points that should be considered when planning a meeting.
3. List six points to consider when selecting a location for a meeting.

ACTIVITIES

1. Call three hotels/motels and ask about charges for:
   a. A meeting room
   b. Sleeping accommodations
   c. A lunch meeting for 50 people
   d. A dinner meeting for 100 people
2. Call three restaurants and ask about
   a. Lunch costs for 20 people
   b. A sample lunch menu
   c. The charge for a meeting room
3. Call a bakery and request prices for donuts, croissants, and pastries to serve 25 people.
4. List 10 facilities in your area where you could hold a one-day meeting.
5. Plan a retreat a couple of hours from your home. Where would you hold the retreat?
6. Ask two administrative assistants how often they plan meetings. Also, ask them to comment about planning large and small meetings. Write a summary of their comments.
7. Make *all* the plans for a informal one-day meeting at a facility other than your office. There will be 15 participants but none of them will be from out-of-town. Submit a detailed list of your plans.
8. Make *all* of the plans for a four-day meeting. There will be 12 out-of-town guests, one out-of-town VIP, and four in-town participants. Submit a detailed list of your plans.
9. Use the Internet to locate information about three restaurants in your city. Write a summary of your findings.

PROJECTS

Project 13

Create the following table. Add a column for the dollar cost of the exhibition space. O'Brien, Community Appliances, and Power each will pay $1,200. Blackstone will pay $1,500, Chamber and Fairdale will pay $2,475, American Donations will pay $1,300, and McFarlin will pay $1,250. Prepare a total cost figure.

CONVENTION EXHIBITORS
CHICAGO
SPRING XXXX

COMPANY	CONTACT	PHONE
American Donations Inc.	Eugene Hartzell	703-439-8613
O'Brien Engineering	Barbara Wilmore	703-946-8153
Chamber Designs	Treva Semanick	703-270-7765
Power Technology	Jody Peerke	202-593-7514
Blackstone, Inc.	Colleen Storch	202-963-2493
Community Appliances	Andrew Knowles	703-854-4487
Fairdale Atlantic	Saba Tollie	202-449-1014
McFarlin Agency	Victoria Gannon	202-686-2556

Project 14

Send this memo to the staff. It is from you, and your title is Training Director. Send a copy to Sharon Barber, Marcia Morton, and Sang Seegars.

Computer training classes will be offered as follows. If you have questions, please call Clifton at extension 6177.

All classes are held from 9 to 4 with a lunch break of one hour. The classes will be held in room 809.

I encourage you to register as soon as possible, as classes fill quickly.

DATE	CLASS	INSTRUCTOR
January 15	Introduction to Access	Hainer
January 28	Intermediate Access	Hainer
February 10	Intermediate Word	Leroy
February 20	Introduction to PowerPoint	Perez
March 4	Introduction to Excel	Zang
March 8	HTML Fundamentals	Anderson
March 15	Advanced HTML	Anderson
March 22	Introduction to Digital Imaging	Powers

HUMAN RELATIONS SKILL DEVELOPMENT

Working with Pessimistic People

In your working environment, you may encounter a person who sees the negative side of everything. When dealing with this person, do not permit yourself to become pessimistic also. If possible, keep your contact to a minimum and encourage other workers to be present when the two of you are together. After being with this type of person, make a list of positive thoughts.

- Who among your acquaintances has a pessimistic outlook?
- Describe your feelings when you are around pessimistic people.

Problems with Your Supervisor

Never take a problem to someone above your supervisor without first discussing the problem with your supervisor. If the situation persists after several unsatisfactory attempts to solve the problem with your supervisor, it can be taken to a higher level. Depending on the circumstances, it may be wise to tell your supervisor that you are seeking a response from another person. Whenever you discuss a problem, respect the other person's opinions and be tactful with your comments.

Before taking your problem to a higher level, decide if the situation is important enough for you to pursue it. Taking a problem to a higher level could alter the relationship between you and your supervisor—no matter how the problem is resolved.

- What tone of voice would you use when discussing a problem with your supervisor?
- Describe your approach when taking a problem to your supervisor's manager.
- Describe three types of problems that are too petty to take to a higher level.
- What are you going to do if the supervisor's manager does not agree with you? What will your reaction be to this situation?
- How would you handle a problem that your supervisor cannot solve? Describe a problem that your supervisor cannot resolve and explain how you would handle it.

SITUATIONS

How would you handle each of the following situations?

- A meeting is continuing longer than you anticipated and everyone is hungry.
- Last night your supervisor took a file home and forgot to return it today. You need the file today so that you can complete a report.
- Last weekend at a party you heard confidential information about a project you are completing.
- Jennie is frequently late returning from lunch. She tells you that she must run errands at lunch and asks you to cover for her.

PUNCTUATION REVIEW

Punctuate each of the following sentences.

1. The community needs affordable housing and a balanced budget
2. Patrick of course understands the importance of completing projects by the due dates
3. I received the Outstanding Employee of the Year award and I was very surprised
4. Cincinnati my hometown is the site of the next annual meeting
5. While Max was in Paris his mail was forwarded to him
6. As you mentioned the minutes of the meeting were incorrect
7. Hedys mother Mrs Hoffman was the director responsible for the revised budget
8. Opal Marshall Executive Manager for Personnel has a large office
9. While the Marketing Department remains on the third floor the Administration Department has been moved from the first floor to the second floor
10. Ed who is active in community affairs is an excellent speaker
11. Rachel who exercises daily has lost 20 pounds as a result of her involvement in the Employee Wellness Program

12. When it comes to management skills demonstration is more important than paperwork
13. In her struggle to combine a career and a personal life she developed health problems
14. This notion of course runs counter to all you have learned in the seminars you have attended
15. Every department has a desk manual and it is your job to locate it and to be familiar with it

▼**8**▼
Travel

OBJECTIVES

After studying this chapter, you should be able to:

1. Read and understand an airline flight guide.
2. Make airline reservations.
3. Make hotel and motel reservations.
4. Determine the rental car that best meets your needs.
5. Apply for a passport.
6. Prepare an itinerary.
7. Prepare an expense report.
8. Use the Internet to plan a business trip.

▼ FUNDAMENTALS OF OFFICE TRAVEL ▼

Travel is an integral part of today's business world. Business trips planned at the last minute are often the norm, not the exception. If your company has a travel department, your only responsibility may be to notify that department of the impending trip including location, date, and travel preferences.

However, as an office employee it often may be your responsibility to make travel arrangements. The first requirement is to be aware of your company's travel policies. The second requirement is to know the preferences of the traveler. Personal preferences might include the method of transportation, particular airline, chain of hotels or motels, room location, time of day of traveling, airline food preferences, and so on. If you do not know your supervisor's travel preferences, you should ask. Usually you will be given information regarding the destination and time for a trip, and you will have to arrange the itinerary yourself.

If it is your responsibility to prepare the travel arrangements, *organize your thoughts, and then proceed*. Arrangements can be made through a travel agent, or you can make arrangements directly with airlines, hotels, and rental-car agencies. Knowing the specifics of the trip are important before proceeding. For example, will the person be traveling by air, railroad, or personal car? In some organizations, a company airplane may be used, so that may also be an option.

Your company may have a contract with an airline, auto-rental company, or hotel chain which provides for discounts from the usual rates. If so, check with the airline, auto company, or hotel chain to see if they serve the area of travel.

Prior to a business trip, check the weather forecast for the area. Weather information can be obtained from newspapers, television weather channels, or from an Internet site.

Travel by rail or air will require ground transportation to a hotel or a business meeting location. Most airports are served by a variety of ground transportation services, including taxis, auto rentals, or shuttle vans to and from downtown locations or the suburbs. Hotels near airports often have free shuttle service between the airport and the hotel.

▼ TRAVEL ASSISTANCE ▼

Travel Agencies

Travel agencies can be very helpful in planning a trip. Instead of your contacting each airline individually, travel agents use their computer systems to review the airline schedules and prices of all the airlines serving a market. They will find different pricing, alternative routes, and wade through the thicket of restrictions that qualify each fare. Through their computer reservation systems, travel agents can also give you information about auto rentals, hotel availability, and prices. You can request that the travel agency make a reservation on a specific flight, at a specific hotel, and with an auto-rental agency.

Many companies have contracts with travel agencies to make their travel reservations for all of their traveling personnel. Fees for these services are part of the agreement between the travel agent and the company. Reductions in the amount of commissions travel agents receive from the airlines for which they book reservations have forced many travel agents to charge processing fees for their services. Before using a travel agency that does not have a contract with your company, ask if there is a charge for services. Many travel agents specialize in certain types of travel. If you find a travel agent who provides current information, good service, and reasonable airline prices, their fees will be worthwhile. A good travel agent can save time and prevent aggravation for your office.

Toll-free Numbers

Airlines, railroads, and car-rental agencies have toll-free numbers for centralized reservation systems. Hotel and motel reservations may be made through toll-free centralized sys-

FIGURE 8-1 Working in a Travel Agency.

tems or directly with the hotel. Hotels catering to the business traveler may also have a toll-free number that can be found in travel directories. An efficient administrative assistant should record frequently called numbers in a personal telephone directory.

Travel Guides

Travel guides include information and recommendations about airlines serving an area, distances from the airport to downtown locations, traffic conditions, parking, hotels, motels, restaurants, and attractions. There are books available for specific cities, regions, and countries. Examples of travel guides are:

- *AAA TourBook* (available to members of travel clubs affiliated with the American Automobile Association)
- *Arthur Frommer's Guides*
- *Fodor's Travel Guides*
- *Mobil Guides*
- *Stephen Birnbaum Guides*

Since there are many other travel books available, check the travel department of your library or bookstore to determine what other travel resources are available.

The Internet

Travel all over the world on the Internet. The Internet can be very helpful for obtaining information on travel and destinations around the world. Whether you are traveling or making arrangements for your supervisor, using the Internet will provide information about travel destinations, and even enable you to make airline, auto, and hotel reservations right from your computer.

Finding travel information on the Internet is usually very easy. Many of the common Internet software programs have sections devoted to travel. Selecting the Travel icon will bring you to a world of travel information. If your computer does not have a travel icon, entering the name of a destination in a search engine will usually bring up many pages about the area. You will be able to find city maps, lists of hotels, city services, and special events. Often, you will be able to link directly to Web sites from the hotels or events listed.

The Internet has made finding airline reservations a quick and easy task. Many airlines have their own sites where you can enter the name of the starting and ending cities and the dates of travel. The Web will search and provide a selection of airline schedules and pricing. Although you can make a plane reservation directly over the Internet, you may want to check several alternatives with your supervisor before actually making a reservation and sending payment over the computer. There are several sites that will provide information from numerous airlines so that you do not have to check each airline's Web site individually. When you deal directly with an airline's Internet site, however, you may be able to enter the passenger's frequent flyer membership number, make seat selection, or request special meals.

Airline tickets, automobile rentals, hotel reservations, and train tickets can all be reserved on the Internet. For some reservations you will have to connect directly to a specific company's Web site. As more companies become committed to the Internet, they will increase their offerings on the Web. Making travel arrangements on the Web is expected to be a major factor in the expected dramatic increase in electronic commerce in coming years.

You should keep a file of useful travel Web sites. These sites can change often, so always be on the lookout for new and interesting Internet sites. To get started, ask co-workers or your supervisor for sites they have found useful. New sites are often recommended in newspapers, magazines, or listed in company's advertisements. You will often find new useful sites as links from older sites. When you find a useful Internet site, you should bookmark the site on your Internet browser so that it is easily available. You should also write the site's address on a list that is *not* kept on the computer. You do not want to lose Web addresses to a computer crash or as the result of an upgrade of your Internet browser software.

Computer Maps

Maps are helpful to orient travelers to new surroundings and are available from Internet sites or on CD-ROMs. People traveling by auto will also be able to use the Internet or CD-ROMs to obtain maps with personalized directions to help them reach their destination. By entering the starting location and the desired destination, a computer program can provide both a map and written directions all along the route, including milage, route numbers, and where to turn. These maps can be printed and used as a guide during the drive. Map programs can also calculate the driving distance and time that should be allotted for the trip. Some computer programs are very detailed in their maps and directions and will pinpoint street addresses and provide such detailed instructions as "Turn left at Rt. 5, drive 1.4 miles, right on Rt. 343."

As computers and satellite technology become more widespread, more automobiles will have built-in display screens that show a map and highlight the location of the car. The computer will calculate the route to be followed, and the driver can follow the car's progress made during the journey.

Automobile Clubs

Automobile clubs offer travel information concerning hotels, motels, restaurants, places of interest, and maps. AAA (American Automobile Association) offers *Triptiks* to its members, which are detailed maps directing a traveler from one city to another city. Automobile clubs offering these services are also operated by other organizations such as Allstate, Amoco, and Exxon.

▼ AIRLINE TRAVEL ▼

In the years since airline deregulation, air travel has undergone a revolution where airlines change fares, schedules, and even cities of service with little advance notice. Some changes are made seasonally in response to travel patterns; other changes are made in response to competing airlines and changing economic conditions.

Although airline travel today is often discounted, there are many restrictions on discount fares. Examples of airline restrictions include issuing nonrefundable tickets, requiring the purchase of tickets 24 hours after the reservation is made, or purchasing tickets 7 to 30 days in advance of travel to get a special fare. A common restriction to secure a discount airfare is the requirement for the traveler to a stay at the destination city over a Saturday night. Since business travelers often do not have advance notice before traveling, they usually are not able to take advantage of the best discounts. Many businesses now require that travelers include a Saturday night stay on their trips in order to obtain a lower fare. The important point to remember is *always* to ask about any restrictions before making a reservation.

If airline reservations are made through a travel agent, the ticket will be issued by the agent. Tickets may also be ordered by calling the airline, or they may be purchased at an airline ticket office. Purchasing tickets at an airport ticket counter should be avoided except for last-minute emergencies, as *long delays* can occur. If a travel agent is not used, the administrative assistant should call an airline and inquire if they serve the desired city. Also, request the names of other airlines that serve the same locality. Ask for information on departure and arrival times, types of service available, which airports in that city they use, and the cost of airfare. After checking with all airlines that service the destination, make a reservation with the most convenient carrier. When calling the airline to make the reservation, have the following information available: travel date, destination, airline, airplane schedule, and method of payment.

As mentioned earlier in this chapter, airline tickets can also be purchased over the Internet. Airlines are moving beyond just using the Internet to reach the consumer through new technologies. Some airlines are installing automated kiosks located at grocery stores, shopping malls, or other locations that sell tickets.

Airline tickets may be paid for with cash, credit card, or check. Boarding passes are issued by the airline to reserve seating and to ensure that only the ticketed passengers enter the plane. Boarding passes may be issued at the airport or may be issued by travel agents. At the airport, the traveler must check in at the airline counter to have the ticket validated prior to boarding. Even with a flight ticket, travelers who do not check in with the airline prior to a flight can lose their seats. The requirement for check-in time varies with the airline, but for domestic flights check-in time is approximately 20 minutes before the scheduled flight departure time. For security reasons, all travelers must show a government-issued photo identification. Due to security concerns, check-in time for international flights can be several hours before the scheduled flight departure time. Always check with the airline regarding how long before the flight they require passengers to check in at the airport counter.

When making reservations, be sure to give the airline the home and office telephone numbers of the traveler. If there is a schedule change or flight cancellation, the airline may try to contact the traveler. Airline reservations should be reconfirmed a couple of days prior to traveling. Airlines try to notify travelers of schedule changes, but it is best to verify flight times and reservations to avoid last-minute problems.

Many airlines offer frequent-flyer bonus programs. These programs encourage a traveler to use one particular airline. By flying one airline often, the traveler accumulates points that may be used toward free travel, upgraded seating, or other gifts. Many airlines have joint programs with hotel and car-rental agencies where the traveler may earn extra points and obtain discounts for using those hotel or car-rental companies. Also, airlines have partnerships with credit card companies which award the traveler bonus points by using the credit card for restaurant meals, shopping, medical bills, and so on. Business travelers often use a particular airline to increase the number of frequent-flyer miles in their account to generate a free trip. Many companies permit the traveler to use the frequent-flyer miles for personal travel, but some companies and the federal government require that frequent-flyer travel be used only for business purposes.

Electronic Airline Tickets

Electronic tickets are cheaper for the airlines than the standard paper forms, and many airlines are encouraging passengers to use electronic ticketing. In electronic ticketing, the passenger receives a confirmation number for a flight itinerary and uses that confirmation number to board an airplane. Electronic ticketing is quicker than using paper forms since the entire booking and ticketing transaction can be done via phone or computer. There is no need to go to an airline or travel agent or wait for a ticket through the mail. If a paper ticket is lost, the traveler absorbs the loss since airline tickets are like money. Depending on the airline policy, lost tickets may be refunded minus a service fee of approximately $70.

Unfortunately, there are some disadvantages for the traveler in using electronic tickets. The traveler loses some flexibility with an electronic ticket. For example, if a flight on airline A is canceled, with a paper ticket the traveler can usually go to airline B and airline B will accept the ticket for a flight. However, airlines will not accept the code numbers that represent an electronic ticket since they do not have access to another airline's computer to verify that the electronic ticket is valid.

Luggage

Airline travelers on a short trip face a dilemma: whether they should take their luggage on the airplane or check the luggage with the airline. The two main reasons for carrying luggage on the plane are to save the time spent waiting for luggage to arrive at the end of the trip and to ensure that the luggage does, in fact, arrive. The price for taking luggage on the plane is carrying heavy luggage, often down endless corridors through airports, through security, and then trying to find a place for the luggage on the plane. Suitcases with built-in wheels are very popular to help people transport luggage through airports. Business people also use catalog carts, which are briefcases on wheels.

There is very limited space on aircraft and airlines are very restrictive on the size and amount of baggage they will permit to be carried aboard aircraft. Most airlines have sizing boxes at airport counters which show the dimensions of luggage that are permitted on the plane. If planes are full, travelers may have to place the suitcase underneath the seat in front of them, thereby using most of their leg space. This can result in a very uncomfortable flight.

When checking luggage with an airline, always have your personal identification tag on the inside and outside of the luggage, and be sure that the airline has placed the proper *airport code* on the suitcase. Each airport in the world has a unique three-letter identifier code. This is done to avoid confusion between airports serving cities with the same names: for example, Charleston, West Virginia (code CRW) and Charleston, South Carolina (code CHS). The code also distinguishes between multiple airports serving the same city. For example, three airports serve the Washington, DC area: Ronald Reagan Washington National Airport (code DCA), Washington Dulles International Airport (code IAD), and Baltimore–Washington International Airport (code BWI). If the wrong airport code is placed on your suitcase, it will have a nice trip without you.

Airport Security

A heightening of airport security is an important safety factor for the traveler. In some cases, the increase in security has caused delays for the traveler. The airlines recommend arriving at the airport at least one hour prior to a domestic flight and at least two hours prior to an international flight. While airport security has safety advantages, it has created a haven for thieves. It is important to watch your personal possessions when passing through the security detection equipment. Pay particular attention to your laptop computer as it moves on the conveyer belt, as computers are attractive to thieves.

Choices of Airline Services

Types of Service

Most airlines offer at least two types of service, *first-class* and *coach*. First-class service is considerably more expensive than coach, the seats are wider, and first-class service provides good-quality food, free alcoholic beverages, and more service from flight attendants. First-class passengers sit at the front of the plane, so they enter and exit the plane before others. Companies usually purchase first-class seats only for top executives, and increasingly, business travelers are not permitted to travel first-class at company expense. Some airlines offer *business class* service, which offers larger seats and more amenities than coach for a price between that of first-class and coach. The discount tickets widely advertised by the airlines are usually for coach seats. Airlines that fly smaller planes, such as commuter airlines, may offer only one class of service.

Personal Preferences

Check with your travelers to determine his or her personal seating preferences when flying. Some people prefer to sit toward the front of the airplane, others over the wing, while others prefer to sit toward the back. Also determine whether a window or aisle seat is preferred. An aisle seat provides more legroom. Always avoid seating a business traveler in the middle seat of a three-seat row if at all possible. Smoking sections are no longer an option on most flights in the United States and Canada, as U.S. and Canadian airlines have banned smoking on domestic and foreign flights. Many foreign airlines, however, continue to have a smoking section for their travelers.

Flights

Airline flights can be classified as nonstop, direct, and connecting. *Nonstop* service means that the flight flies directly between two cities with no intermediate stops. A *direct*

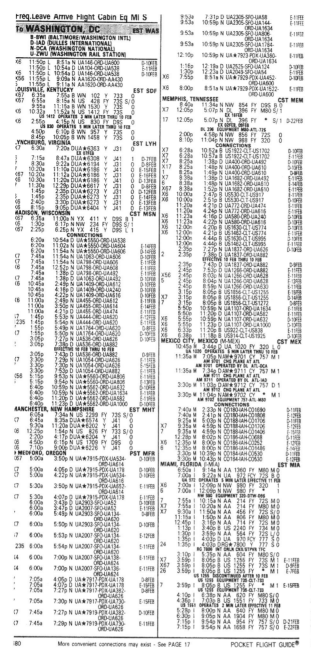

FIGURE 8-2 Excerpt from *OAG Pocket Flight Guide*. (Reprinted by special permission from the February 1998 issue of the *OAG North American Pocket Flight Guide*. All rights reserved.)

flight means that the flight has an intermediate stop but a plane change is not required. A nonstop flight could, therefore, leave at 8:15 A.M. and arrive before a direct flight that left at 7:30 A.M. and makes several stops on the way. The final type of flight is the *connecting* flight, on which the traveler must change planes at an intermediate city.

Many airlines encourage connecting flights by routing passengers through a *hub* where as many as 20 or more airplanes will land and depart within an hour. Each airline has a *minimum legal connecting time* regarding the amount of time that must be available at a particular airport for a passenger to transfer from one flight to another. Airlines will accept only reservations for flights that meet their legal connecting time. However, even with a flight itinerary meeting the minimum connecting time, there is always the danger that a delay in the first flight may cause a passenger to miss a subsequent flight. Connecting flights where both flights are on the same airline enable the traveler to deal with a single airline to resolve missed flight connections.

Meals

Airlines offer special meals, such as kosher, vegetarian, fruit plate, low-sodium, and others. Special meals must be ordered at least 24 hours in advance of the flight. Determine in advance if your traveler wants a special meal.

Airline Guides

Although airline schedules are available via the Internet, it is still important for you to be able to read an airline guide. Many airlines publish seasonal guides of their own flights. These guides are usually sized to fit in a traveler's pocket and are available from travel agents and at airline counters. Seasoned travelers often carry an airline flight guide for information on alternate flights in case they have a change in plans or flights are delayed. Flight schedules for every airline in North America can be found in the *OAG Pocket Flight Guide, North American Edition*. This guide includes schedules on over 100,000 flights to over 500 cities in North America and is published monthly.

Travel agents and travel departments use the *OAG* (Official Airline Guide) *Desktop Flight Guide*, which is published in two thick volumes, a *North American Edition* and a *Worldwide Edition*. Many offices purchase these guides to help employees make flight arrangements. OAG also has an online service, for a fee, which provides full information on flight schedules and can book reservations using a computer. The Official Airline Guides contain the following information for every flight: frequency of service, departure time, arrival time, airline, flight number, airport, fares, type of aircraft, food service, and the number of stops. The OAG also contains information on connecting flights, amount of time required at each airport to make connecting flights, and full listing of each flight's itinerary.

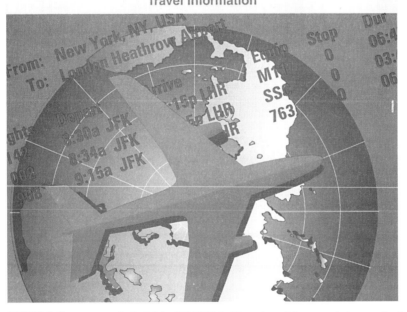

FIGURE 8-3 *OAG FlightDisk*, CD-ROM. (Reprinted by special permission from the *OAG FlightDisk*. All rights reserved.)

Naturally, to be able to present all this information for each flight, the OAG must condense the information through the use of codes. In addition to the *Pocket Flight Guide* edition mentioned earlier, OAG also distributes the *OAG FlightDisk*, a CD-ROM that can be used on a laptop computer.

▼ LODGING ▼

Selecting a Hotel or Motel

Selecting lodging can be the most difficult part of preparing an itinerary. The choice of hotels and motels is usually greater than the choice of airlines or car-rental agencies. In a large metropolitan area, the hotel choices can be overwhelming.

A traveler who visits a destination often has a preference regarding lodging. Travelers attending a convention or large meeting will usually be given information about suggested hotels. If the traveler is visiting a community for the first time, the administrative assistant may be able to contact someone in the destination city for suggestions about suitable lodging. If an administrative assistant is not given specific hotel recommendations, the selection of a hotel is usually based on the following criteria: location, accessibility to clients or meeting sites, accommodations desired, and price.

Location and price are the two most important criteria in selecting accommodations. Usually, except in resort areas, the closer a hotel is to the city's central business district, the more expensive the room rate. Hotels that are convenient to an airport, particularly those hotels with courtesy transportation to the airport, can command a premium room rate. Usually, the most reasonably priced accommodations are on the fringes of cities and are

FIGURE 8-4 *OAG HotelDisk.* (Reprinted by special permission from the *OAG HotelDisk*. All rights reserved.)

near major highways. However, a traveler staying in such a hotel or motel may need to rent a car to reach clients and meeting sites. People with meetings in a city center area can use taxis to travel from the hotel to meetings. Ideally, the hotel or motel should be convenient to the business appointments and to transportation. This, however, is not always possible.

Today, many hotels and motels offer a free continental breakfast, which is convenient for the traveler and saves valuable time. The breakfast usually consists of at least donuts, coffee, and juice. More elaborate breakfasts include cereal, toast, bagels, eggs, and other foods.

Hotels

Hotels that cater to the business traveler are located in a city center, at resorts, or near industrial parks or airports; and they offer a variety of restaurants, meeting rooms, and additional services that are not available in most motels. Hotels are often used by travelers without auto transportation; therefore, they provide a variety of services and entertainment at one location. A hotel may include shops, airline and auto-rental desks, secretarial services, indoor swimming pool, and a health club. These services may be very important or have no value to the individual traveler. You should determine which, if any, of these amenities are important to your traveler.

Motels

Motels are usually smaller than hotels, with an informal atmosphere and limited food services or no food services. Motels are frequently located near major highways, and they usually offer extensive parking. Travelers planning to do a lot of driving to meeting facilities and appointments may prefer a motel convenient to major highways rather than a hotel in the center of a city.

Other Lodging

The overnight accommodation industry is continually developing new variations on the concept of hotels and motels. Some hotels offer two-room suites that may include a sitting room suite or kitchen facilities in addition to the usual bedroom. In addition, bed and breakfast (B & B) facilities, which are usually small inns or restored properties, are also available.

Nationwide Lodging Chains

There are many national hotel and motel chains that specialize in a particular type of accommodation. These chains have toll-free central reservation services and most provide free booklets with maps indicating the location and the services offered at each hotel or motel. Many of the national and worldwide lodging chains own facilities in one or more of the following categories of lodging: luxury, medium priced, and budget. Examples of national chains are Hyatt, Marriott, Hilton, Holiday Inn, Ramada, Hampton Inn, and Quality Inn. In addition to national chains, accommodations are available through regional chains and local hotels and motels. As an assistant who makes reservations for a supervisor, you should keep records for use in future trips regarding the traveler's experiences and preferences and of the hotels or motels used.

Reservations

Hotel and motel reservations are usually made by calling the facility's toll-free telephone number. Although it may be quicker to use the chain's centralized reservations number, cheaper rates can often be obtained by making reservations directly with the hotel or motel. Whether you call the central reservation number or the hotel, never accept the first rate quoted and *always ask if there is a lower rate available*. Ask your supervisor if the supervisor belongs to any organizations that may qualify for travel discounts, such as the American Automobile Association (AAA) or the American Association of Retired Persons (AARP). Many hotel and motel chains have clubs for frequent guests which may qualify the traveler for special discounts, upgrades, or other amenities. Hotels and motels often participate in airline frequent-flyer programs, and this information should also be checked when making a reservation.

The administrative assistant should know the supervisor's preferences in lodging accommodations. Nonsmoking rooms are available in most hotels and motels. Some travelers prefer one large bed or two smaller beds. If the traveler intends to work in the room, you should ask if a desk is included in the furnishings and if the telephone is equipped for a computer hookup.

When making a lodging or car-rental reservation, request either a written confirmation or a confirmation number. Always verify the confirmation number by repeating it to the reservation agent. The traveler should be given a copy of the written confirmation or confirmation number and a second copy should be kept in the office file.

Guaranteed Reservations

Most hotel and motel reservations are held only until 4 P.M. or 6 P.M. on the day of arrival. As a precaution against having a reservation canceled, it is best to make a *guaranteed* reservation by using a major credit card. Giving the credit card number to the hotel guarantees that a room will be available no matter how late in the evening the traveler arrives. This also means that the room must be paid for if the reservation is not canceled by a deadline, such as 4 P.M. or 6 P.M. on the day of arrival. Always ask the hotel's cancellation policy when making a guaranteed reservation and be sure to get a cancellation number from the hotel or motel if you must cancel a reservation. Also, be aware that some facilities have a policy requiring cancellations two or three days prior to the arrival date.

▼ AUTOMOBILE TRAVEL ▼

Personal Car

Many times a personal car will be used for business purposes. In that case, an expense report form will be completed so that the employee will be reimbursed for expenses. Reimbursement is usually based on a per mile rate, usually not more than the Internal Revenue Service allows per mile traveled for business purposes. The employee should keep accurate records of the dates and purposes of business travel and the number of miles traveled.

Auto Rental

There are national and local auto-rental companies and most have toll-free numbers. The rates vary widely and often discounts are offered. Some companies offer free mileage, while others charge for the number of miles traveled. Rates are based on the size of the car and the number of days of the rental. The smallest size auto available for rental, the economy size, often has a trunk too small for the traveler's luggage or a uncovered trunk that can be seen from outside the vehicle. Most business travelers prefer to rent a compact or midsized auto. Auto-rental companies often have coupons for business travelers that provide an upgrade to a larger car for the same price as a smaller vehicle. Cars may be rented by the hour and by the day, but the daily charge is usually the same as a few hours, and the weekly charge is usually equal to the charge for four days. An additional *drop-off* charge is added if a car is returned to a city other than the one where it was picked up.

Date	Beginning Mileage	Ending Mileage	Destination	Parking	Other Expenses
6/1/XXXX	32457	32489	Wood Inc.	2.00	
6/2/XXXX	32489	32529	B. K. Supplies	5.00	1.75 Toll

FIGURE 8-5 An Auto Expense Record.

Auto-rental companies offer and charge for a variety of other services. The major additional charges are for personal insurance and liability insurance on the car. These charges can significantly increase the base price of the auto rental. Many personal auto-insurance policies and credit card company agreements (such as American Express) cover the insurance on a rental car, so additional insurance may not be necessary. All auto-rental companies also charge for gasoline. Some companies ask the traveler to return the car empty of gas, while others ask the driver to fill the car before returning it. The traveler should be aware of which method is used by the rental company. Some companies charge an additional fee for a second driver.

Larger companies frequently have a contract with a specific nationwide rental-car company, and they expect all traveling employees to use that company. In exchange, the company gets a better rate than individuals would get on a single rental.

The primary location to rent a car is at an airport. Since many so-called airport rental agencies are not actually located within the airport terminals, courtesy transportation is often provided from the terminal to the car-rental agency. Car-rental agencies will usually provide a renter with directions and with maps of the area. Car-rental agencies catering to the business traveler usually provide express check-in and returns. If express check-in and/or return is important to the traveler, you should verify arrangements with the agency when reserving a car.

You should also confirm the car-rental agency's operating hours at the auto pickup location. This is particularly important if the car rental is set for very early in the morning or very late in the evening. Most car-rental agencies request the flight number of the incoming flight. If the flight is delayed, the agency will continue to hold the car until the traveler arrives.

Some car-rental companies now have software with maps and directions installed in their cars; thus making travel easier for their clients.

▼ TRAVEL FUNDS ▼

Expense Accounts

Travel can be a major expense for many companies, so companies often limit the travel expenses that they will pay. Usually, companies will only pay for approved travel expenses for such

---

PERSONAL RECORD OF TRAVEL EXPENSES

Date _____

Hotel/Motel _____ Amount _____

Mileage Begin _____ End _____

Breakfast _____

Lunch _____

Dinner _____

Taxi _____

Parking _____

Tips _____

Additional Expenses _____

FIGURE 8-6 A Personal Daily Expense Worksheet.

```
                         TRAVEL EXPENSE RECORD

   Date      Lodging     Meals    Mileage    Misc.     Daily Total

   8/14      $60         $35      _____    $5        $100

   8/15      $60         $42      _____    $8        $110

   8/16      $60         $33      _____    $9        $102


   Method of Transportation      airplane

   _____ miles @ .25    _____

   Airline Ticket                $300_____

   Trip Total                    $612

   Traveler's Signature _____  Date _____
   Supervisor's Signature _____  Date _____
```

FIGURE 8-7 A Travel Expense Record.

items as transportation (including cabs, parking, or tolls), food, and lodging. At the completion of the trip, the traveler completes an expense account report and is reimbursed by the company for approved expenses. Companies often advance employees cash or travelers checks which are used to cover anticipated costs of a trip. At the end of a trip, the expenses of the trip are compared with the funds given in advance to the traveler. The traveler may receive additional money from the company if the approved expenses are more than the travel advance or may refund money to the company if the cost of the trip is less than anticipated.

Some companies allow employees a *per diem*, which is a fixed amount for travel expenses per day. The per diem amount usually includes meals but may also include lodging expenses. Employees usually do not have to submit receipts to their employers for those items covered by the per diem allowance. Some companies permit employees to use a company credit card to pay business travel expenses. When using a company credit card, the employee completes an expense account and payment of the credit-card invoice is handled by the company.

Expense Reports

One of the duties of an administrative assistant is to help the traveler prepare the expense report at the end of a business trip. A detailed list of expenses must be available to complete the expense report accurately. For that reason, a business traveler must make a daily recap of expenses while traveling.

Shown in Figure 8-6 is an example of a personal record of travel expenses that a traveler would complete each day of a trip. Develop a similar sheet for your company and have your supervisor use it while traveling. If receipts are required, they would be attached to the expense record. After a trip, an administrative assistant would complete the company expense reimbursement form using the information the traveler has provided. Company expense report forms will vary, but the information required is essentially the same.

Credit Cards or Traveler's Checks

Traveler's checks can be purchased from a bank, credit union, auto club, or on the Internet. Prior to each trip, verify that the assistant has a list of the numbers of all traveler's checks and credit cards as well as their related toll-free phone numbers. If the traveler's checks or credit cards are lost or stolen, the assistant can notify the traveler's check or credit card companies and obtain replacements.

Special Rates

Corporate Rates

Business travelers often receive corporate rates at hotels, motels, and auto-rental agencies. These are discounted rates offered to frequent users. Often, a corporate identification card is all that is necessary to qualify for these discounts. When making a reservation, ask if your company qualifies for a corporate discount.

Government Travel

The U.S. government has developed a contract rate schedule with specific airlines and hotels and motels. U.S. government employees traveling on business qualify for these government rates.

▼ ITINERARY ▼

An itinerary is a day-by-day travel plan. It includes dates, hotels, telephone numbers, times and locations of meetings, methods of transportation, airline schedule and flight numbers, hotel and car-rental agency rates and confirmation numbers, and any other information necessary to help the traveler. If the traveler is flying, transportation to and from the airport must also be considered; if special airport pickup service is used, it should be noted on the itinerary.

ITINERARY FOR Marcie H. Edwards
6/1/XXXX–6/4/XXXX

June 1	American Airlines flight 347
	Departs Boston Logan Airport at 10:08 A.M.
	Arrives in Los Angeles at 11:57 A.M.
	Avis car rental confirmation number 278234
	3 P.M.: meet with Bill Kodomo at his office at 3000 Western Blvd. (A map is enclosed.)
	Reservation at California Best Western, 3400 Western Blvd.
	Confirmation number GJ39812. Telephone number 213-492-6714.
June 2	Meet with Bill Kodomo at 9:00 A.M.
	Reservation at California Best Western
June 3	Drive to Newport Beach
	Meet at 11:30 A.M. with Rachel Ragman at 2380 Beach Way.
	Reservation at Newport Beach Villa, 1215 Beach Drive
	Confirmation number 2318. Telephone number 562-344-8977.
June 4	American Airlines flight 782
	Departs Los Angeles at 9:45 A.M.
	Arrives Boston Logan Airport at 5:08 P.M.

FIGURE 8-8   An Itinerary.

Some cities are served by more than one airport. When preparing an itinerary, indicate which airport is being used. Copies of the itinerary should be given to the traveler and administrative assistant and be available to the traveler's family if so desired.

▼ PASSPORTS AND VISAS ▼

Travelers to locations outside the United States and Canada require a *passport*. A passport is used by a government to grant permission for international travel and also is the interna-

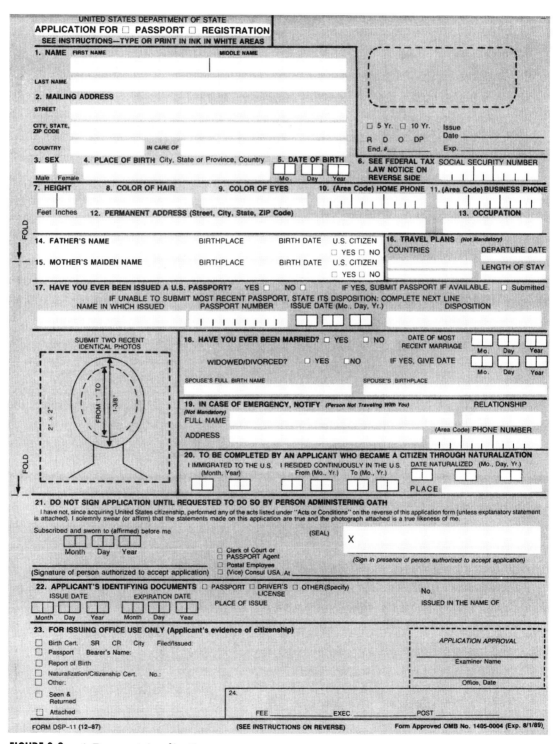

FIGURE 8-9　A Passport Application.

tionally recognized way to identify the traveler. Citizens of the United States obtain passports from the Department of State. Passport applications are available from passport agencies, major post offices, federal and state courts, and probate courts. Applicants for a passport must furnish proof of citizenship (such as a birth certificate), proof of identity (such as a valid driver's license or corporate ID) and two photographs. The first time that an applicant applies for a passport, the applicant must appear in person, but passport renewals may be processed by mail. For persons over 18 years of age, passports are issued for a 10-year period. Passports may be paid for by check or money order and post offices and passport agencies accept cash. Information on obtaining U.S. passports is available via the Internet at http://travel.state.gov. Information on obtaining Canadian passports is available from the Canada Passport Office Internet site at http://www.dfait-maeci.gc.ca/passport/passport.htm.

A *visa* is a document permitting a visitor *entry* into a foreign country. Not all countries require a visa for entry. Information regarding visa requirements can be obtained from travel books, travel agencies, and airlines serving foreign countries. Visas are usually obtained from the embassy of the foreign country a visitor plans to visit. Visas fees and the time required for processing applications varies, so it is best to check on visa requirements as soon as foreign travel is known.

Before traveling to another country, it is prudent to investigate whether any medical precautions may be necessary. The U.S. government's Centers for Disease Control and Prevention (CDC) maintains an Internet site (Internet address: www.cdc.gov) which is the standard reference for medical information of interest to travelers. The CDC Internet site includes information on vaccinations that may be required or medication recommended to be taken as a precaution when traveling to specific countries.

CHAPTER REVIEW

1. Name four travel guides that would be helpful when planning trips.
2. What factors should be considered when renting a car?
3. What is meant by the term *corporate travel rates*?
4. Explain the term *guaranteed reservation*.
5. What information should be included in an itinerary?
6. What is the purpose of a visa?

ACTIVITIES

1. Call three airlines and compare the travel times and prices for a trip from your home to a city of your choice.
2. Use the Internet to determine the time and cost of a trip from your home to the city of your choice. Include in your report three possible time schedules, airlines used, and a cost comparison for your trip.
3. Go to an airport or a travel agency, pick up a flight schedule, and read it. Select five cities you would like to visit and record the best schedules.
4. Call two airlines and request that they send you information about their frequent-flyer bonus travel program.
5. Call two airlines and ask what kinds of special meals are available.
6. Go to a library and look at the travel book section for books by Birnbaum, Mobil, Frommer, Fordor, or others. Select a city you would like to visit. Then select two hotels or motels that appeal to you. Also select three restaurants where you would like to eat. Explain why you made your selections.
7. Select two cities that are in different states about 500 miles apart. Call two auto-rental agencies and inquire about renting a car for a trip between the two cities. The trip should take a week. You have not decided if you want an economy car or a midsized car. You

are going to leave the car in the second city. What are the charges? Remember that you must be concerned with drop-off charges, mileage charges, gasoline charges, and insurance fees. Explain why you made your final selection.

8. Complete an expense-report form for a four-day business trip. Include lodging, food, tips, gasoline, and mileage. Design the form to meet your needs.

9. Get a passport application and complete it. If you do not currently have a passport, you might actually apply for one.

10. Prepare a detailed itinerary for your employer for a three-day trip to a city that your employer chooses. Call several airlines to determine the best schedule and fare. Call several car-rental agencies to compare rental costs. Select a hotel that is a member of a national chain. Ask if there is a limousine service to the hotel from the airport. After deciding on the hotel, call the toll-free reservation number and inquire about room costs and the reservation cancellation policy. Type a complete itinerary, including dates, times, locations, hotel and rental-car rates, telephone numbers, and method of transportation.

PROJECTS

Project 15

Complete the following travel expense report from the receipts shown below.

Travel Expense Report						
Date	City	Lodging	Food	Tips	Taxi	Daily Total

Total amount to be reimbursed _____

Date _____ Signature _____

Date _____ Supervisor's Signature _____

8230 87235 23789 2076
VISA   3 nights $295.00
Lucy R. Castle

Inns of Tomorrow
Tampa, FL 33606
7/27/XX

8230 87235 23789 2076
VISA   Food $23.95
Lucy R. Castle

The Sea's Delight   Tip $4.00
Tampa, FL 33607   Total $27.95

7/26/XX

8230 87235 23789 2076
VISA   Food $27.00
Lucy R. Castle

Hawaii At Night   Tip $5.50
Tampa, FL   Total $32.50

7/24/XX

8230 87235 23789 2076
VISA   Food $21.00
Lucy R. Castle

Pedro's Best   Tip $4.00
Clearwater, FL 33609   Total $25.00

7/25/XX

Receipt

Taxi
7/24/XX
$22.00

Lunch at a fast-food restaurant $4.25
Tampa
I forgot to get a receipt
7/25/XX

Project 16

Prepare the following itinerary.

Mary, I am going to be traveling to Denver on May 1(United Airlines flight 478), which leaves at 10:01 A.M. It arrives at 12:33 P.M. I will be staying at the Sheraton Convention Center (confirmation number 7182409). I will then fly to San Francisco on American Airlines (flight 326) and will stay three nights at the Mark Hopkins Hotel. The flight leaves Denver at 9:02 A.M. and arrives in San Francisco at 11:17 A.M. The confirmation number at the Mark Hopkins is 221684. After two nights in Denver and three nights in San Francisco, I will be returning on the 8:07 A.M. flight arriving at Chicago O'Hare at 3:59 P.M.

HUMAN RELATIONS SKILL DEVELOPMENT

Scents

Men and women who wear perfume, cologne, aftershave, scented hair-care products, and scented cosmetics can offend others without realizing it. Fragrances should be light enough so they do not disturb other workers. Working in close proximity to others and in closed or windowless offices can compound the problem of a heavy fragrance. In addition, people with allergies can become physically ill from breathing strong scents. After using a product for a period of time, the user becomes less sensitive to the smell and may not be aware that the scent is disturbing to others.

- Ask a friend to tell you honestly if your fragrances can be smelled by a person near you. Are your fragrances too heavy or offensive?
- How would you tell a co-worker diplomatically that you find a scent too heavy?

Restoring an Injured Relationship

Getting along with other workers is important, but a relationship can be damaged by a mis-understanding or insensitivity to a situation. If a friendship existed and then cooled because of a problem, the problem must be solved before the friendship can continue. Unfortunately, one person may not be aware of what caused the problem, and getting the other person to talk about the problem may be difficult. To begin solving the problem, remove yourself from the office environment. Suggest meeting for lunch, going for a walk at lunch, or meeting after work to talk. Start by saying that you would like to continue your friendship and explain that you are not aware of what created the problem. Repairing a damaged relationship can take time, but it can be worth the effort.

- Have you ever lost a friendship?
- Discuss a friendship that you lost.
- How would you restore a damaged relationship with your supervisor?
- If your co-worker was not interested in remaining friends, how would you handle the day-to-day work situation?

SITUATIONS

How would you handle each of the following situations?

- Your employer asks you to go to the airport to pickup Ms. Kahn, whom you have never met.

- Your employer is in Cheyenne, Wyoming, and she needs a folder immediately that she did not take with her on the trip.
- Your employer is on the third day of a 14-day trip. You have just received a telephone call informing you that the hotel for day 12 has been destroyed by fire.

PUNCTUATION REVIEW

Punctuate each of the following sentences.

1. He wore a dark blue suit and he impressed the manager
2. The budget office estimated that because of the new regulations the cost of maintaining the equipment would be very expensive
3. Rodney who has a pleasing personality worked in a small office on the tenth floor
4. Because most persons who receive outplacement counseling are anxious to continue working they actively search for jobs
5. Penny has a large office with an impressive view of the city and a private elevator
6. At one time my mentor was Ted Lincoln the manager
7. With all of their credentials the applicants also have many shortcomings that must be considered
8. William I believe received the Outstanding Employee award at last years ceremony
9. Yes I saw the results of the advertising campaign
10. If business takes a hands-off attitude the problem will not be solved by next June said th mayor
11. The reigning theory about career development was discussed at the last board meeting and Samuel said let's stop talking and implement it
12. Such a policy would create what many of our departments drastically need a think tank
13. In our view Thomas Costello took the initiative developed the project and brought it to a successful conclusion
14. The petroleum company which is incorporated in Kentucky transferred the stock to three members of the board of directors
15. Joseph Peerless the witness stated I have never seen a corporation run with such a lack of courtesy

▼9▼

Terminology
of the World of Business

OBJECTIVES

After studying this chapter, you should be able to:

1. Explain market systems.
2. Explain the four types of business ownership.
3. Define and use basic business terms.
4. Define and use basic financial terms.
5. Define and use basic legal terms.
6. Define and use basic accounting terms.
7. Define and use basic real estate terms.
8. Read and use a stock listing.

▼ INTRODUCTION ▼

To climb the business ladder from an entry-level position to a job with greater responsibilities, it is essential for you to understand how the American economic system operates. Business and economic terms are not only important in the business world but also have become an integral part of modern society. An understanding of these terms, therefore, will help you to be successful in your personal life as well as in your professional career. Each business uses its own special terminology. While the professional terms used in a real estate office will be quite different from the specialized terms used in a medical office, both offices will use the same language for general business activities.

In this chapter we review basic economic terminology often used in an office environment as well as general business terms and specialized terms used in several different types of offices. Mastering the language of business will improve your ability to work with greater understanding in an office environment.

Globalization

The *globalization* of the world economy has affected business across the country. Business decisions made in Europe or Asia can affect the availability of raw materials, can provide competition to your company, or can open new markets for your employer's product. Today, businesses often operate in many countries and are no longer limited to one locality. Employees with international business skills and knowledge of the economic systems of other countries are attributes to a company. Not understanding a culture can create barriers to communications. Assistants who can travel to other countries and know how to work with persons of other cultures are assets. Cultural differences exist in oral and written communications. One untactful remark can destroy a relationship that took many months to establish. A joke that you find very funny may offend a person from another culture.

Cultural diversity has become commonplace in today's business environment. Earning the trust and respect of members of all cultures is vital to the business climate.

Prior to traveling to another country or working with foreign businesses, research the customs of that area. Become knowledgeable of the proper behavior and protocol of that country. In some countries shaking hands is not acceptable, while in other countries it is expected. Also, taking business gifts when visiting one culture may be expected, and in other societies it may be inappropriate. Slang should not be used because it may not be understood by persons from other cultures. Learning a few words of another language can show business associates that you are interested in them and their company. Employees who work in a global company must adapt to new customs and economic practices.

▼ SOURCES OF BUSINESS INFORMATION ▼

Reading daily newspapers and business publications will help keep you informed of current events. A political or economic event in another part of the country or in another part of the world may affect the business where you work. A change in economic conditions or new legislation could alter the business environment in which your employer operates, your job, and the operation of your office.

Many offices subscribe to well-known business publications such as *The Wall Street Journal*, which contains news about business ventures, stocks, taxes, politics, marketing, and other subjects that affect the business environment. Other important business publications include *Business Week, Fortune, Barron's, Financial World,* and *Dun's Review.* In addition, there are many specialized services such as *Standard and Poor's* and *Moody's,* which report on the stock, bond, and municipal markets. You should become familiar with these publications and skim them for information related to your business. If your office does not subscribe to the business newspapers or magazines that interest you, check the selection available at your library or purchase your own subscription.

Each industry also has specialized publications and newsletters which contain information directly related to that industry. These publications may be monthly, weekly, or daily, and some are available via electronic mail. Examples of these specialized publications are *Journal of Accountancy, Journal of Taxation, Accounting Review, Administrative Management,* and *Best's Insurance Reports.* These publications are excellent sources of news about the industry specified. By reading these publications, you will be well informed about events in your field.

The television media have entered the field of business and financial information by broadcasting daily and weekly financial television programs. In addition to daily business programs, such as *Nightly Business Report* and weekly financial programs such as *Wall Street Week,* there are several full-time financial television channels such as CNBC and CNNfn distributed by cable and by satellite systems.

▼ ECONOMICS ▼

Economics is the study of how a community manages its income, expenditures, labor, and natural resources. The production, distribution, and consumption of goods and services are all included in the study of economics. Individuals, businesses, and governments continually make choices regarding the acquisition and expenditure of money. No person or government can produce or purchase everything needed. Choices must be made regarding the use of finances and resources. As individuals, we make choices when we decide to spend our money on a movie or restaurant. In the same sense, each business must make choices about how to allocate its resources of money, people, or raw materials. For example, to earn a greater profit, should a business raise its prices or lower its costs to increase market share? As this question implies, economic decisions can be very complex with far-reaching results.

Market Systems

One aspect of economics is the *market system*. A market is a location where buyers and sellers exchange goods or services for a price. In economic terms, a market is not simply one store but includes the entire community.

We live in a *free-market system*. In this type of system, people are free to go into whatever type of business they choose. The variety of goods and services available in a free-market system reflects the interests and ideas of the individual business owners in the community.

Exchange of goods and services in a free-market economy results when consumers and businesses agree on the *perceived value* of an item. An exchange of goods and services takes place when a consumer is willing to buy an item at the same price at which the business is willing to sell it. A business owner tries to attract consumers to products so that the business will earn the owner a *profit*. Profit is the difference between the selling price of goods or services and the costs to manufacture and sell the items.

Consumers have a major role in deciding the types of products manufactured and their selling price. People will not purchase goods or services if they do not need or want them or if the price is higher than they are willing to pay. In a free-market system, both the consumer and the business owner have *freedom of choice*. A manufacturer chooses to make a product in the hope that it can be sold for a profit. The consumer has the final choice—deciding whether to purchase or not to purchase it. Of course, *marketing* influences the purchasing decision. Marketing involves the selling of goods and services and often uses advertising to influence consumers to purchase a product.

When a new product is developed, consumers have no knowledge of the item. Demand is created by advertising the product. Consumers do not know that they want a product unless advertising convinces them that the product is desirable.

The price of most new products is very high because of the expense of developing and producing only a limited number of items. As larger numbers are produced through *mass production*, the price of the products can be reduced. As larger numbers of a product become available, and as more people know about it through marketing, more people will want to purchase it.

The primary motive for operating a business is profit. Since the business owner, or *entrepreneur*, is in business to make a profit, the owner has an incentive to produce items efficiently in response to consumer demand. The more efficiently the product is produced, the greater the profit can be. *Competition* limits the profit of a company because it involves rivalry between companies selling the same products or offering similar services. Competition regulates the price that can be charged for a product or service. The producer or retailer can raise the selling price of a product when there is a lack of competition or when the limited quantity of a product is insufficient to meet consumer demand. If a consumer can find the same item at a lower cost, the consumer will purchase it at the lower cost. The entrepreneur who is the most efficient producer or retailer can lower the selling price and attract more customers. Profits can then be increased by selling more of the item.

The free-market system encourages *specialization*, which results in the most efficient use of time and resources. Specialization is producing one particular item or delivering one type of service. Companies specialize in those products that are most profitable for them.

The government does not directly control the economy in a free-market system. A free-market system, however, does not mean a total absence of a government role in the nation's economy. Governments may regulate some industries, such as requiring the treatment of hazardous waste material or prohibiting the sale of dangerous toys to children. The government's ability to tax business and the government's own spending have a major effect on the nation's economy. The extent of government regulation, the tax policy, and spending levels are major political and economic issues in our society.

Business provides goods and services for the consumer to purchase. The income received from the sale of these goods and services allows a business to pay workers a salary. Workers spend the salaries for food, shelter, clothing, and other products. This spending, in turn, produces other jobs and the money continues to flow through the economic system. This process is called the *circular flow of goods and services*. If jobs are terminated, workers do not receive a salary. Consequently, their ability to purchase goods and services must decrease. This change in spending patterns is felt throughout the business community.

▼ TYPES OF BUSINESS ORGANIZATIONS ▼

As the size of businesses have increased, different types of business ownership have developed to meet financial and management requirements. Business ownership can be divided into four categories: sole proprietorship, partnership, corporation, and cooperative.

Sole Proprietorship

A *sole proprietorship* is a business owned by one person. The owner provides all the money for the investment in the business and receives all of the profits. The owner manages the business, makes all the policy decisions, and is personally liable for all the business's debts. If the business has financial difficulties, the owner can be required to sell personal property to pay the debts. An example of a sole proprietorship may be a small business such as a photographer's studio, a farm, an accountant's office, or a business operated from a person's home.

Partnership

A *partnership* is a business owned by at least two people. While the decisions of the business are made by the partners, each partner may have an area of expertise for which that partner is responsible. Ownership in the business may or may not be equally divided. Ownership and profits are divided according to an agreement between the partners. Each partner, however, is legally liable for the debts of the business and the promises of the other partners. Debts incurred by one partner may force another partner to use personal funds to pay those debts. Examples of a partnership could include a restaurant, an attorney's office, and a supply store. It is frequently difficult for a consumer to know whether a business is a sole proprietorship or a partnership.

Corporation

A *corporation* is a business owned by a number of people called *stockholders*, who each own *stock* in the corporation. The state in which the corporation is organized authorizes a *charter*, which is a license to operate the business. Profits earned by a corporation may be reinvested in the business or distributed to the stockholders. A corporation pays taxes on its profits, and the stockholders pay taxes on the portion of the profits that they receive. Stockholders have no personal liability in the business. If a corporation fails, the stockholders lose only their investment. Their personal money is never used to pay the debts of the business. IBM, General Motors, and Exxon are all corporations, but corporations are not limited to large companies.

Ownership in the corporation is represented by shares of stock. When a person purchases shares of stock, a *stock certificate* is issued. The certificate states how many shares of stock were purchased. Stock may be transferred to another person easily without the consent of the corporation. The stockholder can sell the stock at any time as long as there is a buyer available. People usually buy shares of stock in a company because they expect the company to grow and to earn a profit. The profit can be reinvested in the business or it can be returned to the stockholders in the form of a *dividend*. (A dividend is similar to the interest you earn from a savings account at a bank.) Stockholders purchase stock with the expectation that the stock will increase in value or that dividends will be earned.

The stockholders control the corporation by selecting the *board of directors*, which operates the company. The board of directors manages the corporation and appoints the officers who run the company. The size of the board of directors varies. Corporations have an annual meeting where stockholders vote on policy decisions. Each share of stock represents one vote. Stockholders who do not attend the annual meeting are asked to sign a *proxy*, which gives written authorization for another person to vote on the issues.

There are two types of stock: *common* and *preferred*. Preferred stockholders have preference over common stockholders. When a dividend is declared, preferred stockholders receive their dividends before the common stockholders receive theirs. Preferred stockholders usually receive a fixed rate of dividends, while common stockholders do not receive dividends at a fixed rate.

Cooperative

A *cooperative* is a business that is owned by its members. The members are not liable for the debts of the business, but the profits are returned to the members. Each member of a cooperative votes for the board of directors that manages the business. An example of a cooperative is a food cooperative that provides low-cost food to its members.

▼ BONDS AND TREASURY SECURITIES ▼

Corporations raise money by selling shares of stock that represent ownership in the company and which include the potential of sharing in the future profits of the corporation. Private corporations—as well as the federal, state, and local governments—borrow money by selling *bonds* to investors. Bonds are loans made by individuals or financial institutions and do not represent ownership or a potential share in future profits. Repayment of a bond is the first obligation of a corporation, and bond payments must be made before any dividends or profits are distributed to shareholders.

Bonds are issued with a maturity date that may be 10 or 20 years in the future. The bondholder receives interest payments each year until the *maturity* date. At the maturity date the company pays back (*redeems*) the amount of the loan, which is the face value (*principal*) of the bond certificate. Bonds are often purchased for prices above or below the face value. If the bond is paying an interest rate higher than can be obtained through the purchase of a new bond, people are willing to pay a higher price, a *premium*, to obtain the higher income. However, if the bond is paying an interest rate less than can be obtained through the purchase of a new bond, the bond will sell at a *discount* of the face value. Bonds selling at a discount will be redeemed at full face value if held to maturity.

Corporate bonds are certificates issued by corporations, and they are usually issued in $1,000 denominations. Investment bankers and security agencies sell these bonds to their clients. Bonds represent a company's promise to pay interest to the bondholder. The stronger the financial condition of the company, the better chance the bondholder has of receiving repayment of the money. The financial strength of many companies is rated by independent companies such as Moody's and Standard and Poor's.

When a city, state, or local government, issues a bond, it is called a *municipal bond*. Interest income from municipal bonds are normally not taxed by the federal government or by the government in the state in which the bond is issued. People in high tax brackets have an incentive to purchase municipal bonds since the interest income is free of most income taxes.

One way the U.S. government meets its financial needs is through the sale of government securities. Treasury securities may be purchased by individuals or businesses directly from the 12 Federal Reserve Banks, the Bureau of Public Debt in Washington, commercial banks, and other financial institutions. Purchases made through commercial banks and other financial institutions usually include a fee in addition to the cost of the security.

Treasury securities are very safe investments since both the bonds and the interest to be paid on government securities are backed by the federal government. There is an active market for previously issued securities and they are easily purchased or sold on the open market. Interest earned from Treasury securities is exempted from state and local income taxes.

Types of government securities

- *Treasury bills (T-bills)* are issued by the U.S. Treasury for 13 weeks, 26 weeks, and 52 weeks. The minimum amount of purchase is $10,000, and bills are sold in multiples of $5,000 above the $10,000 minimum.

- *Treasury notes* are similar to T-bills, but the minimum amount of purchase is $1,000. Treasury notes are issued for more than one year but not for more than 10 years.
- *Treasury bonds* are issued for more than 10 years. Bonds may be redeemed by the government before the maturity date, and they are sold with a minimum purchase of $5,000.

▼ TERMINOLOGY IN THE WORLD OF BUSINESS ▼

As an administrative assistant, you will be expected to be familiar with the following business terminology used in an office. Specialized terminology used in finance, law, real estate, and accounting offices follows these general business terms.

General Business Terms

- An *annual report* is a report issued by a corporation each year that reviews the corporation's business activities and financial statements for the year and discusses its future expectations.
- *Business forecasting* provides projections of a business' future. Business forecasting is used to plan budgets, revenues, and expenses under a variety of conditions. Computers and spreadsheet programs are widely used in business forecasting.
- The *Consumer Price Index* (CPI) is an index calculated monthly by the U.S. government showing the change in the prices of the same group of consumer goods and services.
- *Deflation* is a general decrease in the price of goods and services and is the opposite of *inflation.*
- *Depreciation* is the gradual decrease in the value of an item. The value of office equipment such as computers depreciates as it ages.
- *Depression* is a very low point in a nation's economy when there is high unemployment and a decrease in the purchasing of goods and services. (A depression is worse than a *recession.*)
- The *fiscal year* is a 12-month calendar period used for budgeting and planning purposes. For the federal government, a fiscal year begins on October 1 and ends the next September 30. State and local governments usually run on a fiscal year of July 1 to June 30 or October 1 to September 30. A private business can elect to begin its fiscal year with any month, although most begin with January, April, July, or October. A fiscal year is usually referred to by the year that the cycle *ends.* For example, the U.S. government's fiscal 2000 (FY 00) begins October 1, 1999 and ends September 30, 2000. Businesses report their earnings and file their tax returns based on their fiscal year.
- The *Gross National Product* (GNP) is the total value of all goods and services produced by a country in one year. GNP is an index used to compare the size of a country's economy over a period of years or to compare one country's total output with another country's total output.
- *Inflation* is a general increase in the price of products and services. An example of inflation is a house that cost $50,000 twenty years ago now selling for $150,000. The house is the same house, but now many more dollars are required to purchase it. If wages have risen at the same inflation rate as houses, then houses remain affordable even if the price is three times what it was 20 years ago.
- *Liquidating* means converting *securities* (stocks or bonds) to cash.
- A *monopoly* is a situation where there is only one supplier of a good or service or where one supplier is so large that it can control the market. In the United States, monopolies are permitted only where government policy determines that a single provider is in the public interest. Many former monopolies, such as local telephone

FIGURE 9-1 Computers in a Financial Office. (Courtesy of International Business Machines Corporation. Unauthorized use not permitted.)

and electric services, are now being deregulated by the government and are being opened to competition.

- The *Producer Price Index* (PPI) is an index calculated monthly by the U.S. government showing the change in prices of farm products, processed foods, and industrial products.

- A *quarter* is one of four parts of the business fiscal year. Most businesses review their financial status at the end of each quarter of the business' fiscal year. Each of the four quarters of the business year contain three months. The first quarter is the first three months of the fiscal year, while the fourth (or last) quarter is the final three months of the fiscal year. Financial activity often increases near the end of a quarter as businesses try to complete transactions for financial reporting. At the end of the quarter, corporations may issue *quarterly reports* to their shareholders, which report the business activities during the period.

- A *recession* is a slowdown in economic activity, which is often accompanied by a reduction in sales, profits, and employment.

- *Retained earnings* is the money remaining in a company after paying taxes and dividends.

Terms Used in Financial Institutions

- A *bear market* is the time period during which the price of stocks decline.
- The *Big Board* is an informal term used to refer to the New York Stock Exchange.
- *Blue chip* is an informal term for the common stock of a company that is known for long-term, high-quality financial performance. Blue-chip stocks are generally thought of as investments with low risk.
- A *broker* is an agent who handles the sale or purchase of securities, including stocks, bonds, mutual funds, insurance, or annuities.
- A *bull market* is the time period during which the price of stocks rise.
- A *call provision* is a clause in a bond agreement that allows the issuer to redeem (call) the bond prior to the maturity date.

- A *certificate of deposit* (CD) relates to a specific type of account in a bank or other financial institution. A CD is an investment for a fixed term and pays a higher rate of interest than a regular interest account. Usually, the interest is guaranteed during the term of the CD.
- A *commission* is a broker's fee for buying or selling a security for a client.
- The *Dow Jones Industrial Average* is the most common benchmark used for comparing the price level of common stocks on the New York Stock Exchange. The Dow Jones Company, publisher of *The Wall Street Journal*, calculates the value of a stock portfolio of 30 large companies. Changes in the stocks are compared on a daily basis. The Dow Jones Industrial Average, often referred to as the Dow Jones Average (or the *Dow*), is only one of many averages used to track the advances and declines of the stock market. Other averages exist for specific industrial areas, such as banking stocks, transportation stocks, for stocks on the American Stock Exchange, for bonds, and for many other financial securities.
- An *Individual Retirement Account* (IRA) is a special account permitted by the federal government where a person can invest money for retirement. Money may be invested in a variety of items, including CDs, stocks, bonds, and mutual funds. An IRA must be established with an approved financial institution. There are two types of IRA accounts. The money invested in a *regular IRA* can be deducted from gross income for income tax purposes, and payment of taxes on income earned on an IRA is delayed until the person withdraws the money, usually at retirement. A *Roth IRA* is similar to a regular IRA, except that taxes are paid on the funds placed in the Roth IRA, but no taxes are paid on the earnings while they are in the IRA or when they are withdrawn.
- *Junk bonds* are bonds that pay a high rate of interest, due to a low credit rating, which reflects a higher risk of default.
- The *margin* is the amount of money a customer puts down toward the purchase price when buying a security on credit. The remainder of the purchase price is loaned by the broker.
- A *market order* is an order to buy or sell a security (stock or bond) at the best price available when the order reaches the Stock Exchange floor.
- The *market price* is the last price at which a security (stock or bond) was bought or sold.
- The *maturity date* (or *redemption date*) is the date that the bond issuer will pay the *principal* (face value) of the bond.
- *Mutual funds* are investments where a financial firm purchases stocks or bonds from many issuers and sells shares in the fund to the public. The goal of a mutual fund is to diversify investment and therefore reduce client risk. Mutual funds often specialize in the types of securities they purchase or in their investment objectives.
- An *odd lot* is an order for the purchase of stock in other than 100-share units.
- A *portfolio* is a group of securities owned by a person or a company.
- The *price–earnings ratio* is the ratio between the market price of stock and its earnings per share.
- A *prospectus* is a brochure describing securities offered for sale. The Securities and Exchange Commission requires that a purchaser be supplied with a prospectus before a security is purchased.
- A *round lot* is a stock bought or sold in 100-share units.
- The *Securities and Exchange Commission* (SEC) is an agency of the U.S. government that regulates the sale of stocks and bonds. It is the Securities and Exchange Commission's responsibility to ensure that the public is provided truthful information about securities.
- A *speculator* is a person who assumes a large risk in anticipation of receiving a high profit.
- A *stock exchange* is a place where stocks and bonds are traded. Examples are the New York, American, Philadelphia, Pacific, Tokyo, and Toronto stock exchanges. Brokerage

firms that are members of a stock exchange are referred to as having a *seat* on a stock exchange.

- In a *stock split* a company issues additional shares of stock to its stockholders. For example, a company may double the number of shares (a two-for-one split). Each stockholder will then own twice as many shares as before the split. Each share, however, will sell for approximately half the previous value. Companies may split the stock in the hope that a stock selling at a lower price will be attractive to more investors. In a *reverse split*, a company may reduce the number of shares of a stock owned by all stockholders by issuing new stock for each two or three shares previously issued. In a one-for-two reverse split, the new share would be worth approximately twice the value of the old share.
- A *stop order* is an order to buy or sell a stock when it reaches a set price.
- The *yield* is a return on an investment. The yield is usually referred to as a percentage of the purchase price.

How to Read a Stock Listing

Most Americans own securities, either directly through ownership of stocks and bonds or indirectly through participation in a company retirement plan. Following the stock market is easy since most newspapers carry stock quotations. Some newspapers may only print information on those stocks of local interest or the 10 most active stocks of the day, while other newspapers carry several pages listing hundreds of stock transactions.

Most stock tables utilize a format similar to that shown in Figure 9-2. Stock tables are read beginning with the left column.

52-week High	The highest price for the stock during the prior 52 weeks.
Low	The lowest price for the stock during the prior 52 weeks.
Stock	The name of the stock, which is abbreviated.
Symb	A short code assigned to the stock.
Div	The amount of the dividend paid on the stock for the past year.
Yld.	The yield on the stock is the dividend expressed as a percentage of the stock price.
PE	The price–earnings ratio of the stock is the ratio between the market price of the stock and its earnings per share.
Sales	The number of shares sold (in hundreds) during the day.
High	The highest price for the stock for that day.
Low	The lowest price paid for the stock for that day.
Last	The closing price of the stock for that day.
Chg.	The change in price from the prior day's closing price.

52-week High	Low	Stock	Symb	Div	Yld.	PE	Sales 100s	High	Low	Last	Chg.
42	38	NorW	NXC	4.00	10.3	15	189	39	38 1/4	39	-1/2
117	101	Otell	OWT	5.00	4.5	20	256	112	111	112	+3/8
32	19	PlaDa	PRP	.88	2.8	18	123	31	30 7/8	31	

FIGURE 9-2 A Stock Table.

Legal Terms

- *Affidavit:* a statement in writing and sworn before an officer who administers an oath.
- *Appellate court:* a higher court that reviews a lower court's decision.
- *Contributory negligence:* failure to do what was wise and reasonable.
- *Decree:* an order of the court.
- *Defendant:* person against whom a suit or complaint is brought.
- *Felony:* a grave crime punishable by heavy penalties.
- *Habeas corpus:* a *writ* (written order) requiring that a person be brought before a judge before being held.
- *Injunction:* an order issued by a court requiring someone to do or refrain from doing a particular act.
- *Misdemeanor:* a less severe crime than a felony.
- *Perjury:* swearing that something is true while knowing it is false.
- *Plaintiff:* person who brings a suit or complaint.
- *Tort:* a legal wrong that prompts a civil lawsuit.

Real Estate Terms

- *Appraisal:* an estimate of the value of an item, building, or property.
- *Assessment:* a charge by the government against real estate to cover improvements such as a sewer. The assessment is usually a percentage of the appraised value of the property.
- *Deed:* a written form that transfers property from one owner to a new owner.
- *Domicile:* the place where a person has a permanent residence.
- *Easement:* one person's right to use or pass through another person's property.
- *Encroachment:* property that trespasses on another's property.
- *Escrow:* a deed or money given to a third party to hold until an obligation is fulfilled. An example of escrow is giving the homeowner's insurance payment or real estate taxes to the mortgage company to hold until the payment is due.
- *Foreclosure:* the removal of the right to continue paying the mortgage and owning the property.
- *Mortgage:* a contract specifying that a sum of money will be paid periodically for the repayment of a loan.

Accounting Terms

- *Account:* a form that separates business transactions into similar groups.
- *Asset:* anything that a business owns. Examples of assets include buildings, cash, furniture, and equipment.
- *Audit:* a verification of accounting records. An audit is usually performed by a person not affiliated with the company being audited.
- *Capital:* what the business is worth. Capital is found by subtracting the liabilities from assets.
- *Credit:* an entry on the right side of an account ledger.
- *Debit:* an entry on the left side of an account ledger.
- *Ledger:* a group of accounts.
- *Liability:* anything that a business owes. Examples of liabilities include mortgages, credit card charges, and auto loans.
- *Petty cash:* an office cash fund for small expenses.
- *Trial balance:* shows that the debits and credits in the ledger are equal.

Income Statement and Balance Sheet

In your role as an office employee, you may be asked to read, interpret, and keyboard an income statement or a balance sheet. An *income statement* is a financial statement that lists the income and expenses of a business over a particular period of time, often a month or year. A *balance sheet* is a financial statement that lists the assets, liabilities, and capital of the business on a specific date.

Budgets

One of your duties may be to assist with the preparation or keyboarding of a department or office budget. In a large company, departmental budgets may be prepared in addition to company budgets. A budget includes a dollar figure for each anticipated item of income and expense and is usually prepared a year or more in advance. Before budgets are adopted, they must be approved by top management. Past experience, new initiatives, and a percentage of increase in anticipated income and expenses are usually the basis for preparing a future year's budget. The development of computer spreadsheet packages have made budget preparations and revisions an easier task and permit budget forecasting many years in advance. The use of computer spreadsheets in the preparation of budgets was discussed in Chapter 5.

L & K Manufacturing
Income Statement
For Year Ended December 31, XXXX

Revenue

Professional fees income		$150,780

Expenses

Rent Expense	12,000	
Salary Expense	52,000	
Travel Expense	8,000	
Office Supplies	2,000	
Office Equipment	8,000	
Telephone Expense	1,000	
Electricity Expense	1,200	
Gasoline Expense	900	
Maintenance Expense	2,500	
Total Expenses		87,600

Net Income $ 63,180

FIGURE 9-3   An Income Statement.

```
                            C & C Manufacturing
                               Balance Sheet
                             December 31, XXXX

                                   Assets
Cash                              200,000
Office Equipment                   56,000
Building                          350,000
Total Assets                                                    $606,000

                                 Liabilities
Accounts Receivable                75,000
Notes Payable                      30,000
Accounts Payable                   12,000
FICA Tax Payable                    2,800
Federal Income Tax Payable          5,000
Total Liabilities                                               124,800

                                   Capital
C & C Manufacturing Capital                                    481,200
Total Liabilities and Capital                                  $606,000
```

FIGURE 9-4   A Balance Sheet.

```
                          PURCHASING DEPARTMENT
                               Budget for XXXX

Projected Income (Budget Allocation)
Base Operating Support                                         $800,000
Special Funds to Support
     Expansion Project                                           93,400
     Total Projected Income                                    $893,400

Projected Expenses

Rent                                                           $   5,600
Utilities                                                          1,000
Telephone                                                         1,200
Travel                                                           15,000
Insurance                                                           600
Salary                                                          600,000
Taxes and Benefits                                             220,000
Office Supplies                                                 10,000
Office Equipment                                                40,000
     Total Projected Expenses                                  $893,400
```

FIGURE 9-5   A Department Budget.

Taxes are a fact of life in every business. Most businesses must be responsible for both the collection of taxes and the payment of various taxes. Businesses often collect sales and use taxes from customers and are responsible for forwarding these funds to a government agency. Businesses also pay a variety of taxes based on their payroll and income. Business taxes are very complicated and office employees should be aware of any tax collection or reporting within their area of responsibility.

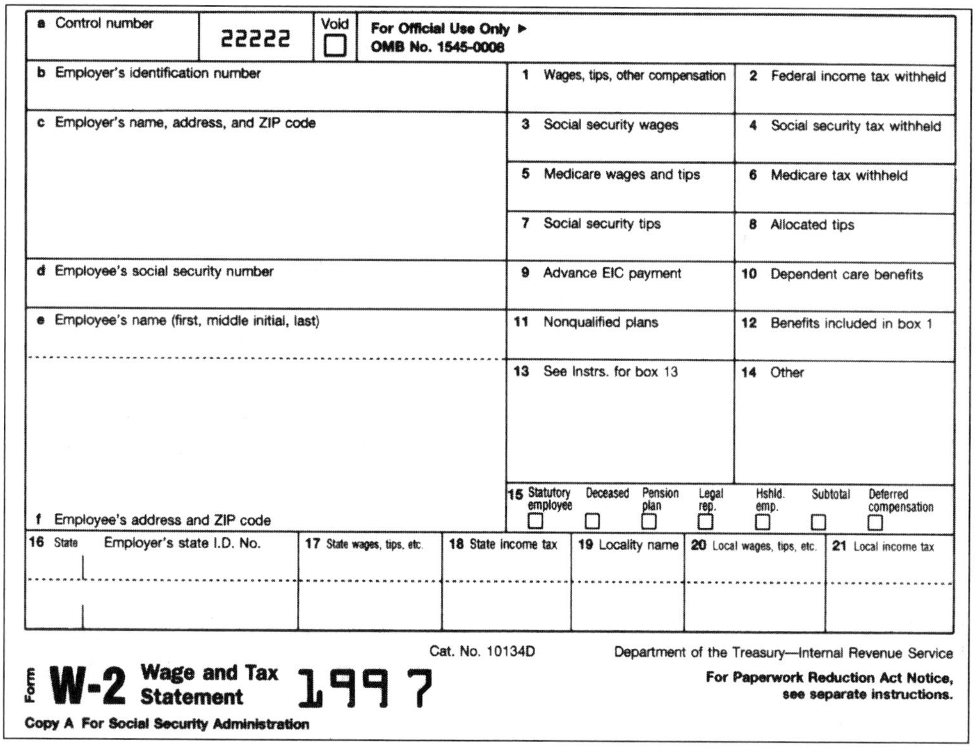

a Control number
22222
Void
For Official Use Only ▶
OMB No. 1545-0008
b Employer's identification number
1 Wages, tips, other compensation
2 Federal income tax withheld
c Employer's name, address, and ZIP code
3 Social security wages
4 Social security tax withheld
5 Medicare wages and tips
6 Medicare tax withheld
7 Social security tips
8 Allocated tips
d Employee's social security number
9 Advance EIC payment
10 Dependent care benefits
e Employee's name (first, middle initial, last)
11 Nonqualified plans
12 Benefits included in box 1
13 See Instrs. for box 13
14 Other
15 Statutory employee / Deceased / Pension plan / Legal rep. / Hshld. emp. / Subtotal / Deferred compensation
f Employee's address and ZIP code
16 State / Employer's state I.D. No.
17 State wages, tips, etc.
18 State income tax
19 Locality name
20 Local wages, tips, etc.
21 Local income tax
Cat. No. 10134D
Department of the Treasury—Internal Revenue Service
Form W-2 Wage and Tax Statement 1997
For Paperwork Reduction Act Notice, see separate instructions.
Copy A For Social Security Administration

FIGURE 9-6 A W-2 Tax Form.

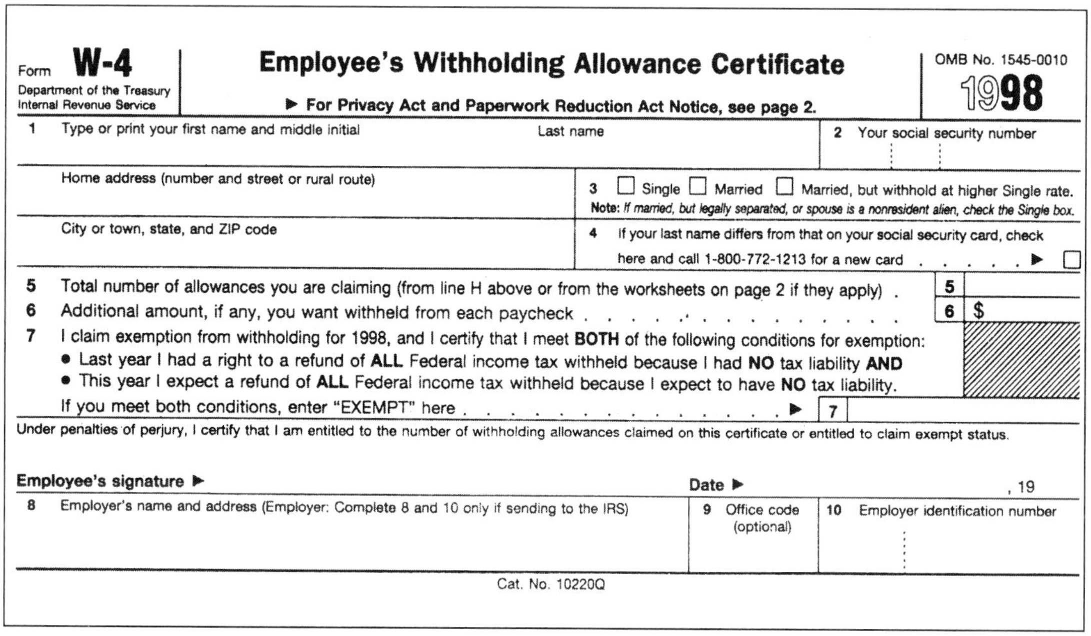

Form W-4
Department of the Treasury
Internal Revenue Service
Employee's Withholding Allowance Certificate
▶ For Privacy Act and Paperwork Reduction Act Notice, see page 2.
OMB No. 1545-0010
1998
1 Type or print your first name and middle initial
Last name
2 Your social security number
Home address (number and street or rural route)
3 ☐ Single ☐ Married ☐ Married, but withhold at higher Single rate.
Note: If married, but legally separated, or spouse is a nonresident alien, check the Single box.
City or town, state, and ZIP code
4 If your last name differs from that on your social security card, check here and call 1-800-772-1213 for a new card . . . . . . ▶ ☐
5 Total number of allowances you are claiming (from line H above or from the worksheets on page 2 if they apply) . 5
6 Additional amount, if any, you want withheld from each paycheck . . . . 6 $
7 I claim exemption from withholding for 1998, and I certify that I meet BOTH of the following conditions for exemption:
• Last year I had a right to a refund of ALL Federal income tax withheld because I had NO tax liability AND
• This year I expect a refund of ALL Federal income tax withheld because I expect to have NO tax liability.
If you meet both conditions, enter "EXEMPT" here . . . . ▶ 7
Under penalties of perjury, I certify that I am entitled to the number of withholding allowances claimed on this certificate or entitled to claim exempt status.
Employee's signature ▶
Date ▶ , 19
8 Employer's name and address (Employer: Complete 8 and 10 only if sending to the IRS)
9 Office code (optional)
10 Employer identification number
Cat. No. 10220Q

FIGURE 9-7 A W-4 Tax Form.

Common tax forms

941	The federal quarterly tax return prepared by businesses.
1040	The personal income tax return, not used by businesses.
1099	A tax form that lists interest earned at banks, savings institutions, and brokerage firms and is sent at the end of the year to each client.
W-2	The federal tax form provided to employees listing wages earned and taxes withheld.
W-4	The employee withholding allowance certificate. This form is completed by the employee and is used by the employer to determine the amount of tax to be withheld.

▼ READINGS ▼

To be informed about business, you should read as many business publications as you can. Following is a list of publications with which you should be familiar.

- *Barron's*
- *Business Week*
- *Business Month*
- *Columbia Journal of World Business*
- *Commerce America*
- *Credit and Financial Management*
- Daily business sections of newspapers
- *Dunn and Bradstreet*
- *Electronic News*
- *Forbes*
- *Fortune*
- *Harvard Business Review*
- *High Technology Business*
- *Industrial and Labor Relations Review*
- *Money*
- *Nation's Business*
- *Quarterly Journal of Economics*
- *Survey of Current Business*
- *The Wall Street Journal*
- *Trial*

CHAPTER REVIEW

1. Explain the term *economics.*
2. Explain the term *freedom of choice.*
3. Explain the term *marketing.*
4. Explain the term *entrepreneur.*
5. List the four types of business ownership and explain each.
6. List three types of government securities.
7. List five general business terms and explain each.
8. List five terms used in a financial institution and explain each.
9. List five legal terms and explain each.
10. List five real estate terms and explain each.
11. List five accounting terms and explain each.

12. List three tax forms and explain the purpose of each.
13. Explain this stock quote:

52-week							Sales				
High	Low	Stock	Symbl	Div	Yld.	PE	100s	High	Low	Last	Chg.
12	7	Hargo	HRX	.25	1.7	7	35	8 3/4	8 1/4	8 1/4	-1/2

ACTIVITIES

1. Visit a stock brokerage firm, and prepare a written report describing what you saw.
2. Follow five stocks for three weeks, and prepare a written and oral report summarizing the progress of the stocks.
3. Select three business publications and summarize one article from each. Also, present one summary orally to your class.
4. Read two articles about the current economic forecast and summarize each.
5. For a two-week period, read your local newspaper and clip all the investment advertisements you find.
6. Watch a financial television program and write a summary of it.
7. Talk with employees of two different types of businesses. Ask what business terms are used in their particular business. Then write a report about the types of companies, terms used, and the advantages of working in that type of business.
8. Watch three television news shows, and prepare oral and written summaries of the business and economic news discussed.
9. Search the Internet for financial information about three companies. Write a report about your findings.

PROJECTS

Project 17

Key in the letter using the appropriate format. Change the style to modified block.

Joyce C. Kaplan
Purchasing Agent
R & W Manufacturing Company
2735 Franklin Lane
Charleston, WV 25311

Dear Ms. Kaplan:

As we have discussed, we are interested in saving your company money. Our office developed a new organization software package last June, and we have installed it in 25 companies in your city. We would like your company to be number 26.

The organization package will allow your company to save over 80 staff hours a week. As you can see, this package will save you the salary of two full-time employees.

Learning to use this package is simple. We will train your staff to use this package in our free one-day seminar. This seminar is offered at your office immediately after you purchase the package.

I will call you next week so that we can arrange a demonstration for you.

S. C. Rosen
Regional Sales Manager

Project 18

Send this memo to the staff and supply all necessary information. The memo is from Rhonda S. Brown, Chairperson, Company Innovation Development Team.

Please accept my congratulations for a job well completed. The Company Innovation Development Team has done an outstanding job, and they deserve our praise. We believe that the report they have created will be a guide to assist us in charting our future. Their recommendations will be discussed at the monthly company forum next week.

Attached is your copy of the final report. Please review the document prior to the forum so that you will be ready to address any issues of concern.

In addition to the printed copy, an electronic version of this report is available on the network in the Innovation Directory.

I look forward to seeing you at the next forum.

HUMAN RELATIONS SKILL DEVELOPMENT

Extra Hours

Depending on the office situation, working extra hours can be a daily occurrence or a peak-time problem. Some employees enjoy working extra hours because of the extra money, prestige, or the chance for advancement. Other employees prefer not to work extra hours. Additional hours may cause personal problems because of schedule conflicts or child-care responsibilities.

- How would you tell your manager that you do not mind working extra hours occasionally but that you do not wish to do so on a regular basis?
- How would you help a manager who frequently does not give advance notice of overtime to understand that you need advance notice in order to make arrangements for care of an elderly relative?
- What would you do if you were asked to work overtime on a Saturday and you had already planned to go away for the weekend?

Another Job

Sometimes one job does not pay enough money to meet all of your financial requirements. While moonlighting at a second job may be an option to meet your financial needs, the stress of two jobs can become overwhelming. People working a second job can become irritable and nonproductive, and an excellent employee can become a mediocre employee at both jobs. Some companies have policies that prohibit moonlighting. Dealing with an overworked employee requires diplomacy.

- As a supervisor, what would you say to an employee who you know is moonlighting and whose production in the office has declined?

SITUATIONS

How would you handle each of the following situations?

- As a supervisor, you have noticed that Mark, Wilma, and Barry are extending the lunch break so they can watch the conclusion of a television show.

- Today you received the sixth call this week from Harry Whitlock. Harry would like to talk with Tim Kendrick, your supervisor, but Tim refuses to talk with Mr. Whitlock.
- Harriet Peckman always arrives at the office by 8:15 A.M., and it is now 9:30 A.M. Dinora Pazimo has a 9 A.M. appointment with Harriet, and she is still waiting. You know that Harriet's husband works until 2 A.M., and he does not like to be disturbed early in the morning when he is sleeping.
- Your supervisor asked you to complete a project, but you do not understand the meaning of the business terms that your supervisor used when explaining the project to you.

PUNCTUATION REVIEW

Punctuate each of the following sentences.

1. As the meeting concluded she contacted the director and arranged another meeting
2. Jack who is retiring in June is going to England France and Germany
3. You will I think like the new line of appointment calendars
4. I do not have in my personal library the book you cited but it should be available from the department library county library or university library
5. However the meeting was rescheduled for next month
6. Before she left for her vacation she completed all the jobs in the basket
7. Ted who recently became assistant director has been with the company for over 20 years
8. When she called I was in conference with Mr Epstein and Ms Chen
9. I am meeting Henry Rosen Junior on Monday and Tuesday I am meeting Henry Rosen Senior
10. The guest speaker is Elliott Jameson III and his topic is Business in the New Century
11. If your total payments to the IRS fall short of your estimate pay the revised estimate by January 15 which is the deadline for the December payment
12. In order to capitalize on the enormous demand for publication 205 Office Environments the price was raised from $15 to $20
13. I bought my personal digital assistant and new computer software at Chips Inc which is located at 7th Avenue
14. The brokers offered advice but the stockholders didnt listen
15. While Joseph was manager he wrote a policy and procedures manual for his department

▼10▼
The Office

OBJECTIVES

After studying this chapter, you should be able to:

1. Handle situations involving the office landlord.
2. Explain security techniques used in an office.
3. Describe a favorable office environment.
4. Explain the important aspects of office design and layout.
5. Describe methods of purchasing office supplies.
6. Explain methods of inventory and their purposes.
7. Prepare a deposit slip, write checks, and reconcile a bank account.

▼ INTRODUCTION ▼

Working in an office can be challenging. While preparing for your profession, it is easy to overlook some hidden activities that are vital to the successful operation of an office. In this chapter we deal with activities related to the office environment. The mastery of these housekeeping activities will keep an office running smoothly on a daily basis.

▼ THE BUILDING ▼

Dealing with Your Landlord

Most offices have a landlord. If your office is part of a large organization, the business may lease a floor of a large office building or may even occupy its own building. In these situations, the business will have a professional staff to deal with landlord–tenant relationships or with the responsibilities of building ownership.

   If the business is small, you or your supervisor may deal directly with the landlord regarding the lease of space. A *lease* is a document that establishes a business's relationship with the landlord. The lease specifies the amount of office space the business will occupy, the rental rate, and the services the landlord will provide. Landlord-supplied services may include heating, lighting, security, and provisions for parking, cleaning, and maintenance of building common areas. The lease will also explain the conditions under which the business may occupy space in the building. The lease may include restrictions about the type of businesses, hours of operation, use of machinery, noise, and the number of people allowed in an office. If you work in a small office and must deal with the landlord, you should become familiar with the terms of your business's office lease.

Building Staff and Maintenance Staff

While most employees do not deal directly with their landlord, every employee should have an interest in the building where they work. The maintenance of the building and of the individual offices will affect the health, safety, and attitude of the people working in it. The *building staff* supervises the building and acts as the landlord's representative. They may or may not have an office in the building. The *maintenance staff* are responsible for the daily functioning of the building, including the heating, plumbing, and electricity. It is always best to develop a good relationship with the building staff and maintenance staff, and it is important to treat them with respect. Some offices even remember the members of the maintenance staff with small gifts at holidays. Keep in mind that people are much more helpful if you are pleasant and ask for assistance rather than ordering them around and demanding service. By developing a friendly, respectful relationship with members of the building staff, you will get better service.

Building Security

One of the major purposes of an office building is to provide a safe and secure environment for a business and its employees. Modern building codes and zoning regulations in many areas address the basic safety requirements of office buildings. These regulations address such items as emergency exits, electric and water requirements, the type of business, and the number of people that can safely be located in a specific type of building.

As an employee, it is your personal responsibility to know where fire exits are and to ensure that those exits are never blocked in any way. If you see anything unsafe taking place in your building or in your office, call the situation to your supervisor's attention at once.

Due to concern for the physical safety of a building's staff and contents, access to the building may be controlled by office guards. Many offices contain confidential commercial information or sensitive government documents. Guards permit only authorized personnel to enter the building, and members of the staff may be required to display photo badges. Visitors may have to sign registers, show identification, and/or be escorted by employees. Doors to some offices may be locked with admission by door buzzer or combination locks.

No business wants a visitor wandering alone through an office where that visitor could disturb employees, "accidentally" see confidential documents, steal documents or equipment, or even have an accident for which the company would be liable. It is important for every employee to follow all office procedures regarding controlled access and security.

▼ THE OFFICE ▼

Physical Environment

Your office will be the single place where you spend most of your waking hours. Your office, therefore, should provide comfort and meet your needs as well as those of your employer. With the changes in office technology, offices have been redesigned. It has become less common for each employee to have a private office. In many offices, a large room is divided into many individual workstations. These stations may be grouped or divided by partitions, shelves, or acoustic panels. This *open* type of office design can be rearranged easily to meet the changing needs of the business. A redesign of an open office is less expensive than modification of a traditional fixed-wall office.

Shared offices, telephones, and office equipment can be a source of noise pollution. Reducing the level of noise caused by equipment, telephones, conversations, and traffic in an open office is a challenge. Acoustic tiles, partitions, carpeting, and draperies are often used to reduce the level of noise.

The quality of lighting in an office is important, especially for employees who spend much of their day working at a computer. Lighting, sun-related lighting problems, and glare on a page or a computer terminal can cause eye strain. To combat lighting problems, fluorescent lights, which create less glare, and window shades or drapes are frequently used. Eye strain may be reduced by taking breaks from the computer, using eyedrops specifically developed for computer users, and using nonglare computer shields.

Another health problem associated with a computer is *carpal tunnel syndrome*. This injury, which is often caused by repetitive motions used in keyboarding documents, results in pain in the hands, wrists, or arms. Carpal tunnel syndrome can be reduced by taking breaks to rest your hands, using correct hand placement on the keyboards, or using wrist supports when keyboarding. Another pain experienced in the office is back or neck pain, which can be caused by incorrectly lifting items or by not properly supporting the back while seated. When lifting items, always use safe lifting techniques, such as lifting from a kneeling position instead of lifting by bending at the waist.

Indoor air pollution has become a problem in some offices because of improperly designed buildings or poorly ventilated air systems. Another source of indoor pollution is caused by office equipment that produces ozone (electrically charged air) which is inhaled into the body. Employees need to be aware of potential indoor pollution problems and alert the supervisor if there is a problem.

Heat and Air Conditioning

Electronic equipment, such as computers and printers, is very sensitive to temperature, humidity, air quality, and cigarette smoke. To control the climate within the office and maintain the health of both the staff and equipment, modern office buildings are usually constructed as closed, controlled environments with sealed windows. Heating and air conditioning may be controlled for the entire building by the building maintenance staff. Some buildings may have temperature controls for specific floors, zones, or offices. Temperature control for individual office areas often is not feasible. Heat and air conditioning may not be available after traditional business hours or on weekends or holidays when the building is not normally used.

Heating and cooling should be set at a comfortable temperature of 68 to 75°F in winter and 73 to 79°F in summer. An uncomfortable employee is not a productive employee. However, a temperature that is comfortable for one employee may be too hot or cold for another. Unfortunately, employees who work in controlled environment buildings must often cope when the office temperature is beyond their immediate control or individual comfort level.

- Be aware of the general temperature of your office in relation to other offices. Because of their placement in the building, some offices may be warmer than other offices. Some offices will be comfortable in winter but not in summer, while others will only be comfortable in summer.
- If your office is consistently uncomfortable, there may be a problem with the heating/air-conditioning unit in your area. The building staff may be able to adjust the unit for a comfortable temperature.
- The temperature in offices that have windows can be regulated by using the window blinds. Opening the blinds will bring in heat as well as light, while closing the blinds will reduce solar heat which warms the office.
- Some employees use small electric fans to cool their offices in summer and electric heaters to warm their offices in the winter. Be careful when using electric appliances not to overload electrical circuits. Electric heaters can get very hot and should be used with caution. Also be careful about placing the electrical cords for fans or heaters so that they are not in a traffic area.
- Many employees dress for the temperature they expect to find in their office. A sweater or suit jacket can be worn or removed as the office temperature changes. Employees will often keep a solid-color sweater in the office for days when the office is cold.

Plants

Plants are used in an office to bring the warmth of the outdoors inside, helping to soothe an office environment and making it seem less harsh. The color that plants bring to the office can enliven a dull decorating scheme. Another function of plants is to separate work areas and create privacy. Because plants need frequent maintenance, they should be placed at an easily accessible level. A lack of water or sun will cause plants to die, ruining the attractiveness of the office. There are plant specialists who make recommendations regarding the type of plants suitable for a particular office, suggest where to place the plants for maximum enjoyment, and maintain the plants. The philodendron and the corn plant require little light and minimum maintenance, and they are frequently used in offices.

Safety

Safety in the office is an important consideration. Items placed in or near walk areas are a major cause of accidents. People walking through an office may not be familiar with the specific location of all office furniture or may be thinking about their work and not watching every step. Electrical wires and cords should be enclosed in tubes, taped to the floor, buried, or placed so that people do not trip over them. Trash cans should be placed along walls or next to furniture away from where people walk. When chairs are not in use, they should be placed close to the desk. If a desk has a pull-out shelf, it should be pushed in when not in use.

File cabinets can be a source of injuries. When not in use, the drawers of file cabinets should not be left open. People can trip over or run into opened file drawers. Only one drawer of a file cabinet should be opened at a time. If several drawers are opened, the cabinet may become top-heavy and tip over.

File Security

Always be aware of the security requirements of your office and be responsible for the security of your area. When computers were first introduced, some people thought the electronic transfer of data would lead to the paperless office. Unfortunately, the ease and speed of information exchange using computers, word processors, photocopy machines, and facsimile machines have lead to more paper in most offices, not less paper. Much of the information that is processed is of a confidential nature. To protect the privacy of individuals and the confidential nature of many business transactions, care must be taken to secure the information used and stored.

Many offices require that files be locked when not in use. Although this may appear inconvenient, it is essential that the employee follow the company policy regarding security. Some organizations will conduct surprise inspections regarding the security of offices and files. Keys to locks should not be left out where they can be found easily. Many people write down the lock's combination somewhere in case they forget it. Then they place the written combination in their desk drawer, where it is easily found. Although this may be convenient for the employee, it decreases the security of the files. If other persons know where the lock combination is located, the files are not really secure. If you have been given the combination of the office safe, do not divulge it to anyone. If you are working on sensitive material and you leave your office—even for a few minutes—secure the documents before leaving.

After confidential documents are no longer needed, they are often destroyed before they are thrown out. A *paper shredder* is used to cut the paper into very thin strips or to shred it to the size of confetti. For destruction of the most sensitive documents, the shredded paper may be placed in special bags and burned.

Computer Security

Computer security is a major issue in the office. The office may have procedures addressing the security of computer equipment, limitations on access to computer files, and the safeguard of computer data. The loss of computer information would be a disaster for most offices, so be knowledgeable and follow the computer security procedures in your office.

Data security has become an important issue in the office. All computer systems are vulnerable to *hackers*, people who make unauthorized entry into computers and who may steal, disrupt, or destroy computer data. Hackers are usually people unknown to the company who enter computer systems through modems via the Internet, but they may also be disgruntled present or former employees. The more information unauthorized people know about the company's computer system, the easier it is for hackers to break into the system and destroy information. Office computer systems frequently require the user to have a log-on code and a password to gain access to the system. Remember that your password is confidential, so do not disclose it to others. Do not write your computer password down where others may see it. Do not tell anyone outside your office how your office computer system operates.

Computer systems are also vulnerable to storms, which can cause electrical surges destroying computers, computer data, printers, and other electrical equipment. *Surge protectors* are devices that protect computer equipment from damage by smoothing over sudden changes in the electric current. Always be sure that the surge protectors in your office are in use and operating properly.

Theft of computer hardware is a common occurrence. Many computer systems have special locks that secure equipment to their desks. Security hardware may be inconvenient, but the loss of a computer and its data can be very damaging to an office. Notebook computers and PDAs are designed to be carried out of the office. In some offices, an employee may need a property pass to document that taking computer equipment out of the office is authorized. If you are authorized to take computer equipment out of the office, the equipment has been placed in your care and you will be held accountable for its return.

All offices should have a plan for recovery in the event that a disaster strikes their computer system. The most common recovery plan involves storing data off-site. Having backup copies of data stored in the same office as the original copy does not prevent loss if the facility is struck by fire, flood, or other disasters. Off-site storage should be attended to on a regular basis, at least once a week.

Securing computers against viruses is also an important part of a computer security plan. As discussed in Chapter 5, scanning for a computer virus is essential to avoid file and system damage.

Cleaning the Office

In some offices, a professional cleaning staff goes through the offices at night when the offices are vacant. In other offices, the cleaning staff cleans the offices during normal working hours. In either circumstance, be pleasant to the cleaning staff and know what you should do to help them in their work. Cleaning staffs are instructed about how to clean offices and under what circumstances not to clean offices. If you make cleaning your office difficult, you will probably not be pleased with the way it looks.

▼ OFFICE FURNITURE AND EQUIPMENT ▼

An administrative assistant's desk should be large enough to accommodate all the work and papers used. The desk should be placed for easy accessibility to the supervisor. It should also be situated so that the administrative assistant can greet clients easily and will not be surprised by an unexpected visitor. In addition, the desk must be away from the office traffic so that work can be completed without being hindered by noise, conversations, and passerbys.

A computer stand or desk is an essential item in the office. The stand or desk should be the correct height for keyboarding documents. Many computer desks have pull-out shelves for keyboards. The printer also needs a stand or desk area.

Employees working in a multiperson office should have some personal space. Plants or filing cabinets can be used to create private areas. Also, employees should have an unobstructed view of persons approaching them so they are not shocked by a sudden interruption. A multiperson office should be designed to accommodate the traffic caused by a large number of employees entering and leaving.

Ergonomics is the study of the human body in relation to its work environment, that is, the study of how the physical environment affects employees. To meet the changing needs of the office environment, office furniture has been developed to make employees more comfortable. Chairs, tables, and printer stands that adjust to individual heights have been developed. A comfortable employee completes a task more accurately, more quickly, and more efficiently.

FIGURE 10-1 An Ergonomically Designed Workstation.

When purchasing a chair, be sure it has an adjustable seat and backrest. The height of the chair should adjust so that a person's arms are high enough for the desk and the person's feet rest on the floor. Short people may require a footrest for comfort. The backrest should include a firm cushion to support the lower back. Chair legs should have wheels to increase mobility.

Before new equipment is purchased, the decision of where to place it and on what to place it must be made. Frequently, equipment is purchased and only later is consideration given about where to place it. Without prior planning, equipment is frequently placed without regard for lighting, height, or comfort.

Studies have shown that color influences employee's moods. Color can be used to create enthusiasm and increase productivity. In addition, color can be used to alter the perceived size of a room. Light colors create the appearance of a larger room; dark colors make a room seem smaller.

▼ PURCHASES AND PAYMENTS ▼

Every office must purchase supplies and equipment to support the operation of the business. Large companies may have a department of several people who do the purchasing of supplies for the entire company. In smaller companies, purchasing of supplies often is the responsibility of an administrative assistant.

Purchasing

Each office has its own specific procedures and forms to be used for purchase of supplies and equipment. These procedures are often outlined in a purchasing handbook. Study the office purchasing handbook to learn your company's purchasing policies and requirements.

The purchasing procedures in most offices have two goals. The first is to ensure that a purchase is made at the best price for the quality of the item required for the job. The second goal is to have a well-documented record to support the purchase. This record will be reviewed by the company's auditor. Companies often require multiple copies of all purchasing documents so that each step in the purchase and payment process can be recorded. Well-developed purchasing procedures guard against employee fraud.

PURCHASE REQUISITION

WILSON HARDWARE
1556 Lindberg Ave.
Jefferson City, MO 67443-9890

Deliver To: Joseph Walker   Requisition No.   672890

Location: Purchasing   Date   June 15, XXXX

Job No.:   12424   Date Required   July 25, XXXX

Quantity   Description

1   Adjustable posture chair
1   Executive desk

Justification: to set up office for new assistant director of the Purchasing
                Department

See attached quotations: Eastman $1,125
                              Blackbird Office $1,400
                              R. J. Hemp $1,750

Signature   _____

FIGURE 10-2   A Purchase Requisition.

Requisition

When the company needs an item, the first step is usually a request for purchase. A *purchase requisition* is completed and sent to the supervisor or to the company's purchasing department. The purchase requisition lists the item required and the reason for the purchase. If the purchase is unusual or the cost is above a preset dollar limit, a detailed justification may be required.

For the purchase of small items, a list of several vendors and the price of each item required often accompany the purchase requisition. Price quotations may be obtained from catalogs or by making telephone calls to vendors. The source of the price quote—including the name, date, and title of the person providing the quote—should be recorded. Each company will have its own policy regarding the dollar limit of purchases that can be made using telephone quotations.

Price information for larger purchases may be requested by telephone, but the vendor must provide a *written quotation* regarding the price and terms of the sale. For the largest purchases, vendors are often mailed detailed specifications of the items required, and they must return their *bids* by a specific date and time. The use of specifications and bids is a very formal process and is usually supervised by a company's purchasing department.

Purchase Order

After a purchase has been approved, a *purchase order* is prepared and is sent to the vendor to order the item.

Payment Terms

In reviewing price quotations, be aware of the vendor's return and payment policies. Some vendors have a *no return* policy, others have a return policy that requires payment of a percentage of the purchase price for reshelving the items, and others issue a full refund.

PURCHASE ORDER

WILSON HARDWARE
1556 Lindberg Ave.
Jefferson City, MO 67443-9890

EASTMAN CORPORATION
3500 Jefferson Drive
St. Louis, MO 67234-7880

PURCHASE ORDER # 91-3434
Date: July 25, XXXX

Deliver To: Joseph Walker

Delivery Required By: Aug. 25, XXXX

Quantity	Item	Description	Cost
1	CH345-A	Adjustable posture chair	275
1	DK8C	Executive desk	850

Total $1,125

FIGURE 10-3   A Purchase Order.

The vendor's policy regarding the receipt of payment can be the source of a hidden savings or it can result in an extra charge. The following payment plans are used by vendors:

- Cash on delivery (COD). When an item is delivered, the purchase price is paid for by cash, company check, or cashier's check. A COD purchase may include a service fee.
- Cash discount. If the item is paid for by a specific date, a discount is applied. The terms of the purchase might be "2/10, n/30." The "2/10" means that a 2 percent discount is applied to the purchase price if the item is paid for within 10 days of the date of the invoice. The "n/30" means that the total purchase price must be paid within 30 days of the invoice date.
- Total payment due at the end of the month.
- Total payment due upon receipt of the *invoice* (bill).
- Total payment due a specific number of days after the date of the invoice.
- Payment due a specific number of days after the date of the invoice with a finance charge applied if the total is not paid by the due date.

You should learn how long it takes to process payments in your office to determine whether you can take advantage of discounts offered for quick payment.

▼ OFFICE SUPPLIES AND EQUIPMENT ▼

Typical Office Supplies

The variety and quality of office supplies and equipment have expanded as a result of the introduction of new technology in the office. Supplies and equipment can be purchased from local or out-of-town vendors.

Sample supplies and equipment used in a modern office

- Selection of rubber stamps with the following imprints:
  - *As per your request*
  - Company's return address
  - *Completed*

- *Confidential*
- Current date and time
- *Faxed*
- *File copy*
- *Final notice*
- *For deposit only*
- *For your information*
- *Paid*
- *Received*
- *Rush*
- *Urgent*
- Binder clips
- Bookends
- Business card holders
- Card file boxes: 3 x 5 in., 4 x 6 in., or 5 x 8 in. with built-in dividers
- Coil pens with stand
- Color-coded labels in a variety of colors, shapes, and sizes
- Color-indexed protector sheets
- Colored markers
- Columnar pads
- Copy holders
- Daily reminders and planners
- Desk and wall calendars
- Desk rack systems for hanging binders and folders
- Electric hole punches
- Expanding accordion file boxes
- Flipcharts and markers
- Get-acquainted badges
- Locator boards to indicate if an employee is in or out of the office
- Magazine and literature storage systems
- Mailing boxes with bubble or plastic peanuts for packing
- Mailing tubes
- Message boards
- Paper clips, regular size and jumbo size, and nonskid paper clips
- Paper trimmers to cut paper to a desired size
- Platform footrests for computer users
- Portfolios
- Postal scales
- Rubber chair mats: mats placed on top of carpets to permit chairs to slide easily
- Scheduling boards
- Staplers, staples, and staple removers
- Stationery trays
- Stick-on notes and flags
- Wall- or door-mounted file folder holders
- Wall-mounted or desk cordless electric pencil sharpeners

Company Storeroom

Large offices often maintain a *storeroom* or *stock room* where supplies are kept. In some businesses, employees must use a form to request supplies stocked in the company storeroom. In other organizations, employees can pick up supplies as needed.

Inventory

A well-run office will include a person who is responsible for ordering and distributing supplies. Essential supplies should always be available. Periodical checks of the supply inventory will avoid discovering that a supply is not available when needed. Some offices keep a perpetual inventory where every item purchased or removed from the supply cabinet is recorded. The advantage of a perpetual inventory is that it is easy to determine how many of an item are still on the shelf, which diminishes the chance of running out of an item. If a supply is needed quickly, it can be purchased from a local store, but last-minute purchases should be kept to a minimum. It is advantageous to maintain a file of supply catalogs from several local suppliers. These catalogs can be useful when determining the types and costs of supplies needed.

Repairs

Office equipment does break and will require repairs. One employee should be responsible for the repair of the equipment. Detailed repair records should be maintained for each piece of equipment. It may be important to know how often and what types of problems occurred on a specific piece of equipment.

Some companies lease equipment instead of purchasing the equipment. A lease contract may or may not include maintenance of the equipment, so you should know the terms of the lease.

Before a repair is requested, the payment of the repair should be considered. Is the equipment under warranty? Is there a maintenance agreement on the equipment? A *maintenance agreement* is a contract for repair of the equipment, and usually a set fee is paid on an annual basis for repairs. Repair for equipment under warranty, under lease, or where a

---

Repair Record

Type of equipment _____

Serial number _____

Model number _____

Purchase date_____

Purchase price _____

Purchased from _____

Terms of the warranty _____

Repair _____

Problem _____

Date repair requested _____

Date repaired_____

Cost of repair_____

Repaired by _____

Comments _____

FIGURE 10-4   A Repair Record.

maintenance agreement is in place will be handled by calling the appropriate vendor. You should have a file of equipment and maintenance contracts. When calling about a repair, indicate the nature of the problem. It may take several telephone calls to have an item repaired. After the repair is completed, you will usually have to sign a receipt indicating that the work was completed.

If an office has no agreements regarding the repair of equipment, you must identify a source for repairs. You could start by contacting the company from which the equipment was purchased, or the manufacturer, or authorized dealer. Many areas have independent shops that can repair equipment. Listings of possible repair facilities can be found in the Yellow Pages of the telephone directory. When contacting a company about the repair of equipment, you will need to determine whether they are qualified to do the repair, how your company will be billed for the service, all costs, and the length of warranty of the repair.

Photocopiers

Photocopy machines make copies of correspondence, reports, and other documents for daily use in the office. The basic photocopy machine makes single or multiple copies of a document. Most machines make copies on at least two sizes of paper: regular size 8 1/2 x 11 in. and legal size 8 1/2 x 14 in. paper. Larger copy machines can reduce or enlarge the size of the copy, collate and staple multiple copies, copy on both sides of the paper, feed a stack of originals automatically, allow interruption of copying at any time, reset the number of copies after the first set has been run, and diagnose and describe machine problems. In addition to having black-and-white copiers in the office, color copiers are becoming more prevalent because of the increased use of colored graphics, pictures, and images to enhance documents. The operating instructions for most copy machines are attached to the machine and are easy to learn. In addition to the general operating instructions, you will need to learn how to replace paper in the machine. Efficient operators should also know how to clear a paper jam in the machine and how to add *toner*—the chemical used to print the text.

An *auditron* is used to count the number of copies made. A company could have an individual auditron for each department so that each department would be charged accurately for the copies made. Operators need to control quantities carefully because costs can be high.

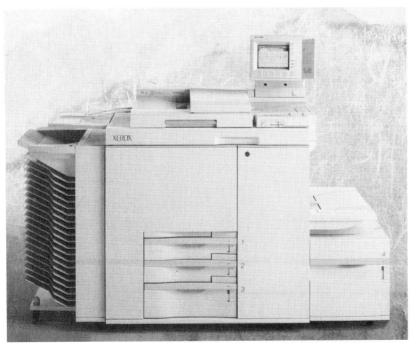

FIGURE 10-5   An Advanced Photocopier with a Display Screen, Automatic Sorter, and Five Paper Trays. (Courtesy of The Xerox Corporation.)

Copying and Shipping Centers

Need an odd-sized package shipped? Want to photocopy a newsletter in red ink? Your office may not have the materials, equipment, or know-how to handle these and many other unusual requests, but there are many businesses that may be able to help in an emergency or to do that "once a year" type of job. If a copy job cannot be completed at your office location because of limited facilities, limited time, or broken equipment, it can be taken to a quick copy store. Copying and shipping centers provide a wide variety of services, but the objective of most of these businesses is to provide quick service at a reasonable cost. The wise administrative assistant should become familiar with the services offered by centers that are convenient to the office.

Copying centers may contain a wide variety of specialized photocopying equipment and supplies not found in many offices. They usually have high-speed machines that can photocopy at high volumes, do color photocopying, or use colored inks. They will often do specialized printing, for example, printing on heavy paper for report covers, and will have machines for binding thick documents. Copy centers can be lifesavers when your regular office photocopier is down and you must finish a critical job. One national chain, Kinko's, is even open 24 hours a day so those last-minute jobs can be completed.

Businesses that specialize in shipping have mailing materials such as boxes, wrappings, and packaging for fragile items. You can buy these specialized supplies or the shipping center can package the item and have it picked up by an overnight carrier service such as FedEx, DHL, or Emery. Many shipping centers have photocopying capability. One national chain, Mail Boxes, Etc., rents mailboxes to a business as an "address of convenience."

Recycling

As society has become more concerned about the environment, many offices have become involved in recycling. Workplaces often have bins to recycle used paper, and many offices purchase recycled paper for copiers, printers, and folders. Recycled printer cartridges are also available. In addition, food facilities purchase recycled napkins and cups made from recycled paper and have bins to collect beverage cans and bottles for recycling.

▼ BANKING ▼

As an administrative assistant, your duties may include making bank deposits, writing checks for payment of bills, and reconciling bank statements.

Bank Deposits

When making a bank deposit, a *deposit slip* must be completed with the date, amount of each check listed on a separate line, an identification number for each check deposited, and the amount of cash deposited. The identification number preferred is the American Bankers Association (ABA) number, which is frequently located in the top right corner of the check.

The ABA number is printed in the following format:

$$\frac{3\text{-}35}{902}$$

The identification number for the specific city and bank on which the check is drawn is "3-35," the number that should be entered on the deposit slip. The number "902" is a routing number used for clearing the check.

While using the ABA number is the traditional way to identify deposits, it may be difficult to identify a check that gets lost in the collection process with this system. Another method is to use the name of the person or company that issues the check.

Deposits can be made in person, by mail, at an automatic teller machine (ATM), and at a night deposit facility. Deposits that include cash should not be made by mail, and coins should not be included in ATM deposits.

Endorsing a Check

Prior to depositing a check, it must be *endorsed*. There are specific rules governing the location of the endorsement of a check. The endorsement should be written on the back side of the check, not more than 1 1/2 in. from the top edge of the check. With the check facing you in the position shown in Figure 10-6 turn the check over and rotate the check so that the short edge is at the top. The endorsement must be written on the reverse side of the end which contains the words "pay to the order of."

The three common endorsements used are restrictive endorsement, endorsement in full, and blank endorsement. A *restrictive endorsement* uses the words "for deposit only" and indicates that the check can only be deposited to an account. An *endorsement in full* uses the words "pay to the order of" the *payee*, the name of the person or company to whom payment is made. After writing "for deposit only" or "pay to the order of (payee)," the check is signed by the person to whom the check is made out. To speed depositing checks, many offices use rubber stamps with "for deposit only," the company name, and the account number. Using this rubber stamp, company checks can quickly be endorsed to the company's bank account. The third type of endorsement is a *blank endorsement*, which only contains the signature of the payee. This endorsement is risky because anyone who has a check with a blank endorsement can cash it.

Writing a Check

When writing a check, the *first* step is completion of the check stub. This is done first because it is easy to forget to write the stub, particularly when there are interruptions in an office. The stub includes the date, the payee (to whom the check is written), reason for the check, and perhaps the account title. If a check was written incorrectly, write VOID on the check and on the stub. Save voided checks for future reference. Payment can be stopped on a check that has been issued by notifying the bank. The usual service charge for this service is $15 to $30.

In addition to handwritten checks, computer software packages are available that write checks and even reconcile the bank account. Using computer software is a quick and accurate way of writing checks. The computer prints the checks and records the payment for accounting purposes. Accounting statements and bank reconciliations are then prepared from the information entered on the check payments. The use of computer-prepared checks has simplified the bookkeeping in many offices.

Paying Bills by Computer

Electronic transfer of funds has long been a common practice. Many organizations direct deposit pay to the employees' checking or savings account. Many organizations have the ability to receive funds directly into their bank accounts. In the near future, the U.S. feder-

$$\frac{3\text{-}35}{902}$$

_____ XXXX

Pay to the
order of _____ $ _____

Dollars

Bank Name _____

675652   82663721

FIGURE 10-6   A Check.

al government plans to use electronic transfers for all payments, whether to employees, vendors, or grant recipients.

Using a personal computer, many organizations can pay bills electronically without writing a check. After setting up an account with a financial institution, the company enters a list of vendors to be paid through the electronic system. When payments are made, the company connects to the bank's electronic bill paying system. Some systems are connected to the Internet, while others require a direct call to the bank's computer. Security is extremely important when paying bills by computer. Passwords and identification numbers are a key to the company's bank account. They should never be left where unauthorized staff or the public can see them.

Reconciling a Bank Statement

Each month the office will receive a report from its bank indicating the deposits and withdrawals made on the company's bank account. *Reconciliation* of a bank statement is a comparison of the balance of the company's checkbook with the bank's records. The following terms will help you to understand the preparation of the monthly bank reconciliation.

- A *bank statement* is a record of your account issued by the bank. It is normally issued once a month and includes all transactions on the account since the last statement.
- A *check printing charge* is a charge by the bank to print the checks.
- A *check stub* is the record maintained by the company of all the transactions, including checks written, service charges, interest earned, and deposits made to an account.
- A *deposit in transit* is a deposit that was recorded in the checkbook but which has not yet been added to the bank account. The deposit may have been mailed to the bank but has not arrived, or it may have been mailed or delivered to the bank after the date the statement was issued.
- An *outstanding check* is a check that has not cleared the bank—this is a check that was written but has not yet been presented to the bank for payment. The check could be in a desk drawer, in the mail, or in a wallet waiting to go to the bank.
- A *service charge* is a charge the bank places on an account for providing service.

L. L. Rosen Corporation
Bank Reconciliation
May 11, XXXX

Bank balance	$1302.02
Outstanding checks	
#293 20.07	
#299 30.17	
#305 34.59	
Total outstanding checks	-74.26
Deposit in transit	+39.50
Adjusted bank balance	$1267.26
Checkbook balance	$1277.26
Service charge	-10.00
Adjusted bank balance	$1267.26

FIGURE 10-7   A Bank Reconciliation.

Preparing a bank reconciliation

1. Checks processed by the financial institution are *canceled checks*. Put all returned checks in numerical order. On the check stub, place a check mark beside each canceled check that was returned by the bank. Those stubs without a check mark are *outstanding checks*. Also place a check mark beside each deposit that appears on the bank statement. Deposits without check marks are *deposits in transit*. If the bank does not return canceled checks, a list of checks processed will be shown on the bank statement.

2. List the amount of the balance as shown on the bank statement.

3. List each outstanding check with its number.

4. Total the outstanding checks and subtract the total from the balance as listed on the bank statement.

5. Add any *deposits in transit*.

6. The new total is the *adjusted bank balance*.

7. Record the balance as listed in the checkbook.

8. Subtract any *service charges* or *check printing charges*. These charges must also be recorded on the check stub.

9. If the account earns *interest*, add the interest. Interest must also be recorded on the check stub.

10. The new total is the *adjusted checkbook balance*.

11. The *adjusted bank balance* and the *adjusted checkbook balance* should be the same. If they are not the same, an error was made in reconciling the account; and it must be found.

Petty Cash

A *petty cash fund* is used to pay for small expenses that occur in the office. Offices usually set a maximum amount for withdrawals from the fund. Depending on the office, the limit can be for purchases below $25, $50, or $100. When an expense is incurred, the purchase receipt is given to the petty cash officer. After signing a petty cash voucher, the employee is reimbursed for the expense, and the receipt is attached to the petty cash voucher. Typical expenses include postage due on an item, emergency supply purchases, taxi fares, and inexpensive office purchases.

```
Voucher number_____

Date _____

Paid to _____

Purpose _____

Account title _____

Amount _____

Approved by _____

Signature of recipient_____
```

FIGURE 10-8   A Petty Cash Voucher Form.

CHAPTER REVIEW

1. How can the noise in an office be reduced?
2. List three suggestions to improve safety in an office.
3. Why are plants used in an office?
4. Define *ergonomics* and explain how it is used in the office.
5. Explain the procedure for purchasing items in an office.
6. Describe three methods of payment used in an office.
7. Define a *restrictive endorsement*, an *endorsement in full*, and a *blank endorsement*.
8. Explain how a petty cash system is used in an office.

ACTIVITIES

1. Visit an office supply store and write a report describing 10 office supplies or pieces of equipment that you were not aware of prior to your visit. Include in your report how each item would be used.
2. Review several periodicals and write a report on the features and brand names of photocopiers.
3. Visit two offices and prepare a written report describing the office layout, use of color, use of plants, sunlight, and placement of equipment. Be prepared to give an oral summary of your report to the class.
4. Reconcile the following bank account:

Bank statement balance	4,437.75
Check stub balance	4,191.48
Outstanding checks	
#4820	30.00
#4839	56.00
#4843	74.84
#4850	37.80
#4853	29.82
Interest	17.81

PROJECTS

Project 19

Send this letter to Mr. A. J. Lockreim, 1142 Madison Heights, Albuquerque, NM 87109. Use the modified block style with open punctuation. Make a file copy and send a copy to Diane Pecorrari, Associate Director. Set the columns up attractively and spell in full all the abbreviations. Use an appropriate closing and sign it from Fred E. Evanski, Manager.

We received your Oct. order and have attempted to fill it immediately. Unfortunately, some of the items are out of stock, but they will be sent by the end of the month.

The following items will be sent immediately:

ITEM	STOCK NUMBER	QUANTITY
Chairs	357NM02	6
Desks	982SRC2	10
Lamps	7243KR1	2

The following items are back ordered:

ITEM	STOCK NUMBER	QUANTITY
Stands	432158JM	2
Charts	21256CC5	5
Fans	41694PS41	8

We appreciate the opportunity to serve you.

Project 20

Send this memo from Joyce R. Stuart, Budget Director, to all department heads.

I have considered the expenditures that you submitted in September. After careful consideration, the budget team and I have developed a projected expense budget for the next several years. The projections are listed below.

CURRENT YEAR	PROJECTED YEAR 1 ($)	PROJECTED YEAR 2 ($)	PROJECTED YEAR 3 ($)
Rent	8,400	10,500	12,000
Utilities	1,800	2,200	2,500
Travel Expense	12,400	15,000	18,000
Administration	40,000	45,000	49,000
Temporary Assistance	5,000	7,500	9,000

HUMAN RELATIONS SKILL DEVELOPMENT

Worker Who Has Too Much to Do

Keeping up with all job responsibilities can be difficult. Improving organizational skills, becoming more knowledgeable about the job, increasing efficiency, and eliminating wasted time all enhance the ability to complete more work in less time. Unfortunately, it may be impossible to complete all the work to be done because the workload is too heavy for the amount of time in the workday. If this is the case, the workload should be reviewed with your supervisor. Before discussing the problem, view the situation from the supervisor's viewpoint and prepare a detailed list of all your duties. Several questions to consider are: (1) Can some job duties be dropped because they are no longer necessary? (2) Can some job assignments be delayed? (3) Can job duties be assigned to another employee? (4) Can a new employee be hired?

- What criteria would you use to determine if you have too many job responsibilities?
- You approached your manager and discussed the overload in your work. Your manager said that your job responsibilities are not too heavy, but you waste too much time. What would you say to the manager?

Do Not Underestimate Your Supervisor

Appearances can be deceiving, so it is easy to underestimate the importance of your supervisor. It is possible to have a preconceived idea of the "important" supervisor. Do not permit your conceptions to rule your thoughts. Remind yourself that in your job as a new employee you are not in a position to judge your supervisor's power and influence.

- Describe what you believe to be the appearance of the "important" supervisor. Include a description of the supervisor's office.

- Have you met an influential businessperson who did not meet your idea of an influential businessperson? Describe the appearance of this person.
- From the company's viewpoint, list three criteria that would demonstrate the importance of a supervisor.

SITUATIONS

How would you handle each of the following situations?

- You have requested several times that an electrical cord be removed because of a potential safety problem. Today, a client tripped and fell because of the electrical cord.
- You have an assigned parking spot at your office. Mark, a co-worker, frequently parks in your spot, and you have difficulty finding a place to park.
- As you walked past the petty cash drawer, you saw Daniel take money and not sign a petty cash form.

GRAMMAR REVIEW

Select the correct word from the words in parentheses.

1. Alexis (is, are) the director of the new project.
2. Bob and Malcom (is, are) attending the seminar at Georgetown University.
3. Audrey (was, were) late for the staff meeting.
4. Ms. Moore and Mr. Wong (was, were) qualified for the new position.
5. Alan and Allison (is, are) members of the Boston Business Association.
6. The bus (was, were) late arriving downtown.
7. All of the managers at the meeting (was, were) trained last year.
8. Everybody (was, were) satisfied with the results of the research.
9. What (is, are) the result of the advertising campaign?
10. Either Herbert or Carlos (was, were) a management trainee at the bank.
11. Both of the managers (was, were) ready to go to the airport.
12. Chan (write, writes) a newspaper article each week.
13. Hung and Jennifer (donate, donates) to the office flower fund.
14. Vicky and Mary (represent, represents) the department at the annual meeting.
15. Each of the employees (is, are) responsible for a segment of the budget.

▼11▼
Seeking Employment

OBJECTIVES

After studying this chapter, you should be able to:

1. Conduct a job search.
2. Write a letter of application.
3. Write your résumé.
4. Complete a job application.
5. Conduct yourself in a professional manner during an interview.
6. Write a thank-you letter after an interview.
7. Explain the types of health insurance discussed in this chapter.
8. Explain *EAP.*
9. Explain a *stock option.*
10. Be familiar with government regulations pertaining to employment.

▼ PLANNING FOR YOUR CAREER ▼

Job Satisfaction

A career choice is not an easy decision to make. Your decision should be based on both personal satisfaction and economic satisfaction. In addition to salary, your career must satisfy your personal goals. Does your job make you happy? Do you leave at the end of the day and want to return to work the next day?

The First Step

The first step in seeking employment is to determine what kind of a job you would like. If you do not think through this question carefully, you may not find a job that will suit your needs. The correct answer to the question, "What kind of job would I like?" is not "Any job that pays well."

Before beginning your job search, ask yourself the following questions:

- Am I interested in part-time or full-time employment?
- What are my career goals?
- Do I have personal interests that I would like to incorporate into my job (for example, music, art, finance, politics, or journalism)?
- In what kind of office do I want to work: legal, medical, insurance, advertising, real estate, and so on?
- Do I want to work for a large, medium-sized, or small company? Is the size of the company important to me?

- Do I want a job with many responsibilities?
- Do I want a job with a defined path for advancement?
- Can I work under pressure? Which jobs would have more pressure?
- Do I want a job near my home?
- Am I willing to commute farther for a higher salary?
- Am I willing to move to another city? If so, where?
- Am I willing to travel overnight on business? Am I willing to be away from my family for several days at a time?
- Do I want to work overtime?
- Am I willing to work overtime occasionally to complete a project?
- Do I need advance notice of overtime because of personal commitments?
- Can I work on an established time schedule or, because of personal requirements, must I have flexible hours?
- Can I work equally well with a male or a female supervisor?
- Do I have difficulty working with certain personality types? If yes, what personality types create problems for me?
- What salary do I expect? What is the least salary that I would be willing to accept? (This is an important issue that must be thought through carefully.)
- What benefits are important to me?
  - Is medical insurance coverage especially important? Do I or does someone in my family have a medical problem that must be considered?
  - Are investment benefits important?
  - Is the type of retirement plan important?
  - What amount of sick leave or vacation time would I expect?
  - Is educational assistance important for my future goals?
  - Are recreational or exercise facilities at the office important to me?

Take the time now to answer each of these questions accurately. Then review your answers. Your answers should provide guidance in selecting the job that will satisfy your needs.

▼ TYPES OF OFFICE POSITIONS AVAILABLE ▼

There are a variety of positions available for the office assistant, and they all require good office skills, good grammar and punctuation skills, attention to detail, and good human relations skills. There are positions in law, medicine, education, government, real estate, accounting, retailing, science, and many other fields. Also careers are available in small businesses such as auto repair, lawn service, or construction. Jobs are obtainable in most fields because every company, regardless of size, needs to manage its operations. While a good background in office procedures is essential for getting the job you want, it is also helpful if you are knowledgeable of the terminology used in that business and, better yet, have some prior experience in the field. As you search for the types of companies where you would like to work, learn some of the terminology used in those fields. Suggestions on how to become familiar with terms used in various fields and examples of some business terms were discussed in Chapter 9. For example, an assistant in a law office must be knowledgeable of legal terminology, while an assistant in a medical office must be knowledgeable of medical terminology. Displaying knowledge of the business where you are applying for a job will help you during jobs interviews and will increase your chances for obtaining the job you want.

One way to gain a background in a particular field is through working for a temporary employment agency. Working for a temporary employment agency also gives an employee the flexibility to determine when, where, and how long to work. A job as a temporary worker may last from one day to six months or more. A temporary employee also has the opportunity of working for a variety of companies. This can be an opportunity to gain valuable experience in a particular field, it can be a method of deciding what kind of a job you want, and it can be an opportunity to meet people in your field. A temporary worker must be adaptable and knowledgeable. Studies have indicated that jobs for temporary workers will grow because companies are using more temporary workers to meet their peak-time staffing requirements. Many employment agencies provide temporary workers with benefit packages and other opportunities that in the past were only associated with full-time employment.

Each community has a different variety of businesses which reflects the economy of that area. Your goal in finding a job will be to match your interests and skills with an employer's needs. Finding the "perfect" job may require you to reevaluate your goals and to accept a position that is "almost perfect." Do not be afraid to take a chance on a position. It may be your path to success.

▼ HOW TO FIND EMPLOYERS ▼

There is no single method that is the "best" way to find an employer. There is some truth in the adage that a successful applicant must be at the right place at the right time. You must therefore expand your job search to contact the largest number of potential employers. When seeking employment, find companies that are hiring. Look in the local newspapers for companies that are "hot" or "growth companies." Using a variety of methods will help you find a job that meets your goals quickly and easily.

When seeking employment, it is wise to work for a company with a stable future. Before accepting a position at a company that has recently experienced restructuring or downsizing, try to determine the business climate for that company and the morale of its employees. Does the company have a future, and do the employees enjoy working there?

Friends

Tell everyone you know that you are looking for a job. When you tell people that you are looking for a job, also tell them about your skills and training. Ask people to pass your name on to others. Since some jobs are never advertised, contacts through friends are good ways to hear about available positions.

College Placement Offices

Most educational institutions have a placement office to assist you in job hunting. Many colleges have on-campus recruitment or job fairs. When you talk with recruiters, have a copy of your résumé with you. A meeting with an on-campus recruiter should be treated the same as an interview at a company. You should wear your interview outfit for this meeting. Job fairs are usually more informal, but you should dress in office attire.

Employment Agencies (Free and Fee Paid)

The purpose of an employment agency is to bring together the job seeker and the employer. Most employment agencies screen applicants before referring them to employers for interviews. Employers do not want to waste their time talking with unqualified applicants. In some of the larger cities, the best jobs may only be handled through an employment agency. If the employment agency is not a government-sponsored agency, either you or the employer will pay the agency's fee. Many jobs are listed as *fee-paid*, which means that the employer pays the fee. If the job is not listed as fee-paid, you, the job applicant, must pay the fee.

Read any contract with an employment agency carefully before you sign it. While you should talk with the employment counselor in great detail before you sign anything, remember that only what is in the written contract is binding. Be sure to ask in advance if the jobs are fee-paid by the employer or if you will pay the fee. If the fee is paid by the applicant, the fee is normally a percentage of the first year's salary. Ask employers and friends to recommend reputable employment agencies to you.

Newspaper Advertisements

The classified section of city and local newspapers can provide the job seeker with information about a wide selection of jobs. Carefully read the qualifications required for each position. Often, telephone numbers are included so that you can arrange an interview quickly. Prepare in advance what you are going to say during the telephone call because the employer may use the call as a screening device to eliminate some applicants. If the newspaper advertisement requests a résumé, send it immediately. A cover letter should always be enclosed with the résumé. Newspaper advertisements often ask that a response be sent to a post office box. This is a device used to keep the name of the company confidential and to allow the company to screen applicants. Today many employers request that the résumé be faxed to them. If you do not have a fax machine, copy centers offer faxing for a nominal fee.

Job Search through the Internet

Another way to search for a job is through the Internet. Jobs can be located on the Internet in several ways. There are Internet sites that provide for interactive career counseling, and many companies will post job openings on their Web site pages. If you think you are interested in working for a specific company, go to its Web page and see if it lists job openings. While at the company Web site, carefully review its pages to obtain background information about the company and its services.

Many government job services use the Web to post openings. There are also private Internet sites that post thousands of jobs from across the country. Professional organizations may offer job openings at their Web site. Some newspapers are placing employment ads on their Web pages. Since these postings change daily and can be accessed by many job seekers, check the Web site daily if you are seriously interested in getting a job.

Some companies may take applications and résumés over the Internet. Be careful about sending personal information over the Internet even if you think you know the company. Depending on the circumstances, it may be better to send a well-written résumé and cover letter through the mail than to submit an application via the Internet.

Professional Organizations

Many professional organizations are active in matching employees and employers. Job announcements in a monthly publication, a job fair at a convention, and job leads from the members of the professional organization are all possible methods of job hunting.

Professional Journals

Professional journals list positions that are available locally or nationally. These publications are found at the library or through professional organizations. Examples of professional journals are *The Chronicle of Higher Education* and *Broadcasting and Cable Magazine*. Entry-level positions are not usually found through professional journals, but these journals may provide information on companies that are expanding and may also be helpful when seeking career advancement.

Chambers of Commerce

Many communities have a chamber of commerce and business organizations will be included in its membership list. You could call or send letters of application to businesses listed as members of the chamber of commerce. Since unsolicited applications are considered a *cold call* on a business, the rate of response will be low. On the other hand, you may find the one company that is interested in you.

The Telephone Directory

If you are interested in working for a particular type of business, the Yellow Pages of the telephone book provides a list of businesses by the type of service or product they offer.

Specific Companies

If you know that you want to work for a specific company, contact that company and arrange an interview.

▼ LETTER OF APPLICATION ▼

Whenever a résumé is sent, a letter of application must accompany it. The letter of application should *never* be sent on the letterhead of your current employer. Since you may not be using letterhead stationery for your letter, you must be sure that your address is at the top of the letter, as shown in Figure 11-1.

A letter of application should include:

- The position for which you are applying.
- Where you heard about the job.
- Why you think you are qualified for the job.
- A *brief* description of your qualifications.
- A request for an interview.

A letter of application should be short and to the point. It should encourage the reader to read your résumé and contact you to arrange an interview. Give enough details in the letter to create interest, but save information for the résumé and interview.

If possible, address the letter to a specific person. If you do not have the name of a specific person, call the company and ask for the name of the person who will receive the application. When writing the letter of application, be careful to spell the company's and person's names properly.

The letter of application must sell your skills and abilities, and it must focus special attention on your résumé. Emphasize what you can do for the company, not what you want the company to do for you. Remember that the company is interested in the service it performs or in the product it sells and in making a profit. The focus on profit is a key issue in today's business climate.

Be specific about your accomplishments, but be brief. Details can be included in your résumé or they can be discussed at the interview. Do not overstate your skills because discrepancies on your application will place your credibility in doubt—always be honest.

The letter of application should look attractive, and it should be one page in length. A page crammed with type, with long paragraphs, and with small margins will not make a good impression on the reader. Proofread the letter for spelling, grammar, and punctuation. Always keep a copy of everything you submit to a prospective employer, including a copy of the letter of application.

▼ REFERENCES ▼

Selecting references is very important because what the people you select as references say about you can help or hinder your ability to obtain a job. When you select a reference, choose someone who knows your work ability. Do not ask your minister, friends, or next-door neighbor unless these people are familiar with your work, job skills, or business accomplishments. Instead, you should seek references from teachers, co-workers, or people you have worked with in a volunteer organization. Former supervisors are usually listed on a job application, so they should not be used as references.

Talk with your references and obtain permission before you use their names. It could be very embarrassing to you if a reference does not remember who you are. If a person who you want to use as a reference is not familiar with all of your accomplishments, send the person a copy of your résumé. The better informed your references are, the better chance

Your Street Address
Your City, State, and ZIP Code
Today's Date

Name of Person Receiving Applications
Company Name
Address
City, State, ZIP Code

Dear _____ .

Please consider me an applicant for the position of office assistant as advertised in the May 2 edition of *The Cincinnati Enquirer.*

While pursuing office technology studies at Midwest College, I have worked part time in an insurance office. In that position, I processed claims, performed general office duties, and keyboarded letters and reports. I am also familiar with computer spreadsheet and database application software. Next week I will receive an Associate of Arts Degree in Administration Technology.

I believe that my job experience and my education have prepared me for an office assistant position with your company. I have enclosed my résumé for your review.

Please call me to arrange an interview so that I can discuss my qualifications with you personally. I can be reached after 2 P.M. at 513-297-5222.

Very truly yours,

Your name

Enclosure

FIGURE 11-1   A Letter of Application.

you have for the job. If your references are not listed on your résumé, take to the interview a printed sheet with their names, addresses, and telephone numbers.

▼ RÉSUMÉ ▼

A *résumé* is a summary of your background, education, work experience, accomplishments, and interests. The terms *résumé* and *data sheet* are used interchangeably. Most résumés for entry-level jobs are limited to one page, but a person who has been employed for many years may have a two-page résumé. Since your résumé may be the major initial contact a prospective employer has with you, it must convince the employer that you are the right person for the job.

Formatting the Résumé

There are computer software packages and word processing templates that assist in the creation of a résumé. Do not, however, just fill in the blanks in these programs.

Analyzing your strengths and deciding what information to include are the key to a successful résumé.

Many companies now scan the résumés they receive and use computer software to conduct the initial screening of job candidates. For résumés to be properly scanned into the computer, they must be prepared in a scannable format. Guidelines for preparing résumés for scanning may be found on a company's Internet home page or included with their application.

In general, computer scanning of résumés relies on the computer's recognition of keywords appropriate to the position. Prior to submitting your résumé, ask if it will be scanned. A company may use résumé scanning software with specific guidelines as to the order the information should be placed on résumés. If you prepare a scannable résumé, be sure your résumé contains enough detail of your skills and background and the keywords appropriate for the position you are seeking. Scannable résumés may require that skills and education be described in only a few words, not complete sentences, so they will be recognized by the computer software. When preparing a résumé for use for scanning, use short phrases such as *wrote manual, designed system, planned meetings,* and so on. Educational degrees should be written as A.A., not Associate of Arts degree.

Suggestions for formatting a résumé

- Place the résumé on standard 8 1/2 x 11 in. white bond paper.
- Print the résumé on one side.
- The résumé should be one or two pages long.
- Use a good printer.
- Use plain type fonts such as Helvetica, Arial, Courier, or Times New Roman.
- Avoid using italics, underlining, lines, shadows, or graphics, which may confuse a computer scanner.
- Make the appearance attractive.
- Make the résumé easy to read.
- Make sure that the copy is clear and professional.
- Proofread—*never* send a résumé with misspelled words or grammatical errors.
- Use action verbs such as the following:

developed	evaluated
organized	represented
wrote	established
unified	created
expanded	improved
formulated	coordinated
enlarged	analyzed
completed	administered
increased	analyzed
generated	performed
processed	arranged

What to Include in Your Résumé

The standard résumé usually consists of seven parts, each of which is discussed in this section. Since a person's résumé reflects that person's background, the type of information included on a résumé will vary widely from one individual to another. Your résumé should be tailored to present your life experiences to a prospective employer. A résumé prepared by someone who has had many years of work experience or by someone who is returning to the workplace after not working for many years may look very different from the résumé of someone who has recently graduated.

The résumés shown in Figures 11-2 and 11-3 later in the chapter are very different. Each person wants to create enough interest so that an employer will want an interview and each item included or omitted from a résumé tells the employer something about the person. As you review the sections of the résumé, consider how you are going to use the résumé to present yourself to prospective employers.

Personal data

The personal data section includes your name, street address, city, state, ZIP code, E-mail address, and telephone number. The personal data section is usually centered at the top of the page, but it can be keyed at the left margin. You should not include on a résumé your marital status, gender, height, weight, or age.

Objective

You should write an objective that will show the employer the type of job you are seeking, but the focus of the objective should not be too limiting or you may be eliminated from consideration. The following are examples of job objectives:

An administrative assistant's position with growth potential and the opportunity to use office technology skills.

An office assistant's position with a large legal firm where my legal and office administration skills would be used.

Education

Include any information pertinent to the job. List schools with the most recent experience first.

College	Include the following for each college attended:
	Name of college; date of graduation or dates of attendance
	Course of study (list specific classes pertinent to the job)
	Degrees or diplomas received
High school	Include the following:
	Name of high school, community, date of graduation
	Course of study (list specific classes pertinent to the job)
	Degrees or diplomas received
	(This section is included only by recent high school graduates)
Other	List any other relevant educational experiences, such as:
	Seminars
	Short courses
	Evening classes
	Courses sponsored by equipment manufacturers, software companies, and professional organizations

Skills

Include specific information such as:

- Keyboarding speed
- Knowledge of specific software programs
- Any unusual skills that may be of interest to an employer

```
                          Mary S. Williams
                          8725 Churchill Drive
                       Rochester, New York 14238
                            716-820-4522


OBJECTIVE:        To obtain an office assistant position in an organization where
                  my office and computer application skills can be utilized.

EDUCATION:        Associate of Arts degree, 1997
                  Western Community College
                  Major—Business Computer Applications

                  Major Courses:
                      Keyboarding              Word Processing
                      Computer Theory          Psychology
                      Office Procedures        Accounting
                      Computer Applications    Management
                      Web Design               Computer Presentations

                  Seminar XXXX, Changes in Office Computers

SKILLS:           Keyboarding 80 wpm
                  Knowledge of computer software:
                      WordPerfect, Word, Excel, Access, and PowerPoint

EXPERIENCES:      1998–Present     Memorial Community Hospital
                  Assistant to Vice President
                  Duties: planning conferences, writing and editing reports, and
                  general office jobs. Wrote a desk manual for the new computer
                  application software.

                  1996–97          Lawrence Health Center
                  Part-time position while in college
                  Duties: greeting clients, answering telephones,
                  keyboarding, and filing.

INTERESTS:        Tennis, jogging, and classical music

REFERENCES:       Available upon request
```

FIGURE 11-2 A Résumé for a Recent Graduate.

Work Experience

List your work experience and dates of employment, with the most recent experience first. If most of your experience is not full time, include part-time experience and indicate that it is part time. Since employers are interested in the job duties you have performed, explain the duties of each job that you list.

Personal Interests and/or Accomplishments

Some people feel that listing your interests is a waste of time. Others feel that your personal interests describe you to an employer. Whether or not to list your interests is your

Deborah P. Shadow
812 Oakmont Drive
Missoula, MT 59801
406-788-9807

Objective: An administrative assistant position using my computer application skills in an office environment.

Profile:
- Willing and eager to learn
- Mature and dependable; can work without direct supervision
- Professional work ethic
- Conscientious
- Knowledge of grammar and punctuation rules
- Knowledge of Word, Excel, Access, and PowerPoint

Recent Work Experience
- Receptionist, Michael Communications
  Answered telephone, operated fax and copier machines, and processed mail.

Previous Work Experience
- Receptionist, Strickland and Castle, Law Firm
  Part-time position
  Duties: operated switchboard, greeted clients, and delivered documents.

- Secretary, Friedman and Associates
  Secretary to Director
  Duties: made appointments, answered correspondence, ordered supplies and equipment, and managed the office.

Additional Experiences
- Managed charity ball for five years
- Treasurer of garden club
- Volunteer at elementary school

References available upon request.

FIGURE 11-3 A Résumé for a Person Returning to the Workforce.

decision. If you decide to list your interests, try to include activities that show that you are able to work productively both alone and as a member of a team. For example, volleyball is a team activity and reading is a solo activity, so listing both on a résumé demonstrates that you function well as a member of a team as well as in individual activities. Any awards or recognitions that you have received should be listed under accomplishments. If you are fluent in more than one language (speaking or reading), include this information.

References

If you have space on your résumé, include three references. If space is not available, indicate "References available upon request." Some employment consultants say that references should always be separate—never included on a résumé.

P&P Communications

Name   Mary S. Williams

Address   1226 Tulip Lane

City   Hollywood   State   FL   ZIP Code   33021

Telephone Number   813-998-0665

Job for which you are applying   Receptionist

When can you start work   Immediately

Part time   Full time   X

WORK EXPERIENCE—List the last three jobs you have held.

     Company   State Insurance

     Address   298 North Simpson Drive

     Supervisor   Tom Rodkins   Telephone   813-926-4800

     Dates of employment   July XXXX to October XXXX

     Job duties   filing, data entry, and word processing

     Company   Bloomberg Industries

     Address   3877 Belkin Drive

     Supervisor   Clara Schwartz   Telephone   813-770-6652

     Dates of employment   October XXXX to May XXXX

     Job duties   answering telephone, word processing, and general office duties

     Company

     Address

     Supervisor   Telephone

     Dates of employment

     Job duties

EDUCATION

     College or University   Florida Center for Education

     City/State   Jacksonville, Florida

     Degree Received   A.S.   Date   May XXXX

     College or University

     City/State

     Degree Received   Date

     High School   Hoover High School

     City/State   Portland, Oregon

     Graduation Date   June XXXX

SPECIAL SKILLS

     Keyboarding   80 wpm

     Fluent in Spanish and French

FIGURE 11-4   An Application Form.

FIGURE 11-4   An Application Form *(continued).*

▼ APPLICATION FOR EMPLOYMENT ▼

If you are asked to complete an application for employment prior to the interview, make a copy of the application before you begin keyboarding it. Practice keyboarding on the copy to determine how many words fit on a line. This practice will indicate if you must omit something or abbreviate words.

When you have completed keyboarding the entire practice application, key the original application and proofread it carefully. Before submitting the application, make a copy of it for your files.

▼ THE INTERVIEW ▼

Planning for the Interview

Most interviews are scheduled by telephone. Be calm and polite when making the appointment, and be sure to obtain clear directions to the business's location. You should also ask if the company can send you an application form to complete prior to the interview. The following information should be placed in your file so that it is readily available when you go to the interview.

- Name of the interviewer
- Name of the company
- Date and time of the interview
- Location of the company, including its street address
- Building and room number of the interview
- Directions to the company
- Directions to the building if it is in a large complex

Before you go to an interview, learn about the company. Never walk into an interview without knowing something about the employer. Doing research on the company will not only give you background for the interview but will also demonstrate to the interviewer your initiative and interest in the business. Knowing about the company will help you to relate your experiences to the company's needs during the interview.

The same sources used in researching the position can be used to obtain information about the company. Many companies have sites on the Internet. This is an excellent resource for current information about the company. If it is a national company, the reference department of your local library should have information in the business reference books. The chamber of commerce and the library may have information about local businesses. Newspapers are also a good source of information about local businesses through both news columns and advertisements. Ask friends who work at the company for information. Also, search the Internet for information about the company. As a last resort, call the company's main telephone number and ask about the company's business and obtain their Internet address.

Use a folder, portfolio, or small briefcase to carry your résumé and your list of references. Several copies of the résumé should be taken to the interview. The résumés *should not* be folded.

Go *alone* to the interview. Do not make plans to meet friends after the interview because you do not know how long the interview will last. You may be asked to complete an application, take a test, or tour the company's facilities as part of the interview process. If you have a friend waiting for you after the interview, you may hurry through the interview and you may not make a good impression.

Preparing for the Interview

The interview is your opportunity to sell yourself to the company, and you must sell yourself quickly because most hiring decisions are made during the *first few seconds* of the interview.

Personal appearance for the interview

- Your hair should be combed.
- Your clothing should be pressed.
- Both men and women should wear a suit for the interview.
- Shoes should be polished and heels must not be worn down.
- You should appear rested. Get a good night's sleep the night before the interview.

Prior to the interview do a practice session in front of the mirror. Dress as you would dress for the interview and look at yourself in the mirror—at your clothing, facial expressions, and *body language.* Body language demonstrates your feelings and attitudes by gestures and posture. For example, sitting forward demonstrates interest and attention; folding your arms across your chest demonstrates a defensive attitude.

Later in this chapter you will find a list of possible questions that an interviewer may ask. Practice answering questions that you think the interviewer might ask you. Also, review your résumé and try to determine what questions it may prompt.

If you hope to work for a specific company, do not interview with that company first. Interview with several other companies so that you are less nervous when you go to interview with your targeted company. By talking with other companies first, you will also have a better perspective regarding the favored company.

Arrive at the interview fifteen minutes early. If you arrive before that, walk around outside or sit in your car. You do not want to be too early, but *never* arrive late for an interview. A day or two before the interview, make a trial run. Locate the building and determine how long it will take you to travel to the company during typical business-hour traffic.

When you arrive at the building, locate a rest room and straighten your hair and clothing.

Take the following items to an interview:

- Social security number
- Pen
- Pencil
- Small notebook

- Résumé
- List of references
- Copy of grades
- Proof of citizenship or work permit

During the Interview

Do not carry any more to the interview than you absolutely need. Leave as much as possible in the car. If you are nervous (most applicants are nervous), you could drop everything, which could be extremely embarrassing. It is better for female applicants not to carry purses. Put your résumé and personal essentials in a small briefcase or portfolio. If possible, leave your coat in the reception office. Never put your personal items on the interviewer's desk.

If at all possible, complete an application form at home so that you can type it. If the application must be completed at the office, complete it with a pen. Print your answers carefully so that the application can be read easily. Interviewers are becoming concerned about handwriting legibility, and some interviewers are concerned with how handwriting reflects a person's personality.

Interviews may be conducted by one person or a team. Some interviews will present the applicant with a situation and ask for a response. The applicant is then judged on the ability to respond quickly to a difficult situation.

If an employer does not have an opening that fits your qualifications, ask if the employer knows of another company that might have a job for someone with your qualifications.

Many businesses now require drug testing of perspective and current employees. Substance abuse is a concern to the employer because persons using drugs or alcohol perform below expected work levels and may cause harm to other employees. Drug testing may be discussed at the interview, and you may be asked to take a drug test as part of the interview process.

Always be pleasant to the receptionist and anyone else you meet. These people may have been asked to evaluate your suitability for the job. Never ask indiscreet questions of, or gossip with, other employees.

During the interview:

- Do not sit until asked to sit.
- Smile.
- Be pleasant.
- Do not smoke or chew gum.
- Look the interviewer in the eye.
- Listen carefully to the interviewer.
- Do not allow nervous gestures to show.
- Do not giggle (this is a sign of nervousness).
- Do not slouch in the chair.
- It is better not to accept coffee or a soft drink—you could spill it.
- Use positive, not negative, body language.
- Do not interrupt the interviewer.
- At the end of the interview, ask specific questions about the job or the company. (*Do not* ask questions about benefits, sick time, vacation, pay, etc. These questions should be saved until a *specific job offer* is made.)
- When the interview is over, leave immediately.
- If the interviewer wishes to shake hands, do so with a firm handshake.

Some people who conduct interviews know the techniques of interviewing, whereas others are not aware of them. As discussed later in this chapter, civil rights legislation prohibits discrimination in employment based on the applicant's race, gender, age, or handicaps. Most employers today are familiar with antidiscrimination laws and ask only job-related questions. If you are asked questions on the following topics, you will have to decide how to respond. You could say that the question is illegal or that you would rather not answer it. However, such statements could come across as negative to the interviewer. Keep in mind that your decision to answer or to not answer these questions could affect the interviewer's decision to offer or not to offer a job.

Questions on the following topics are *not* usually relevant to the position and, therefore, may be illegal:

- Age
- Skin color
- Religion
- Limitations because of gender
- Marital status
- Number of children
- Race
- Ethnic background
- Credit rating
- Employment of spouse

Most interviewers have techniques that they use to encourage you to answer their questions. Some will be very pleasant and make you relax so that you do not realize how much you are telling about yourself. Other interviewers are very rude. Rude behavior may be used to see how you react in a stressful situation. When you go to an interview, be aware of your positive characteristics and skills and emphasize those characteristics and skills to the interviewer.

Questions That May Be Asked during an Interview

The following questions are often asked during interviews. How would you answer each of these questions?

- Tell me about yourself.
- Why should I hire you?
- What can you do for me?
- Why did you choose this company?
- Where do you plan to be five years from today?
- Why did you select this field?
- What was wrong with your last job?
- Why did you leave your last job?
- Did you get along with your supervisor and co-workers?
- Are you punctual?
- What personal characteristics are necessary for success in your field?
- What were your favorite subjects in school?
- What were your least favorite subjects in school?
- How do you spend your leisure time?
- What are your strengths?
- What are your weaknesses?
- What was the last book that you read?
- What do you know about my company?
- What are your future plans?

- What have you learned from other jobs?
- What personal characteristics do you have that will help you in this position?
- What have you done that shows initiative?
- How did you learn about this job?
- What salary do you expect?
- Do you like to work?

Answer all questions honestly. Try to emphasize positive characteristics, not negative ones.

Questions Applicant Might Ask

During the interview, you should be given an opportunity to ask questions regarding the position. The questions you ask should reflect your interest in the job and the company.

Questions to ask

- Who would be my supervisor?
- How would my work be evaluated?
- How often would my work be evaluated?
- What are the opportunities for advancement?
- Are there educational opportunities?
- Was my predecessor promoted?
- What would my duties be?
- Please describe a typical day.
- How would I be trained for the job?
- What duties are most important for the position?
- If hired, would I fill a newly created position, or would I replace someone?
- What is the next step in the interview process?

Questions to be deferred until after the job is offered

- What is the salary for the position?
- What are the hours?
- Is there overtime?
- What are the medical benefits?
- What are vacation and sick-leave policies?
- What other benefits are there?

Reasons Applicants Are Not Hired

The following are reasons that applicants for jobs are not hired. How would you measure up during your interview?

- Insincere
- Too interested in money
- Too interested in what the company can do for them
- Poor appearance
- Inability to speak clearly
- Not interested in working
- No enthusiasm for job
- Spoke badly of past employer
- Lack of skills

- Late for interview
- No job goals
- Too aggressive
- Failure to look at the interviewer
- Lazy
- Poor responses to questions
- Too nervous
- Did not smile
- Past history of job hopping
- No experience

▼ AFTER THE INTERVIEW ▼

Interview Review

Since you should not take notes during an interview, shortly after arriving home, record your impressions of the interview. It will be easier for you if you develop an interview review sheet to use.

Thank-You Letter

Within a couple of days after each interview, you should write a thank-you letter to the interviewer. This is your opportunity to express interest in the job and to emphasize any qualifications that are pertinent to it. Emphasize a qualification to which the interviewer seemed particularly responsive. It is also an opportunity to mention anything that you forgot to express at the interview. Do not wait too long to write the letter. Thank-you letters impress employers, so this letter may be the slight push you need to obtain the job.

Call Back

At the end of the interview, most interviewers say they will call you. If you have not heard from the interviewer in a couple of weeks, you could call and ask if a decision has been made. (*Caution:* Some interviewers indicate that *frequent* telephone calls are overly aggressive.)

▼ JOB OFFER ▼

If you are offered a job, you must then make the decision whether or not to accept. If you have interviewed with several companies, you may be offered a job that is not your first choice. Within a day or two of being offered the job, you may have to make a decision about accepting the offer.

Questions to ask yourself before accepting or declining a job offer

- Is this job right for me?
- Do I have the knowledge and skills to perform the duties of the position?
- Does the job fulfill my needs?
- Would I be happy with this job?
- Would I be happy with this company?
- Do I think that I can work with the supervisor and the other employees?
- Am I satisfied with the salary offer?
- Is the company financially stable?

```
Name of company _____

Address     _____

Phone _____

Name of interviewer _____

Title of interviewer _____

Duties of job _____

Beginning date _____

Salary _____

Benefits _____

Atmosphere of company _____

Transportation/parking _____

Positive aspects of job _____

Negative aspects of job _____

Would I like to work there? _____

Do I think the position would be offered to me? _____

Date of the interview _____

Date I sent thank-you letter _____

Personal evaluation

    Was I nervous? _____

    Did I answer all of the questions effectively?_____

        Did I look the interviewer in the eye? _____

        Did I sell myself? _____

        Was I courteous? _____

        What did I do right? _____

        What did I do wrong? _____

        What could I have done better? _____

        Did I ask questions? _____
```

FIGURE 11-5   An Interview Review Sheet.

Fringe Benefits

Whether you are seeking your first job or considering a job change, there are many things other than just a salary that should be considered. When most people consider a job offer, the first thing they often focus on is the starting salary. People then may consider other items, such as the working hours, how far the job is from home, or the quality of the working conditions.

Although these items are important, you should also consider the other benefits that a job has to offer, such as medical benefits, retirement plans, life insurance, and leave policies. Even if these benefits are not an important consideration in accepting a job offer, you should carefully review the benefits material that is usually given to new employees. As a new employee you may be asked to make a decision about these benefits that cannot be changed while you work for that organization.

```
                                        Your Street Address
                                        Your City, State, and ZIP Code
                                        Today's Date

Interviewer
Company Name
Address
City, State, ZIP Code

Dear _____ :

        Thank you very much for the opportunity to interview for the administrative
assistant position you have available. The position sounds interesting to me. I
believe my education and job experiences have prepared me for responsibilities of
your administrative assistant position, and I am eager to become a member of your
team.

        As I mentioned at the interview, I feel my recent experience in writing the
manual for the computer applications software at my company demonstrates my
ability to use many computer software programs. I would like the opportunity to use
office skills and my computer software knowledge for your company.

        If I can provide you with additional information, please call me at 513-297-
5222. I hope that you will consider me for the position of administrative assistant in
the marketing department.

                                        Very truly yours,



                                        Your Name
```

FIGURE 11-6   A Thank-You Letter.

Cafeteria Benefits

Some employers offer a variety of benefit plans, which are called *cafeteria benefits*. Cafeteria-style office benefits allow the employee to choose which benefits they will receive from a group of benefits. For example, an employer may offer an employee $1,000 in benefits, and let the employee choose to use the money to purchase a more expensive medical plan, pay child care expenses, or invest in a retirement plan. With this type of plan, the employee can tailor the benefits to best fit the employees' needs.

Medical Insurance

The major benefit frequently provided to employees is *medical insurance*. The employer often contributes a portion of the cost of a medical insurance plan with the employee paying the balance. Some companies have a single health plan or you may be given the option of selecting from a number of medical insurance plans, which may include health maintenance organizations (HMOs), preferred provider organizations (PPOs), and direct-pay plans. You will usually be given the option of selecting medical insurance for yourself (single plan) or to include members of your family (family plan). The costs and type of medical coverage will vary widely. You may only be given 30 or 60 days in which to make a choice, so this is something that you should consider promptly when given the opportunity.

Retirement Plans

An important benefit of most jobs is being able to participate in a *retirement plan.* You were just hired, why worry about retirement? You won't have to worry about how you will live during retirement if you regularly save money through a retirement plan. Although it is best to start saving money while you are young, its never too late to put money into a retirement fund. Someone who won't retire for 30 or 40 years can benefit from the miracle of *compounding.* If you can save $1,000 and invest it at only 5 percent for 40 years, it will grow to become $7,000. If the $1,000 is invested at 7 percent it grows to become $14,000. Many employers contribute money toward a retirement plan in addition to paying your basic salary. Money in a retirement plan will earn tax-free income until it is taken out, although there may be a penalty to withdraw the money before you retire. Often, the employer will match contributions made by the employee. Some companies run their own pension plans, while others offer plans in conjunction with banks, mutual funds, or other financial institutions. Perhaps the best type of retirement plan is known as a 401(k) plan, which refers to a section of the Internal Revenue Service law. Under a 401(k) plan, you can ask your employer to make a deduction from your salary for a contribution to the pension plan and the deduction reduces your salary for tax purposes. So if you invest $500 in a 401(k) plan, not only does your money earn tax-free income over the years, you also save the income taxes you would have paid on the $500 for that year. If your employer does not have a pension plan, you may be eligible for an *Individual Retirement Account* (IRA). Information on several types of IRA accounts was contained in Chapter 9.

Other Benefits

The range of other fringe benefits can vary widely. Some employers provide *low-cost life insurance.* You can purchase life insurance, usually in multiples of your salary, for a low cost, usually without having to undergo a physical exam. Some employers offer plans through which you can have deductions taken from your salary for your *medical expenses, child-care expenses,* or *elder-care expenses.* These deductions are taken before taxes, which means that they will reduce your salary for income tax purposes. However, in some instances, you must use the amount deducted within the calendar year. If you deduct $500 for child-care expenses and do not use the $500 within the year, you lose the balance. If you know you are going to have certain types of expenses, these plans are a good way of putting money aside for the expense; and in addition they will reduce your taxes.

As companies increasingly realize the importance of happy and well employees, employee assistance programs (EAPs) are becoming popular. These programs may offer counseling (personal or business), day care, elder care, health benefits, wellness programs, and training programs.

Employee Stock Options

A *stock option* is an increasingly available benefit that gives an employee the right to buy company stock at less than the market price. The employee is given the right in the future to purchase the stock at a fixed price. When using or *exercising* the stock option, the employee purchases the stock for the set price and then can keep the stock or sell the stock on the open market, hopefully for a higher price. Stock options permit employees to share in the success of the company. The more successful the business, the higher the stock price, and the greater the profit the employee can make on exercising the stock option.

▼ ANTIDISCRIMINATION PROTECTION IN THE WORKPLACE ▼

Several federal laws protect employees and applicants for employment from discrimination or harassment in the workplace.

Race/Color Discrimination

Title VII of the Civil Rights Act of 1964 protects employees and applicants for employment against discrimination because of race or color with regard to hiring, termination, promotion, and any condition of employment. Job policies that disproportionately exclude minorities and that are not job related are also prohibited by Title VII. Title VII also prohibits harassment on the basis of color or race which creates intimidating, hostile, or offensive working conditions.

National Origin Discrimination

Title VII of the Civil Rights Act of 1964 protects employees and applicants for employment against discrimination because of national origin with regard to hiring, termination, promotion, and any condition of employment. National origin includes a person'a birthplace, ancestry, culture, or linguistic characteristics. A workplace rule requiring employees to speak only English on the job may violate Title VII unless the employer shows that it is necessary for the conduct of business.

Religious Discrimination

Title VII of the Civil Rights Act of 1964 protects employees and applicants for employment against discrimination because of their religion with regard to hiring, termination, promotion, and any condition of employment. Employers must also make reasonable accommodation for the religious practices of employees unless the accommodations would cause an undue hardship on the employer.

Gender Discrimination

Title VII of the Civil Rights Act of 1964 protects employees and applicants for employment against discrimination because of their gender with regard to hiring, termination, promotion, and any condition of employment.

Sexual harassment is also prohibited by Title VII. Sexual harassment is defined by the Equal Employment Opportunity Commission as unwelcome sexual advances, requests for sexual favors, and other verbal or physical conduct of a sexual nature when:

- Submission to such conduct is made either explicitly or implicitly a term or condition of a person's employment.
- Submission to or rejection of such conduct by a person is used as the basis for employment decisions affecting that person.
- Such conduct has the purpose or effect of unreasonably interfering with a person's work performance or creating an intimidating, hostile, or offensive working environment.
- Sexual harassment can occur between co-workers as well as between employees and supervisors. Both forms are against the law.
- Sexual harassment is unwelcomed verbal and physical conduct of a sexual nature. It is a hostile or intimidating work environment created by sexual comments or jokes.
- The harasser can be a man or a woman and can be of the same gender as the victim.
- The law requires all employers to provide their employees with a workplace that is free from sexual harassment. The law also requires employers to give prompt attention to sexual harassment complaints.

Age Discrimination

The Age Discrimination in Employment Act of 1967 (ADEA) protects employees and applicants for employment over age 40 against discrimination based on age. The Older Workers Benefit Protection Act of 1990 amended the ADEA to prohibit employers from denying benefits to older workers.

Pregnancy Discrimination

The Pregnancy Discrimination Act is an amendment to Title VII of the Civil Rights Act of 1964 and protects employees and applicants for employment from discrimination on the basis of pregnancy or childbirth. An employer cannot refuse to hire a women because of her pregnancy and must treat a women who cannot perform her job because of her pregnancy as any employee temporarily disabled.

Disability Discrimination

The Americans with Disabilities Act of 1990 protects qualified persons with disabilities from discrimination in hiring, termination, promotion, and any condition of employment. Disabilities are defined as mental or physical impairments that substantially limit one or more major life activities. Employers must make reasonable accommodations for disabled workers unless accommodations would impose undue hardships on the operation of the employer's business.

The Equal Employment Opportunities Commission

The Equal Employment Opportunities Commission (EEOC) is the federal agency that enforces the antidiscrimination laws described above. Many states also have state agencies that provide protection to employees and applicants for employment from discrimination.

Information about the EEOC and discrimination protection for employees can be found at the EEOC Internet Web site at www.eeoc.gov. This Internet site also provides information on how to file complaints with the EEOC.

Family and Medical Leave Act

The Family and Medical Leave Act of 1993 does not refer to discrimination but permits employees to take unpaid leave up to 12 weeks for family- and health-related circumstances without losing their jobs.

CHAPTER REVIEW

1. Name three fields in which office assistants are employed.
2. Name four methods of finding a job.
3. What should be included in the letter of application?
4. List five of the suggestions given in this chapter for preparing a résumé.
5. List the types of information that should be included in your résumé.
6. What items should you take to the interview?
7. What types of questions are illegal for an interviewer to ask?
8. What types of questions might an applicant want to *ask* during an interview?
9. List five reasons that applicants may be rejected for a job.
10. Discuss medical insurance as explained in this chapter.
11. Discuss three types of anitdiscrimination protection in the workplace.

ACTIVITIES

1. Find a partner and practice a firm handshake. A weak handshake often indicates that you have no interest in the person.
2. At home, practice your interview in front of a mirror. Watch your body movements, gestures, and facial expressions.
3. Listen to an audiotape of your voice. If your voice is whiny or high pitched, it may be

necessary to lower the pitch of your voice. Notice words that you may continually repeat, such as "ah," "huh," and "ok."

4. Videotape a mock interview and then critique it either privately or in class. Use a partner and trade being the interviewee and the interviewer. Prepare a list of questions that you will ask when you interview the other person.

5. Practice sitting. Are your sitting in a graceful, professional way? Is your body slouched? Is your body language demonstrating positive or negative actions?

6. Practice smiling. Remember that a friendly employee is valued.

7. Practice walking in an assured manner. Keep your head high.

8. Talk with a member of your class and look the person in the eye.

9. Make a list of the questions you plan to ask the employer.

10. Ask a friend in business to do a mock interview with you and then critique it. Write a summary of the interview and the critique.

11. Invite a wardrobe consultant to talk with your class.

12. Go to two stores and look at appropriate clothing for an interview. Select two interview outfits and determine their cost. Talk with a sales representative about building an appropriate work wardrobe for yourself and determine the cost of this new wardrobe. Decide which purchases you would make immediately and which would be deferred to a later date.

13. If you have responsibility for the care of a child or elderly parent, decide how you will handle last-minute illnesses or problems. Locate a backup person if your regular care provider is not available.

14. Even if you plan to drive to work, investigate the potential of using mass transportation. Your car may not always be operable.

15. Research the local newspapers for jobs for which you are qualified. Write a summary of the qualifications, types of jobs, benefits, salary, and locations.

16. Select a job from the newspaper and prepare the following for that job:
    a. Letter of application
    b. Résumé
    c. Thank-you letter

17. Complete the sample application for P & P Communications found on pages 215 and 216.

18. Ask a company about the accommodations it has made for disabled persons.

19. Ask a company how it handles family-leave situations.

PROJECTS

Project 21

Prepare the following letter and make all decisions concerning the letter style. Supply any additional information required to complete the letter. Send this letter to Thomas O'Malley, Attorney at Law, 710 Cherry Hill Court, Denver, CO 80204. The letter is from Robert Rosenblot.

Dear Tom:

My friend's daughter is moving to Denver, and I thought you might be able to help her. I have known Terri Tabber and her family for years. Terri's father and I attended college together and have continued our friendship all these years. Terri is getting married in April and is moving to Denver after the wedding.

She graduated from college with a degree in business and a 3.4 average. Terri's experience has been during the summer working for temporary agencies. She is intelligent, willing to work, and creative.

I think she would be a benefit to your company because she has the ability to grow and learn with you. I hope you will call her and arrange an interview. Her phone number is 716-766-8924.

Tina and I send regards to you and Suzanne. We should plan to get together again soon.

Project 22

Send this letter to Tanya Troll, Office Manager, Sade & Uriz, Inc., 5207 Colony Lane, Nashville, TN 37901. The letter is from Emanuel W. Giegerick, Plant Director. Use block style with mixed punctuation.

Are you aware of the health benefits of plants in your office? Plants remove harmful pollutants from the air and make our office a healthier environment. Now that we are environmentally conscious, we are aware of the pollutants that grow in our offices.

Our plant service will plant, arrange, water, and maintain your plants. All you have to do is enjoy the plants.

We base the charge for our service on the number of plants in the office. If you have more than 12 plants, we have a special plan. Below is a sample of our costs.

Number of Plants	Costs Per Visit
1-3	$10
4-7	$12
8-12	$26

We have contracts with many businesses in your area and would like you to join our family of customers. Please call us at 615-337-7844 to make arrangements for a free consultation. We hope to hear from you soon.

HUMAN RELATIONS SKILL DEVELOPMENT

Bragging Workers

An office environment where one person is constantly bragging about something can become uncomfortable for others. Learning to tolerate a person who boasts is easier than attempting to change the other person's personality. Sometimes people brag to gain attention. Agreeing with and listening to a person is a passive way to tolerate the situation. Also, changing the subject, but allowing the other person to speak, may solve the problem.

- How would you handle the situation where co-workers constantly tell you how brilliant their children are?
- What would you say to a co-worker who brags about job successes?
- What would you say to a supervisor who wastes time telling you about job successes?

Increasing Your Self Confidence

Increasing your self-confidence is important for your professional growth. A low opinion of yourself can be transmitted to others, and they can adopt the same opinion of you. To increase your self-confidence, make a list of your attributes, review past evaluations, review your letters of recommendation, and review favorable comments that you have received from employers and peers.

- Name three people who believe that you are a success.
- Do you have confidence in your abilities?
- List five of your successes.

SITUATIONS

How would you handle each of the following situations?

- Next week the office is having a retirement party at 3 P.M. for Bart, and everyone wants to attend. Your supervisor has said that the office must be staffed, and since you are the receptionist, you will be the person staying at the office. What options do you have?
- Ms. Kathryn Leadman, the director, has asked you to plan the annual picnic again this year. You are very busy with your high-priority assignments and you feel that you do not have enough time to do everything.
- It is 12:30 P.M. and everyone is at lunch. Your supervisor's 1 P.M. appointment has arrived, and the client only speaks a language that you do not understand.

PUNCTUATION REVIEW

Punctuate each of the following sentences.

1. Linda Meyers president of Golds Inc was my mentor
2. Dr Levitt cannot see you at 12 however she can see you at 1
3. The computer disk price is very good therefore I will take two boxes
4. Charleston West Virginia Columbus Ohio and Harrisburg Pennsylvania are all capitals of states
5. His finances are in poor condition however he is not concerned
6. The cost of living is increasing and interest rates are rising
7. There are many jobs available in the computer industry therefore Bill decided to attend several seminars
8. The new telephone system was installed however there are problems with two office telephones
9. Limited partnerships were purchased for the tax advantages but the tax laws have been changed
10. Robert keyboarded the letter therefore the mistake is his
11. I just met Mr Hoover who is the assistant
12. The adjustable chair which is the most comfortable one is the chair my office bought
13. Would you rather meet at 10 AM or would you rather meet at 12 noon
14. Most savings and loan institutions are solvent but a few fail each year
15. Jennifer Minks the lawyer questioned the witness than she requested a delay in the trial

P&P Communications

Name _____

Address _____

City _____ State _____ ZIP Code _____

Telephone Number _____

Job for which you are applying _____

When can you start work _____

Part time _____ Full time _____

WORK EXPERIENCE—List the last three jobs you have held.

    Company _____

    Address _____

    Supervisor _____ Telephone _____

    Dates of employment _____

    Job duties _____

    Company _____

    Address _____

    Supervisor _____ Telephone _____

    Dates of employment _____

    Job duties _____

    Company _____

    Address _____

    Supervisor _____ Telephone _____

    Dates of employment _____

    Job duties _____

EDUCATION

    College or University _____

    City/State _____

    Degree Received _____ Date _____

    College or University _____

    City/State _____

    Degree Received _____ Date _____

    High School _____

    City/State _____

    Graduation Date _____

SPECIAL SKILLS

_____

_____

(continues on next page)

AWARDS

_____

REFERENCES

Name _____   Title _____

Address _____   City _____

State _____ ZIP Code _____   Telephone _____

Name _____   Title _____

Address _____   City _____

State _____ ZIP Code _____   Telephone _____

Name _____   Title _____

Address _____   City _____

State _____ ZIP Code _____   Telephone _____

.12.

Continuing to Grow in Your Profession

OBJECTIVES

After studying this chapter, you should be able to:

1. Understand downsizing and outsourcing.
2. Obtain a promotion.
3. Understand the procedures of changing jobs.
4. Negotiate a raise.
5. Work with a new supervisor.
6. Define and use the term *networking*.
7. Describe the duties of a manager.
8. List suggestions for becoming an effective supervisor.

▼ CHANGES IN YOUR COMPANY ▼

It is rare today for an employee to spend a lifetime of work with only one company. Even if you intend to work with a firm for many years, changes in your personal life may result in the need to change jobs. Organizations also experience change, and while some companies grow financially stronger over the years, others weaken. A company that was financially secure a few years ago may experience financial problems due to increasing competition, a slowdown in the economy, or other changes in the business climate. Companies restructure and *downsize*, or lay off, employees to reduce their costs and remain competitive with other companies in their industry. Restructuring of a company creates an uncomfortable working environment for the employees. Employees who remain after a downsizing often must not only complete their own jobs but must also perform the duties of departed workers. The morale at companies that have experienced restructuring may be very low.

To continue the operation of the business, some firms will hire independent contractors, who are not paid full benefits, as a way to reduce operating costs. A company may also engage in *outsourcing* job duties. Outsourcing is a method of shifting an office function from regular staff to an outside company. The intent usually is to reduce costs and sometimes also to increase the level of service. For example, a small office may shift its payroll function from a clerk to a business that specializes in processing payrolls. The outsource organization may be better experienced in processing payrolls, and because it prepares payrolls for many organizations, it can charge each organization less than the original company would have to pay to complete its own payroll. Outsourcing often results in loss of jobs for the company's employees, although employees may be given the opportunity to join the firm with whom the company is contracting with for service.

In a rapidly changing business environment, no employee is guaranteed a job. Always be aware of your options for growth, training, advancement, and change. Keep your opportunities open and plan for your future.

With the passage of time, your career goals or job duties may change. You may decide that the first job you accepted was perfect at the time, but as you grew in job knowledge and proficiency, it no longer meets your expectations. Moving to a new job can be a *lateral* or *vertical* career change. A lateral change is a change in duties but with the same level of responsibility as the current job, while a vertical change is the acceptance of a position with more responsibilities than your present job. Both lateral and vertical career changes can result in an increase in salary.

Your education should not stop because you have a job. Employees must upgrade their skills continually. Some employers encourage personnel to take courses, while others require that a specific number of courses be taken each year, and many even pay for retraining. There are many avenues available for retraining or updating your knowledge. They include college courses, seminars, workshops, CD-ROMs, Internet courses, and audio- and videotapes. Being successful in the workplace depends on a lifetime of learning.

Perhaps you have continued to grow in your profession by taking courses or attending seminars. It is reasonable that you now want to use the knowledge that you have recently acquired. You may have to inform your employer about your new skills and your desire to use them in the office. If you cannot use these new skills in your current position, you may have to obtain another position either with your current employer or at another company. Listed below is the framework for planning your career.

Develop your own career plan

- Identify new duties that you would like to perform.
- List courses that you have taken.
- Summarize knowledge that you have gained.
- Search for courses that you should take to advance in your career.
- Determine the knowledge that you must obtain through on-the-job training.
- Set your future goals.

This is not a once-a-year project but a continuous process that you should conduct throughout your professional career. When you have reached your goals or when you have become bored with your job, it is time to seek a change. A job without a challenge can be humdrum and dull. If you are not challenged, you will not produce to the best of your ability. The most important point to remember is that you do not want to become stagnant in

FIGURE 12-1 Advancing in Your Career. (Courtesy of International Business Machines Corporation. Unauthorized use not permitted.)

your job. The potential for advancement is up to you. You must show initiative and desire in order to be promoted to a new and challenging job.

The opportunity for professional advancement is only one reason for you to seek a new assignment. You may have taken your present job knowing that it was not the career of your dreams, but you had to accept it for financial reasons. There may be a personality conflict between you and your supervisor or between you and a co-worker. Your present job may not be giving you enough responsibility, or you may be disenchanted with the duties. Your personal situation may require that you have a position with a higher salary. Any of these reasons may be motivation for your desire for advancement.

Before you talk with your employer, decide what kind of a change you desire. Do you want new responsibilities with your current firm, or do you want to move to a new company? By analyzing your career plan, you will present your case to your supervisor in a well-planned manner.

Demonstrate Your Excellence

Not everyone deserves a promotion. In today's business climate, you must *prove* that you deserve any promotion, job change, or raise. To obtain the change you desire, you must demonstrate outstanding performance in two critical areas—initiative and excellence of work.

To establish a reputation for initiative and excellence of work:

- Read and comprehend the information you work with on your job. This is a good way to learn about the company and its projects.
- Offer to draft reports for your supervisor. Also offer to edit reports written by other employees.
- Be financially responsible and develop money-saving techniques that increase efficiency.
- Do not be a clock watcher. Be willing to arrive early or stay late if necessary to complete an important project on time.
- Be courteous to the clients and to all employees regardless of their job status.
- Take advantage of company training programs to learn new skills. Also, update your present skills as technology changes.
- Learn about something that no one else wants to learn. After you become an expert, you can train the other employees.
- Learn new software packages and offer to train other employees in their use.
- Let your supervisor know that you are active in professional activities.
- Always be professional in the way you dress and act.
- Complete each project accurately and promptly. Always meet every deadline.
- Read professional journals so that you are aware of developments in your field.
- Be consistent with your excellent performance. Do not allow yourself to slip even for one day.
- Tell your supervisor that you are ready for a new and challenging project. Then develop the project and obtain the desired results.

As you establish a reputation for initiative and excellent work, make yourself more visible to management by letting others know about your accomplishments. When you meet a goal or complete a project successfully, diplomatically let your co-workers know about it. Management usually hears news through the grapevine. If your company has a staff newsletter, send a note to the editor listing your recent achievement.

Indicate that you are planning to stay with the company for a long time. Diplomatically inform your supervisor that you have no desire to find a new job because you enjoy your current and anticipated responsibilities. Talk with your supervisor about your desire for advancement and your willingness to try other challenging assignments. Present your supervisor with a detailed plan for your advancement, and include in your plan, projects on which you would like to work so that you may grow in your job responsibilities.

Carefully analyze your present job description and work with your supervisor to redesign your current position into the career you want. Then rewrite the job description, including the new tasks you plan to complete, but omit the tasks that you feel are no longer important. With a thorough explanation, recommend that those tasks be omitted entirely or reassigned to another colleague.

Asking for a Raise

A *raise* is an increase in salary and a *promotion* brings such changes as better benefits, a preferable job assignment, a more desirable office, a new title, or improved working conditions. These changes may occur with or without a salary increase.

Before you ask for a raise, research the market to determine the accepted salary range for the duties you perform. As you research salary ranges for the type of job you have, remember that salary ranges can vary considerably from one geographic area to another. Also, survey the job market to determine what types of jobs are available for people with your qualifications. Then prepare a detailed list of your achievements. The list should include how you solved problems; and projects that you organized, developed, and completed. Hand your list of achievements to the supervisor when you discuss the potential for a raise.

When you make the decision to negotiate a raise, consider all of your options first. Do not go into your supervisor's office and ask for a raise without considering the fact that you may not get want you what. Listed below are issues to think about prior to requesting a raise.

- If you do not get the raise you want, how would you feel?
- Would not receiving the salary increase cause a strained relationship between you and your supervisor?
- Would an improvement in benefits be an acceptable alternative to you?
- Would the promise of a raise in a few months be acceptable to you?
- What is acceptable to you in terms of a raise, and what is not acceptable?
- What other alternatives would you consider?

If you did not receive the salary increase you expected, do not resign immediately. There are many considerations to be made before resigning a job.

▼ MAKING A JOB CHANGE ▼

Starting off on the Right Foot with a New Supervisor

Employee turnover at all levels is very common in modern offices. At some time in your career, it is likely that your supervisor will change jobs while you remain in the same position. A new supervisor will have different ideas about how to handle situations. You will have to relate to the new supervisor's operating style and personality, so give yourself time to adapt to the new office environment.

Suggestions for success with a new supervisor

- Do not indicate that the former supervisor did something in a certain way and that you believe that method is the only correct procedure. Accept the fact that two managers do not work in the same manner. You should realize that there are many ways to reach the same goal.
- Do not gossip with co-workers about the prospect of a new supervisor. Accept the change and decide that you will profit and learn from the new situation.
- As soon as possible, make an appointment to talk with the new supervisor about your job responsibilities. Have a copy of your job description with you. You and your

supervisor can compare your current job description with the new supervisor's expectations for you.

- Let your supervisor know that you are ready and willing to work as part of the team. Offer to answer any questions you can to acquaint the supervisor with ongoing projects.
- Do not relay stories about your impressions of the new supervisor to other co-workers. Always be courteous and pleasant.
- Give the new supervisor time to meet the challenges of the job. If you are unhappy with the situation, wait. Time may resolve the situation. When you have a new supervisor, it is a good idea to wait at least six months before you consider looking for a new job.

Is it Time to Change Employers?

If you are thinking of resigning your job, do not make a hasty decision to leave. Everyone has bad days and thinks of quitting. Make a list of the positive and negative aspects of the job. Which list is longer? Which list contains the most important items? Weigh the decision to leave very carefully.

Before changing a job, ask yourself the following questions:

- What do I expect from a new position?
- Am I satisfied with my present job? Why?
- What changes would I like to make?
- What do I like about my supervisor?
- What do I dislike about my supervisor?
- What characteristics would I like to see in a supervisor?
- Is my present salary reasonable?
- What should my salary be?
- What types of projects do I like doing?
- What types of projects do I dislike doing?
- What opportunities are there for advancement in my present job?
- Which companies have better opportunities for me?
- Whom do I know who works for a company that might provide opportunities for me?
- Am I satisfied with my job location?
- Would a better job location be important enough to cause me to change jobs?
- Am I willing to commute longer for a better job?
- If I have a personality conflict with my supervisor or with a co-worker, is it serious enough to cause me to seek another job?

Thoroughly research other positions in the same company and decide if there are other positions attainable. If the reason you are leaving is for more money, discuss this with your supervisor because you may be offered a higher salary. If you are leaving because of a problem with a co-worker, job responsibilities, or working conditions, discuss the problem with your supervisor, who may be able to resolve the problem so a job change is not required.

If you do decide to leave, wait a few days before you notify anyone because you may change your mind. Quitting immediately will not solve all your problems; you will then have the "job search issue" to resolve. After you announce your decision to leave, stick with the decision. You will appear ambivalent if you constantly change your mind about leaving and will weaken your credibility if you stay.

Looking for a New Job

After you have made the decision to seek other employment, you must decide whether to give immediate notice of resignation or to begin your job search while you are still employed. Most people simply cannot go without a salary for a long period of time between jobs and must begin their search for a new position while continuing with their current job.

Your job search should include the techniques discussed in Chapter 11. Talk with others in your field and let your contacts know that you are ready for a new challenge. You should also use two techniques discussed later in this chapter: using networking skills and becoming active with professional organizations.

Your job search must, however, be handled with discretion. You should not tell co-workers you are looking for other employment, work on your résumé at the office, or use the office telephone to set up interviews. Job-seeking phone calls can be made during your lunch break from a pay phone outside your office complex. Once your decision to seek other employment is known, you may not receive choice assignments. People will think you are no longer interested in your current job, and your supervisor's attitude toward you may change. Therefore, keep the news of your job search away from your co-workers as long as possible because it may take an extended period of time to find the "perfect" new job.

The Trailing Spouse

In a two-career family, a problem occurs when one person's career requires relocation to another city. The remaining spouse may be perfectly content with the current job but will usually want to move to be with the spouse. Large companies that relocate employees often will provide assistance to the trailing spouse in finding a job. Even if the relocation is not due to a transfer but is to accept a position with a new employer, that employer may offer assistance to place the trailing spouse in a suitable position.

▼ LEAVING THE OLD JOB ▼

Letter of Resignation

Since considerable time and money is spent training employees, most employers would like you to stay in your job forever. That is not a realistic situation in our mobile society. Although job hopping is frowned upon by employers, it is acceptable to change a job after two years. In large metropolitan cities, it may be acceptable to stay in a job for only one year. However, a record of constant job hopping may jeopardize your chances of future employment.

When you do decide to change employers, do it courteously and graciously. When you leave a job, do not voice all your grievances and past problems with the office and your co-workers. You may need help from your co-workers as future references, or they could eventually be employed at the same company where you work.

Before you tell your friends and co-workers that you are quitting to take a new job, tell your supervisor about your decision to leave. It would be embarrassing for you if your supervisor heard about your decision to leave from another source. Select the right time and atmosphere in which to tell your supervisor of your new job. Indicate that you have enjoyed working with the supervisor and the company, but you have received an employment offer that you cannot refuse. Since your leaving may present a problem for the supervisor, be prepared for the possibility that your supervisor may not be happy with your decision to leave.

It is customary to give at least two weeks notice before leaving a position. To demonstrate your professionalism, always offer to train your replacement and complete any projects in progress. A letter of resignation should be given to your supervisor when you resign. The letter should express your satisfaction with the company, demonstrate your professionalism, and indicate the date you intend to leave. It is not essential to include the name of your new company or when you will begin working at the new job.

Leaving a job is not easy—whether you enjoyed the job or hated it. Because of emotional attachments at your current organization, you probably have a feeling of belonging to the company, pride in your job, and comradery with your colleagues. Leaving a job and moving to a new endeavor can create stress and a sense of uncertainty, but the promise of a blossoming new future is yours.

September 12, XXXX

Mr. Jerry Edens, Director
Watson, Inc.
3000 Running Brook
Forest Grove, OR 97116

Dear Mr. Edens:

I have enjoyed the three years that I have been employed by Watson Inc., but the time has come for me to accept another position. I have been offered a position too promising for me to decline. My last day of employment at Watson, Inc. will be September 27.

I will be glad to train my replacement. I realize how important it is to have continuity for my projects so they will be completed in a satisfactory manner.

Because of the many opportunities I have experienced here, I have grown a great deal in my field. I know that I will miss everyone at Watson's. Thank you for your help and consideration during the last three years.

Sincerely,

Alicia Webster

FIGURE 12-2 A Letter of Resignation.

Job Dismissal

In today's complex business world, people are released from a job for a variety of reasons. Cost saving by companies often results in layoffs. Reorganization of companies often results in a change of duties and dismissals, and poor work habits or personality conflicts may result in an employee being fired.

If you are released from your job, assess why you lost the job. If the situation occurred because of circumstances that you could not control, such as companywide layoffs, accept the situation and seek another position.

If you were fired because of problems you could change, you should evaluate the situation carefully and alter your behavior. For example, if you lost your job because you were rude to someone, make an effort to improve your personality. Do not carry the same problems to a new job. If a prospective employer asks why you were fired, be honest. State the reason for the dismissal and then state how you have corrected the problem.

▼ OBTAINING ASSISTANCE ▼

Networking

Growing in your chosen career includes meeting other professionals. One of the terms used today for meeting and forming your own group of professional contacts is *networking*. A network is an informal association of business associates who can provide assistance to each other. A group of business associates meeting and sharing ideas at a business meeting, at home, or at a party can be a network. A network is not a formal organization and may consist of only one or two other people, who, in turn, will know a few other people. When you attend business or social meetings and parties, talk with other professionals and exchange business cards. Then arrange to meet for lunch or after work. When you or another member of your network need business assistance, you have friends, or friends of friends, to contact who can make helpful suggestions and recommendations. A network would be advantageous to you if you are looking for a job because people in your network can recommend companies and employers to you.

Professional Organizations

A professional organization can help you to grow in your field. Professional organizations expose their members to new and changing ideas, provide discussions on, and solutions to, important problems, and provide a means of meeting other professionals in your field. There are professional organizations for persons interested in many fields, and attending meetings of professional organizations is an excellent opportunity to network. Professional Secretaries International (PSI) is a professional organization for secretaries and office personnel.

▼ CERTIFIED PROFESSIONAL SECRETARY ▼

One avenue for advancement in your career is to become a Certified Professional Secretary. CPS is a professional title granted only to those individuals who meet the educational and work-experience requirements developed by Professional Secretaries International (PSI). To become a CPS, a candidate must complete a comprehensive exam developed by PSI.

The areas tested in the exam are:

- Finance and Business Law, covering economics, accounting, and business law
- Office Systems and Administration, covering office technology, office administration, and business communications
- Management, covering behavior science in business, human resources management, and organizations and management

This exam is given twice a year in May and November at 250 locations in the United States, Canada, Jamaica, Virgin Islands, Puerto Rico, and Malaysia. There is a future plan to offer the exam over the Internet at more frequent intervals. Prior to taking the exam it would be wise to take a CPS review course and to study the CPS review modules.

Information about qualifying for the CPS exam and other information about the exam is available from Professional Secretaries International, 10502 Northwest Ambassador Drive, P.O. Box 20404, Kansas City, MO 64195-9404. Telephone 816-891-6600. Fax 816-891-9118. Web address http://www.fhpw.org/whcpsi/certifie.htm.

▼ BECOMING A MANAGER OR SUPERVISOR ▼

If you are in an entry-level position, your goal may be to advance to a position of *supervisor* or *manager*. The two terms are often used interchangeably. Both terms refer to people who direct or administer the activities of a business. Some businesses have many layers of management, with each level of management responsible for increasingly larger divisions of the organization. But whether a person manages a division or just a single project with no employees to supervise, managers at all levels must deal with many of the same concerns.

As you advance to a position of supervision, your perspective, your duties, and your responsibilities will change. Many of the techniques discussed earlier in the section "Demonstrate Your Excellence" will help build the experience, reputation for excellence, and initiative you will need to move into management.

A manager's duties

- *Managing the office*, which includes overseeing the daily activities of the office and planning for the future.

- *Motivating subordinates* is a human-relations technique that encourages employees to work to the peak of their abilities.
- *Establishing and enforcing office rules* requires foresight into problems and situations and a tactful person to mediate office problems.
- *Delegating work* requires established work procedures and an equitable division of the workload. A *team approach* is necessary when dividing the workload.
- *Disciplining subordinates* is a difficult job and requires diplomacy and objectivity. It is easy to become involved in the personal life of an employee and overlook negative work situations.
- *Purchasing* supplies and equipment is necessary for the efficient operation of your office.
- *Planning office work schedules* so that all work is completed by the due date requires knowledge of the project and the ability to determine realistically the amount of time necessary to complete a project.
- *Maintaining safety* is a constant concern in the office. One lapse in safety could result in a catastrophic personal injury that might bring about a huge law suit and astronomical financial loss for the company.
- *Designing and implementing a budget* may be the responsibility of the supervisor. This includes coping with anticipated as well as unexpected expenses. Operating within a framework of a budget is a fact of business life.
- *Hiring and evaluating employees* requires selecting the best person for the job. Selecting the best person for the job includes knowing the objectives and skills necessary for the position. After a person is hired, a periodic review is used to determine if the employee is meeting the objectives of the position. Employee evaluation may require the development of objective forms and a personal conference with the employee.
- *Making decisions* after weighing the positive and negative aspects of a problem.
- *Planning and supervising training* for employees in a fast-changing technological world is important.
- *Leading employees* during normal daily business activities and through periods of chaos is necessary. Most people like to be led gently and not forced in a harsh way to reach a goal. Therefore, diplomacy is important. Employees also want someone to help them to solve problems in their daily work.
- *Using effective human relations skills* is very important for success in the office. A good supervisor should have the ability to solve employee problems that relate to the office environment. Employee problems might include personality conflicts, being unqualified to complete some jobs, having negative feelings about the office, and allowing personal problems to affect the employee's ability to produce effectively on the job. Employees' personal problems can sometimes be referred to a counselor or physician.
- *Listening to employees' suggestions* and accepting the best ideas and rejecting less favorable recommendations without damaging employee morale is essential.
- *Before the completion date of a project arrives,* the manager should review the project with the employee. Then, if additional assistance is needed, time is available to complete the project.
- *Periodic review of all projects* reduces the chance of a last-minute crisis. If the project is not following the established goals, if the employees needs assistance, or if the project requires additional staff so that it will be completed by the due date, a manager who is on top of the project will have the time to solve the problems.

Problem Solving Techniques

It is important for an office supervisor to understand problem-solving techniques. A manager who cannot solve problems is ineffective.

EMPLOYEE EVALUATION FORM

Name _____

Job Title _____

Date _____

Supervisor _____

Complete the following for each duty in the job description
1 = Unsatisfactory   2 = Marginal   3 = Acceptable
4 = Commendable   5 = Outstanding

Duty _____ Rating: 1 2 3 4 5
Comments: _____

Duty _____ Rating: 1 2 3 4 5
Comments: _____

Duty _____ Rating: 1 2 3 4 5
Comments: _____

Duty _____ Rating: 1 2 3 4 5
Comments: _____

Duty _____ Rating: 1 2 3 4 5
Comments: _____

Work Habits _____ Rating: 1 2 3 4 5
Comments: _____

Cooperativeness _____ Rating: 1 2 3 4 5
Comments: _____

Flexibility _____ Rating: 1 2 3 4 5
Comments: _____

Overall Rating _____ Rating: 1 2 3 4 5
Comments: _____

FIGURE 12-3   An Employee Evaluation Form.

Suggestions for solving problems

- Define the problem.
- List on paper the positive and negative points of each possible solution to the problem.
- Analyze and consider each point.
- Study the ramifications of each possible solution.
- Make a list of the people who will be affected by the decision.

- Consider how this type of problem was solved in the past.
- Consider whether the solution being considered may set a precedent.

Suggestions for the Supervisor

Listed below are hints to make you an effective supervisor.

- Recognize that employees may have personal or family problems that may occasionally interfere with their performance in the workplace.
- Encourage employees to trust you.
- Discuss your plans and goals for the company with employees. Make them aware of any changes you anticipate.
- Involve employees in the planning stages of any changes you propose.
- Involve employees in the responsibilities of operating the business.
- Be objective, not critical, when an employee discusses a concern with you.
- Do not betray a confidence given to you by an employee.
- Motivate the employees to reach their personal aspirations and objectives.
- Encourage employees to communicate with you. Always have an open-door policy.
- Encourage employees to retrain and update their skills.
- Do not show partiality or favoritism to any employee.
- Treat each employee with dignity and courtesy.
- Understand the duties and skills involved in all the projects that you assign to your employees.
- Accept innovation, do not reject it.
- If a conflict arises, listen to each employee's comments before making a decision.

Evaluation

One of the duties of a supervisor is evaluation of employees. Evaluations should be based on realistic criteria, not on subjective thoughts. Positive and negative comments should be documented and kept in an employee's file to be reviewed prior to the evaluation. Figure 12-3 shows a sample evaluation form that could be used in the office. The specific duties of each employee would be placed on that employee's evaluation form. Company policy determines how often a review is conducted. Standard times for reviews are three months, six months, or yearly.

CHAPTER REVIEW

1. List three suggestions for obtaining a promotion.
2. List five questions that employees should ask themselves before changing jobs.
3. Define the term *networking*.
4. Describe two reasons why employees are dismissed from jobs.
5. List five duties of a supervisor.
6. List five suggestions, as discussed in this chapter, for a supervisor.

ACTIVITIES

1. Review local newspapers for meetings of professional organizations. The chamber of commerce and library may have a list of professional organizations in your area. Contact three organizations that interest you and ask for information concerning the scope of the organization, frequency of meetings, location of meetings, cost of membership, and requirements for membership.

2. List 10 people who are members of your network. Indicate how you have helped them and how they have helped you. Also, indicate the future assistance you expect to receive from them and how you expect to help them.

3. Describe the type of office environment in which you would like to be a supervisor. Include the number of employees, type of business, description of the office, and the duties of the supervisor.

4. Observe an office environment and write a report describing either how time was used efficiently or how time was wasted.

5. Videotape a role-playing situation where you request a raise in salary. Include the following situations: the raise is given; it is denied; it is denied, but a job-title change is offered with the promise of a raise later.

6. Prepare a videotape of a role-playing situation in which you notify your supervisor that you have accepted another job.

7. Write a letter of resignation for a position you have held for three years.

PROJECTS

Project 23

Write a memorandum to the staff requesting completion, by the end of the month, of the following survey form. The memo is from you and your title is Benefits Officer. Create a survey form that provides space for responses to the questions. If possible, insert an appropriate graphic on your survey form.

DO YOU NEED CHILD CARE OR ELDER CARE?
Name
Home address
Home telephone number
Department
Department telephone number
How many children need care?
Ages of children
How are children cared for now?
What arrangements have you made if a child is ill?
Is your spouse employed?
Does your spouse's employment offer child/elder care?
Do you need elder care?
Age of adult
Comments

Project 24

Send the following letter to Danielle Levine. It is from Robert T. Shaw, Director of Employee Development. Provide any information necessary to complete the letter and use a modified block style with open punctuation.

Developing your management skills is essential to your professional and personal growth. We are offering several seminars to help you reach your potential and grow professionally.

Listed below are titles and dates of the seminars.

Assertiveness Training	Sept. 2, 3, 4
Decision Making	Sept. 18, 19, 20
New Computer Techniques	Oct. 2, 3, 4
Review of Basic Skills	Oct. 10, 11, 12
Writing for the Future	Nov. 6, 7, 8

Contact Sharon McKinley at 800-286-5175 to reserve your place at the seminar.

HUMAN RELATIONS SKILL DEVELOPMENT

Anger

The ability to control anger is an important skill to develop. There are many situations in an office that can cause the most even-tempered person to become angry. A temper tantrum, however, is not professional behavior for an office. Removing the frustrations that a person feels can be a healthy release for the body; internalizing anger can cause problems including physical illness. Outlets for anger include tearing up paper, physical exercise, talking with a friend, writing a nasty note *and destroying it*, performing an activity that you enjoy, or deciding that the anger is not worth the bother. In the office, do not allow others to see your anger. If you are furious about something, go for a walk, get a drink of water, or close your door and rest for a few moments. Understanding your own anger and learning to handle it and the anger of others will create a better working environment.

- Do you lose your temper easily?
- What causes you to lose your temper?
- How are you going to handle your anger in the office?
- In your role as a manager, an employee approaches you in a fit of anger. How are you going to handle the situation?
- Describe an incident where a co-worker showed great anger.

Emotions in the Office

Some people are very sensitive and become hurt easily. They may have difficulty accepting criticism—either justified or unjustified. A negative comment about a project may be taken personally although the comment was meant to be constructive criticism. A nasty remark from a co-worker may make a person feel worthless. All of these situations can cause a person to cry. Telling someone to control their emotions is easy, but it may be difficult for them to do so. If you feel that your emotions are out of control and if you feel you are going to cry, walk quickly to the rest room. This should give you the privacy you need to regain your composure. If the rest room does not give you privacy, walk to another floor, walk outside, or sit in your car. Most supervisors do not like to deal with tears and do not know how to handle them.

- How would you handle the situation if your supervisor screamed at you in front of a client?
- How would you handle the situation if your supervisor has personal problems at home and takes the frustration out on you by telling you that everything you do is wrong?
- In your role as manager, you reprimand one of your employees and the person begins to cry. How would you handle the situation?

SITUATIONS

As the supervisor of the department, how would you handle each of the following situations?

- Katie used to be a good team worker and would do her share of the work. For the last three months, she has not been doing her share of the work, and other employees have begun to complain to you.
- Daniel is habitually late for work. During the last seven days he has been late four times. When he arrives, he always has an excuse.
- Marsha has a negative attitude and she constantly exhibits it by being rude and snapping at clients and co-workers.

PUNCTUATION REVIEW

Punctuate each of the following sentences.

1. Did the computers arrive Mary asked
2. Yes Ms Cheung we can repair the copying machine before 2 PM on Friday January 16 so you can print the report by your due date
3. Ms Patterson the realtor works most weekends but she enjoys her job
4. After work we are going to a professional meeting
5. Our efficient easy to learn computer software package will take only eight hours to learn and you do not need prior computer experience to understand it
6. My vacation time has been changed from August to September
7. Mr Tilton called and I made a 3 PM appointment for him to see you
8. Mr Ford said I had approval to take my vacation in July
9. If you study the Martin Report carefully you will see the error on page 12 therefore you will understand the problems we are now experiencing
10. When the computer crashed I lost the document I was creating
11. Dr Mason cannot see you on Wednesday but Dr Johnson is available then
12. Our work schedule is now full therefore we will have to work on the weekend
13. Todays staff meeting is canceled but we will reschedule it for tomorrow
14. When I travel on business I usually fly Northern Airlines
15. Because of the court decision the company changed its name

▼13▼
Tips of the Trade

OBJECTIVES

After studying this chapter, you should be able to:

1. Improve your office efficiency.
2. Handle office stress.
3. Dress appropriately for the office.
4. Improve your map-reading skills.
5. Handle work-related problems.

▼ INTRODUCTION ▼

This final chapter is different from the other chapters in this book. Rather than discussing another specific area of office procedures, in this chapter we concentrate on *you* and how you can improve your office efficiency and handle work-related problems. The chapter is filled with hints and techniques that usually come only with years of on-the-job experience. Many of the techniques discussed in this chapter are as applicable to your personal life as they are to your professional career. Mastery of these skills will aid in your personal as well as professional growth.

▼ PERSONAL HINTS ▼

- Be a productive member of the team.
- Anticipate problems so that you are ready to solve them.
- Prioritize your jobs and constantly review your priorities.
- Look for projects that will spotlight your talents.
- Avoid statements that trigger a negative response.
- Change your mind-set to see obstacles as opportunities to succeed.
- Keep yourself focused on your objectives.
- Use feedback from co-workers to fine-tune your projects.
- Be a catalyst for innovation.
- Build a consensus for implementing your ideas.
- Repair damaged professional relationships before it is too late.
- A smile can help you win the support you need for an idea.
- Always be nonjudgmental.
- Always have a positive attitude.
- Redirect anger in a positive way.

- Inspire creative thinking and inspire employees.
- Understand that learning is an ongoing process. Do not limit yourself to what you know today. Learn for the future. Realize that your skills are quickly outdated and need to be updated frequently.
- Expect interruptions and do not allow them to irritate you. Interruptions are a daily occurrence in the life of an office employee. Do not allow interruptions to sabotage your productivity.
- In your role of office assistant, people will think you have answers for everything. They may expect you to be able to answer questions that are not pertinent to your job. Never be rude to anyone; always answer questions in a courteous manner and to the best of your ability. If you do not know the answer to a question, indicate that you will try to locate the information requested.
- Read the newspaper daily to be informed about the political situation and business environment in your area. The business world changes so frequently that it is essential that you read articles in professional journals. Read about your competitors to learn as much about them as you can. Learn what they are planning, their goals, their image, who their clients are, and their financial position.

▼ HINTS FOR YOUR OFFICE ▼

Write It Down

One of the most important hints for the office is *read, watch, listen, and take notes on everything.* Pay particular attention to details. If you do not take notes, you will not remember how to do something the next time the same situation occurs. Write yourself notes about a project and, most important, organize your notes so you can find them later. To organize your notes use a 3 x 5 in. card file box, a notebook with dividers, or a computer software package. Hand-held personal digital assistants are very helpful for note taking and for reference because they are easily accessible. A year later you may have a question about something you did. If you cannot find your notes, it is as if they were never made.

Know Your Office Location

Be able to explain to others the location of your office by describing the distinctive features and color of your building as well as the landmarks, restaurants, and stores near it. Be able to give directions to your office from main roads or interstate highways.

Leaving

Do not be the first person to leave the office each day or the first to leave office-related functions such as holiday parties or luncheons. You may appear too eager to depart.

Elevators

An elevator conversation can be overheard by everyone riding in the elevator. If your conversation can be overhead by others, discuss only casual, nonsensitive subjects. Conversely, if you are with only one person in the elevator, it may be the perfect opportunity to discuss a project or reinforce an idea.

The Lost Supervisor

Be able to locate your supervisor at all times. If the supervisor is going to be out of the office, know when the supervisor is expected to return.

Food at Your Desk

Do not eat at your desk. If a client walks in, food scattered across your desk looks messy and can have a strong aroma. Also, you might spill food on important papers or on the computer. If you must munch something, keep it in your desk drawer and remove a bite at a time. Keep all food out of sight.

Unknown Title

It can be difficult to determine if a name is male or female. If you are unsure of a person's gender when writing a letter, call the person's office and ask. Also, if you are unsure of a person's title, verify your information. Some people are offended if an incorrect title is used.

Checking the Desk

Because of illness or unanticipated problems, an employee may not come to work. Always check the person's desk, in-basket, and out-basket to determine if there is a project that must be handled or a telephone call that must be made. The absence of an employee should not be an excuse for delay in a project. Courtesy in checking a desk is important.

List of Employees

A list of all employees should be available to whomever answers the telephone. Use the list so that you do not have to ask important company officials what their titles are or how to spell their names. Also, be able to pronounce correctly the names of all employees.

Commitments

When you say you will do something, do it. Make a commitment and stick to it. Be responsible.

Remembering People

Prepare a card file or computer software with names and addresses of all clients, business associates, and co-workers. Include important information about these people, such as their preferences about restaurants and foods, their spouses' and children's names, descriptions of the people (so you will recognize them the next time they come to the office), and important dates in their lives. People like to feel important. Review the information prior to the person's next visit at your office.

Computers have made remembering easier. Develop an employee birthday list. Send computer-designed or store-purchased cards. People like to be remembered. Some offices have birthday parties for each person or monthly parties for all persons with a birthday in that month. Other offices have the birthday person bring the food to the office to celebrate the birthday.

Addressing Clients by Name

When clients call on the telephone or visit the office, call them by name. Say, "Good morning, Ms. Sanchez. It is nice to see you."

Toll-free Telephone Directory

Prepare your own directory of toll-free telephone numbers. You can use a telephone address book or you can use a computer software package. Include any toll-free numbers that you might want to call in the future. These could include car-rental agencies, hotels, and businesses. When you use a new number, add it to your directory.

Smoking in the Office

Since many people today are concerned about indoor air pollution and health, smoking in the office is becoming unpopular. Many organizations now restrict smoking in office areas. Be aware of your company's policy regarding smoking. Knowledge of this policy is important if you smoke or if you have clients who smoke.

Reference Materials

In your office you should have the following types of reference materials:

- Almanac
- Atlas
- Book of quotations (this is helpful when writing speeches)
- Computer reference books for the software packages you use
- Computer software packages for ZIP codes, addresses, telephone numbers, encyclopedias, and maps
- Dictionary
- Dictionary of misspelled words (this book lists words the way you think they should be spelled, not how they are spelled)
- *National Five-Digit ZIP Code and Post Office Directory* (USPS Publication 65)
- Office reference manual
- Specific references for your industry
- Telephone directories of cities called frequently
- Thesaurus

Desk Organization

Organize your desk for easy accessability. Always be able to quickly locate supplies and working materials, such as project files. Use desk organizers and dividers to arrange supplies in your desk. Place dictionaries and frequently used reference materials on the top of your desk or in another easy-to-reach area. Dictionaries and reference manuals should not be hidden in the bottom desk drawer. You may not be motivated to use these reference materials if they are not easily accessible.

Serial Numbers

Maintain a list of serial numbers and model numbers for equipment and computer software. To upgrade software, the serial number of the current version is frequently required.

Work Area

Keep your work area neat. Some people believe that a neat workplace means a neat and efficient person. Do not allow your desk to accumulate stacks of papers and folders. Use a file drawer as a temporary location for folders used frequently.

Place only a couple of personal items on your desk. These items should reflect your personal taste but continue to demonstrate your professional image. Your office and desk are good display areas for certificates or awards you have received.

Proofreading

Proofread everything even if you use a computerized spelling or grammar package. Read the document in the normal order. Then read the document backwards—reading from the bottom right of the page to the top left of the page. It is easier to spot an error if the words are not in their proper context. Proofread the third time in the proper sequence. Other techniques are to proofread the document again another day or to exchange proofreading duties with a co-worker.

Comments

It is important to read an entire document before making comments on it. Do not make handwritten notes to yourself on the document. The last paragraph may change your original thoughts.

Envelopes

Remember that all correspondence needs an envelope. Since schools do not always require an envelope for each assignment, students sometimes forget that envelopes are required for mailing documents. When keyboarding a document, prepare an envelope for it.

Pinch Hit

In any office, but particularly a small office, be prepared to do any job. If someone is absent or if there is a rush job, be willing to help complete the project. Be a team player and work together with others. Getting along with people in the office and advancing in your position means doing any job that is necessary.

▼ YOUR DAY ▼

Plan Each Day

You should always have a *to-do list* or *task list*, which includes major as well as minor projects. Computer software can be used to create task lists, and computer calendars can be used to plan your day. Computer organization software helps list and prioritize your projects and can be used on hand-held or desktop computers.

Prepare a schedule of your work each day, listing the projects you will work on, and set realistic time lines for each item. It is often wise to add additional time to each task as a contingency for office interruptions and unscheduled events. Review the schedule during the day and revise it as needed. At the end of each day prepare a work schedule for the next day.

Learn to juggle your regular job responsibilities while completing major projects. People often do not get to the major projects because they become involved in minor projects and the time disappears. If you have a major project, plan to work on a portion of it every day. Set a specific time each day for the major project and adhere to the schedule.

Efficiency

Always prioritize your work assignments. If necessary, ask your supervisor to help you prioritize your work. Review and update the list at least once a day.

If possible, arrange appointments or meetings for specific times or specific days. This method eliminates wasted time and moves people quickly from one appointment to another. An example is scheduling appointments and meetings only on Tuesday and Thursday afternoons. This scheduling technique can be used when arranging appointments and meetings for your supervisor or for yourself.

When the projects are too numerous, decide if a project could be eliminated or if the project could be completed by another staff member. Do not continue to do a job just because it was always done. Question the need to do the job if it appears unnecessary. Jobs that cannot be eliminated can often be streamlined.

Deadlines

Keep your supervisor informed of all deadlines. Set up preliminary checkpoints to measure progress. When the due date arrives, it is too late to make adjustments. If you are not going to be able to meet a deadline, inform your supervisor early, not at the last minute. This gives both you and the supervisor time to revise the deadline or to add additional resources to meet the deadline.

In-Baskets

Keep a separate *in-basket* for yourself and a separate in-basket for items from your supervisor. Review and process items in the in-baskets several times a day.

Pending Folder

Prepare a *pending folder* for all items for which you are waiting for an answer. Check your pending folder daily. If possible, decide on a specific time each day to check the folder. The best time to review the pending folder is at the end of the day when you make up the next day's to-do list.

Bring-up Folder

Meet with the employer once a day to discuss problems and review your assignments. If possible, establish a specific time each day for the meeting and adhere to it. Go to the meeting with a prepared list of items to be discussed. Use a *bring-up folder* to store your problems and questions until the next meeting. This meeting is a good time to compare your version of the employer's calendar with the employer's version of the calendar.

Business Cards

An administrative assistant and the executive should have business cards printed. The cards should be placed in a business card holder on the top of the desk so they are easily accessible when a client is in the office. Also, each person should have a business card carrying case which will fit in a pocket or purse.

Business cards should include the following:

- Company name and logo
- Person's name
- Title
- Address
- City, state, ZIP code
- Telephone number
- Cell telephone number
- Pager number
- Fax number
- E-mail address

When attending meetings outside the office, carry your business cards so they may be exchanged with other colleagues.

If you are mailing a document to someone outside the office, clip your business card to the document. You may also write a short note on the back of the card.

Business Lunches

Business lunches are part of the working day. Do not feel that a business lunch infringes on your personal time. Use the opportunity of a business lunch to your advantage. Meet co-

Marilyn W. Payne
Communications Manager
Globe S. Communications
2788 Roosevelt Drive
Albany, NY 12186

Fax 518-886-0769   Telephone 518-886-2276
E-mail MPayne@GlobeC.com

FIGURE 13-1   A Business Card.

workers and supervisors in a nonoffice environment and demonstrate your knowledge and skills. This may also be an opportunity to show that you have interests outside the office. Mention a book you recently read or a play you attended. You want the office to know that you are a well-informed and social person. Business lunches are also an important opportunity to network.

Do not order the same thing as your supervisor unless it is something that you really would like to have. Use some originality. Eat slowly. Nervousness may make you eat too fast, and then you will have nothing to do while the others are eating. Order something that you can eat easily, not a messy food. It may be better to order sparkling water instead of an alcoholic beverage. Do not be the only person to order dessert. If it is a small group, speak with everyone at the table, not just the person seated beside you.

Security

If you must arrive early, work late, or work alone, be aware of your personal safety. Lock your office and car doors. Always have your keys in your hands when going to your car. If there are security guards, inform them of your schedule. If you must go to a dark parking lot, try to walk with someone. Have a flashlight easily accessible and always be alert to any danger.

Strains Caused by Computer Video Terminals

If you use a computer terminal for several hours each day, it is necessary for you to take breaks often. Every 15 minutes look away from the terminal for a few seconds, and every couple of hours take a 10-minute break from the terminal. Take a walk or stop for a drink of water. Neck and back muscles also need a break from the terminal. Every few hours, loosen tight muscles by rubbing them or doing some stretching exercises.

▼ YOURSELF ▼

Personal/Office Life

Leave your personal life and problems at home, and leave your office life and problems at the office. Make a conscious effort to separate the two phases of your life. Taking your office problems home everyday will interfere with the enjoyment of your personal life. The relaxation and stimulation that you receive from your personal life will enhance your ability to handle office problems. Separating office problems and home problems is not easy, but with practice it can work.

Pick Yourself Up

Everyone has days when nothing seems to go right. To boost your moral, remember your strong points and the positive comments you have received. Also, remind yourself that there will be good days again.

Do not become upset or defensive after receiving constructive criticism; accept it and learn from it. Consider the validity of the comments and modify your behavior accordingly.

Stress

Unfortunately, stress can be a part of your everyday work life. Learning to handle stress is important to your physical and emotional well-being. Surveys have indicated that office assistants work in a stressful environment. Some factors that cause stress in the office are interruptions, too much to do and too little time to do it, lack of advancement opportunities, little input into decisions, lack of communication from supervisors, conflicting assignments from several supervisors, and the constant interruptions caused by the telephone.

Symptoms of stress

- Upset stomach
- Breathing rapidly
- Heart pounding rapidly
- Heavy perspiration
- Tense muscles, often in the neck, back, arms, or legs
- Exhaustion
- Inability to sleep
- Irritability
- Lack of appetite
- Weight gain or loss
- Nausea
- Sweaty palms
- Crying
- Fears
- Lack of attention to details
- Perfectionism
- Feelings of worthlessness

Stress can be controlled by you or by a professional with the use of medicine or psychological assistance.

Techniques to avoid stress before it starts

- Attack stress at its source.
- Exercise.
- Eat a well-balanced diet.
- Recognize stress before it is too late.
- Create a balance between work and home.
- See the humor in a situation.
- Do not create stress by procrastinating on a project.
- Do not try to do everything at the office. Delegate responsibility and permit other employees to work on projects.

FIGURE 13-2 A positive attitude is a key to reducing stress. (Courtesy of International Business Machines Corporation. Unauthorized use not permitted.)

- Learn to relax.
- Find something you enjoy and then do it.

Techniques to deal with stress

- Stop and tell yourself to relax when you feel stress.
- Ask yourself why you are upset. Then alter or accept the situation that causes the stress.
- Ask yourself why you are hurrying.
- Ask yourself if what your are doing is really essential.
- Tell yourself to laugh about the problem that is causing you anxiety.
- Stop and ask yourself if the problem is really worth all the trouble it is causing you. If the problem is not worth the trouble, modify the situation or ignore it.
- Exercise—walk, run, dance, bike, do aerobics, or do any exercise that relieves the tension.
- Develop a hobby that captures your attention and relaxes you.
- Remind yourself that today's problems will probably be unimportant next week.

Etiquette

Social and personal relations skills are important to your ability to handle any situation in the office. Knowing the right time and the proper way to do something may mean the difference between success and failure.

The following are office situations that may require your knowledge of social and business etiquette:

- Expressing your condolences to someone who has experienced the loss of a family member
- Expressing congratulations to a supervisor or co-worker upon receiving an award, recent engagement, marriage, or birth of a child
- What to say to the newly separated or divorced co-worker
- Customs of the visitor from a foreign country
- Who pays the restaurant bill
- How to pay the restaurant bill
- When and how much to tip
- Religious customs of clients and co-workers
- Conduct during an office party
- Attending a business banquet
- Purchasing appropriate business gifts
- Writing thank-you letters for gifts and meals

If you are not comfortable handling any of the situations above, there are many books on etiquette which are available in bookstores and libraries.

Compliments

If someone gives you a compliment, accept it and say thank you. Some people respond with a denial of the compliment. Do not say, "I did not think that I made a good presentation."

Rumors

Use rumors to your advantage. For example, if you hear that your department or company will be restructuring, talk with your supervisor about accepting responsibility for a new project that will allow you to gain skills and demonstrate your capabilities. Then when a new opportunity arises, you will have the required knowledge to step into the job.

Mentor

A mentor is a person who advises and guides. Usually, a mentor is a person who has obtained a position higher than yours and who is willing to provide advice. A mentor can make your career advance more quickly and can steer you in the proper direction when a choice must be made. The selection of a mentor is an informal process, and the relationship is not directly stated between the parties. Rather, the mentor relationship gradually develops through mutual understanding and trust.

Office Attire

Let your voice, appearance, and personal characteristics create the stage for your professional image. A professional is aware of the importance the business community attaches to appearance. When first entering the working world, you may have to adjust your wardrobe from that of a college student to clothing appropriate for a working person. It is wise not to completely change your wardrobe at one time. Buy a few things and decide if they are appropriate. Look at how the others in your office dress, giving special attention to the wardrobes of people who have jobs to which you would like to advance. Do the men wear ties, suits, or sport coats? Do the women wear suits, dresses, blazers, or separates—slacks, skirts, sweaters? Then try to dress like those who have the job you would like in the future rather than dressing for your present job. Executives may see that you are a candidate for advancement if your professional appearance supports your professional work.

In the last few years, the clothing worn in the workplace has become more casual. In some offices where the employees dress in traditional business attire, employees dress casually on Fridays. On Fridays the employees wear *business casual*, casual clothing with a professional appearance—not jeans or sweat outfits. Dress-down days have become more popular, particularly in the summer months. Offices that have a casual Friday policy may have a provision that states if there is a meeting with clients on a Friday, traditional business attire is appropriate instead of casual attire.

FIGURE 13-3   Professional Office Attire. (Courtesy of International Business Machines Corporation. Unauthorized use not permitted.)

Some employers feel that the clothing worn today is too casual and inappropriate for the office. In most offices jeans are not acceptable. T-shirts with ludicrous remarks are not appropriate either. For women, skirts that are too short or blouses that are cut too low are not office attire.

Always dress appropriately for the office. The one day that you dress in a nonbusiness manner will unexpectedly be the day that it will be important for you to look professional. In bad weather, some people dress in a sloppy manner. Do not allow yourself ever to dress in nonprofessional attire.

Plan your outfit the night before so that you do not waste precious morning hours selecting an outfit. Also, organize your closet so that it is easy to coordinate outfits.

Buy good-quality clothing that will last rather than fad items that quickly go out of style. Update your wardrobe each season with accessories such as ties for men and scarves and jewelry for women.

An important aspect of appearance is a rested body. Always allow sufficient time for rest and sleep, because you cannot function properly in the office if you are drowsy and exhausted.

Some offices have a definite dress code. The following is a sample of a dress code of an employer in a large metropolitan area:

- Jackets must be worn by men and women. Sometimes the jacket is removed while working, but if a client comes in, the jacket must be worn.
- Women should not wear heels higher than 2 in.
- A minimum of jewelry is worn. Jewelry should be simple and classic in appearance. If you can hear the jewelry, too much is being worn.

▼ YOUR JOB▼

The New Job

During the first week of any new job, you should carry a pad of paper and a pen with you at all times. Try to make notes constantly since you will not remember everything. Write notes to yourself so that you can remember names, faces, and instructions that you are given. Review your notes each night so that you will feel more comfortable with your new job every day.

Be friendly with everyone, but do not form intense friendships too quickly. In a new environment, introduce yourself and be pleasant to everyone. Give yourself time to become acquainted with all the workers in your office. Establishing close friendships with some co-workers may be seen as excluding others or attaching yourself to a group. Later, it may be difficult to withdraw from the group.

Employees should not gossip. Not only is gossip impolite and unprofessional, but it can be dangerous for a new employee who does not know the relationships of the people involved or the sensitivity of the information being discussed.

The new employee wants to be accepted as a credible, professional member of the staff, so demonstrate that you consider your job important. Arrive early and do not rush out the minute the workday is over. If you have nothing to do, at least look busy. Look through the files and become familiar with the company or read professional publications that are in the office. As soon as you complete one project, ask for another job. Do not wait for the supervisor to bring you another assignment.

If you do not know how to do something, ask questions so that you will be able to complete the project correctly. Always appear interested in learning all of your new duties even if you think that they are boring and inefficient.

Changing Jobs

When seeking a new job, changing jobs, or changing fields, ask friends to introduce you to people who might be able to help you. If you want an entry-level job, do not just ask to meet the head of the organization. Ask to meet supervisors, because people at this level might be better able to help you meet your job goals.

Clipping Service

Begin a clipping service for your supervisor. Read the daily newspaper, out-of-town newspapers, and professional publications. Then clip and mark articles of importance for your supervisor or company.

▼ CO-WORKERS ▼

Sharing Ideas

"I would like to share this information with you" is a tactful way to tell someone something.

Making a Group Decision Stick

Before you leave a meeting, verify that everyone is satisfied with the decision. Reinforce the decision with both an oral and a written summary of the meeting.

Cross Training

Each employee should be encouraged to learn as much as possible about each department and the duties of the department's employees. Knowledge of other jobs, whether in your department or in other departments, will help you grow professionally and may lead to a promotion. You will also be able to better answer questions for clients. It is very frustrating to both you and to clients when you must say, "I do not know the answer. Jane is the only person who knows, and she is out of town."

Death in the Family

It may be the responsibility of the administrative assistant to notify employees of the death of an employee or family member of an employee. Notification can be made by E-mail or by posting a notice. It is customary to send a gift of flowers or a tray of food to the family or to make a charitable donation in memory of the deceased. Money for these purposes may be collected from the staff or may be taken from an office fund. It is always proper to send a letter of condolence to the family. Also, it may be necessary to notify clients of the death of an employee and indicate who will handle the job in the future.

Delegate

If possible, assign work to other employees. Do not feel that you are the only person who can do a job correctly or who should be able to do a specific job, even if you can do the job faster than another employee. You should train other employees so that you will have time for more challenging projects.

Negotiate with Your Supervisor

Understand your supervisor's personality, and know when it is the best time to approach your supervisor. Some people are more responsive in the morning, others in the afternoon. Perhaps the best time to approach your supervisor is after the supervisor has had coffee or read the mail. Timing could be the key factor in receiving the response you want.

Begin a negotiation with a compliment. The compliment sets the mood for the discussion, and it is more difficult to turn down a request that is begun with a compliment. Always be honest and realistic with your compliment. For example,

I have always enjoyed working for this company because of the help and guidance you have given me.

Be flexible, know what can be negotiated, and know what the options are. Present the benefits the company will receive by granting your request. For example,

> By allowing me to begin my day an hour later, I will be at work an hour later. Therefore, after everyone else leaves, I will still be here to help clients.

Discuss one point at a time. Do not overwhelm the supervisor by requesting too much at one time. You have a greater chance of success if you make only a single request.

Dealing with Problems

When you are given a project, analyze it carefully. Outline the project, list possible problems and solutions, and develop a timetable for completion. Try to anticipate the problems that might occur and also allow extra time for unanticipated problems.

Do not run to your supervisor each time you have a problem; try to solve it yourself, instead. If you cannot solve a problem, review your outline and list possible solutions before you talk with your supervisor. This preparation will organize your thoughts and prepare you to answer your supervisor's questions.

There are some problems for which there are no easy answers. Accept the fact that you cannot solve them. If problems do not have a deadline, try to let them solve themselves. Put these problems in a pending file, but do not forget about them. Monitor the situation periodically. An example of an unsolvable problem is that of two employees who do not get along but must work together. Perhaps time will solve the problem and the two employees will work out their differences.

An Indecisive Supervisor

If your supervisor will not make decisions, you will have to assist in the decision-making process. When you present the supervisor with a problem, also present a solution. If the supervisor says, "I will get back to you later," write a note to yourself on your calendar. Then you will know when to ask for an answer.

Crisis Management

Some offices seem to operate by *crisis management*. That means that management only seems to respond to a crisis and often runs from one crisis to another in a panic. Although it is fine for an office to solve problems immediately, it is better to resolve problems before they occur by careful planning. Unfortunately, not all situations can be anticipated

Job Competition

Competition between co-workers is a natural occurrence. Competition may occur for a promotion or for a special project. While everyone hopes to be selected for the promotion or to be given the favored assignment, learning to deal with disappointment is also a part of professional growth. If someone received the promotion you wanted, congratulate the person and work with him or her in a professional manner.

The Unwanted Project

You may be given a project to complete that you do not want to do. You may find the project uninteresting or distasteful, or you simply may not have the time to do it. You should never flatly refuse to do a project, but the following suggestions may be helpful.

- Explain to your supervisor that you are too busy because you are involved in other projects.
- Explain that you have already had the opportunity to learn this duty, so someone else should have the same opportunity. Explain that it would be beneficial to have another person know how to do this job, and offer to assist the colleague.
- Ask for help from other co-workers to complete the project.

Mistakes

Everyone is human and makes mistakes. If you made a mistake, talk with your supervisor, acknowledge the mistake, and apologize. Do not hide the mistake or try to blame someone else. In addition, tell the supervisor what action you will take to ensure that this mistake is avoided in the future.

How to Respond to a Nasty Memo

You may at some time receive a memo or E-mail that is negative in tone and that even may be rude. Do not write a nasty memo in response. It is better not to write anything. Instead, arrange a meeting so that the problem can be discussed. If the memo writer is still angry at the time of the meeting, let the writer talk until the anger is released. Then attempt to solve the problem. You may not agree with the writer's position, but you should try to maintain a good working relationship with the person.

▼ BUSINESS STRATEGIES ▼

Conflict Resolution

As management styles change, business terms become popular or *buzz words*. *Conflict resolution* is a buzz word for solving conflicts. In your role as supervisor, solving conflicts may be a daily occurrence. Listed below are suggestions for solving conflicts:

- Be objective.
- Identify the issue.
- Identify the concerns of each person.
- Do not become emotionally involved in the issue.
- Offer suggestions to solve the problem.

Become an expert at conflict resolution. Learn to use a nonaccusatory and constructive approach to resolve problems. A cooperative workplace is a more productive workplace. Solving conflicts can be a step toward advancement.

Critical Thinking

Critical thinking is a thought process often used to solve problems. In critical thinking, the first step is to define the issue and then to design a creative preliminary solution to the problem. A statement of the problem is very important, because if the problem is not defined correctly, the solution would not solve the problem and would fail. Since all colleagues may not see the problem the same way and may not agree on what problem really is, it is often difficult to define the problem clearly.

After the problem is defined, the next step is to develop a solution. Critical thinking uses a unlimited imagination to create inventive alternatives to problem solving rather than being limited to an obvious solution to a problem.

Mission Statement

Companies write mission statements, which describe the purpose or reason the company is in business. A mission statement might include the following:

This company was organized to provide the highest-quality bicycle parts that represent the best value for our customers.

Total Quality Management

One of the many management techniques used in businesses is *total quality management* (TQM). TQM stresses a process of analysis and continual improvement of procedures so that work is done correctly the first time, thereby saving the time and cost of making corrections. TQM recognizes that each employee involved in a process, whether processing a payroll or assembling a computer, is an expert in that job. Each employee shares decision making with employees to help improve the final product or service. TQM often involves detailed record keeping, which helps identify problem areas to be improved. Customer feedback is important in an organization using TQM. Customer feedback helps identify areas of the business that need improvement. Customer feedback on products and services can help the company identify desired service improvements or new uses for products.

Common Business Acronyms

There are many acronyms that are often used in informal communications such as E-mail messages and internal memos. A few of these are listed below.

Business acronyms

ASAP	As soon as possible
BTW	By the way
COB	Close of business
CEO	Chief executive officer
COO	Chief operating officer
CFO	Chief financial officer
FAQ	Frequently asked question
FYI	For your information
FWIW	For what it is worth
TIA	Thanks in advance

▼ TRAVEL ▼

Business Travel

When traveling on business, check the weather forecast for your destination. Weather information is usually available on television, on the Internet, or in newspapers. Since the weather may be unpredictable, it is wise to take a folding umbrella when you travel.

Select appropriate clothing, but take the least amount possible. Select items of clothing that are coordinated so they can be worn interchangeably. Carrying your luggage with you on the plane is the only way to guarantee that your luggage will arrive at your destination. Carrying your luggage also eliminates the delay of having to wait for the luggage to be unloaded. Most airlines allow one or two pieces per person of carry-on baggage.

Many hotels offer dry cleaning services or have irons available for last-minute touch ups. However, you can eliminate the need for ironing by packing clothes carefully. To avoid wrinkling your jacket while traveling, remove it and hang it or fold it carefully.

It is wise to carry a small snack with you on a plane. On a long flight, meals are usually served a couple of hours after the departure time. If you have a 12 P.M. departure, you may not be served until 2 P.M. It is also a good idea to carry something to read. With the reoccurring delays of airplane travel, your travel time may be several hours longer than you anticipated.

Always take a map with you even if you are not going to drive. The map will assist you in becoming familiar with the area. You should carry small bills and change for tips and be aware of your company's policy on telephone calls home. Some companies will reimburse employees, within set limits, for calls made to the traveler's family.

Map Reading

Since you may be asked to drive to an unknown location or to give directions to a client, map reading skills are important. It can be intimidating to travel alone to a strange city. The fear of the unknown can be eased by having and being able to read a good map. Try, if possible, to get a map of the city or area you will be traveling to *before* you leave on your trip.

- Road atlases are sold in most bookstores. These maps may have a small map of the city you will visit with major streets and items of interest indicated.
- Your auto club may have detailed city maps that will be helpful.
- If you have enough time, you can call the chamber of commerce of the city you will visit and request that they send you a map.
- Maps of many cities can be found on and printed from the Internet.

If you have a map, review it before your trip. Look at how the city lies in relationship to major geographical features such as mountains, rivers, or the ocean. Try to locate the airport, train station, or highway you will use in arriving. Locate the interstates, numbered routes, and major local roads, which are usually shown in thick lines.

Maps can be obtained after you arrive at the city.

- *Auto rental.* If you rent a car, the rental agency usually has a map of the area. Be sure to ask for the map if it is not offered.
- *Hotel/motel.* These places usually will have a map of the immediate area. Inquire at the front desk when you check into the hotel or motel.
- *Information centers.* Many communities have tourist information centers with maps and brochures of the area. These centers may be located with the chamber of commerce or at the airport. Also, information centers are usually located on interstate highways soon after the highway enters a new state.
- *Gas stations.* Many gas stations will sell maps for a few dollars.

CHAPTER REVIEW

1. List 10 hints that you can use in the office.
2. Define the word *mentor* and explain how a mentor may be helpful to you.

ACTIVITIES

1. Plan your school or work day for the next five days. Include your assignments, classes, meetings, future projects, employment, and personal responsibilities.
2. Write exact directions to your:
   a. School
   b. Home
   c. Favorite shopping center
3. Find a partner and have each person give oral directions to a building in your area. Take notes as the oral directions are given. Can you now locate the building?
4. Write a description of the physical appearance of each of the three locations used in Activity 2.
5. Select three friends. Prepare a 3 x 5 in. information card on each and include the following information:
   a. Name
   b. Favorite restaurant
   c. Birthday
   d. Information about family: names, likes, dislikes, and so on
6. Read your daily newspaper or a magazine. Clip articles of interest to office employees. Circulate the articles by sending them to four of the members of your class.

7. List four occasions when you have felt stress. Describe how you felt. Explain how you should have handled the stress.
8. For the next week, select your clothes in advance. Write a description of your weekly selections.
9. Look at your state map and write directions from your school to the state capitol.
10. Role play how you would handle the following situations:
    a. Your supervisor's mother just passed away.
    b. A co-worker has become engaged.
    c. You have just met the president of the company at an office party.
    d. A co-worker has received a promotion and will leave the department.
    e. A client from another part of the world has just walked into your office.
    f. You are meeting your supervisor's spouse for the first time.
11. Select a person who you think would be a good mentor and explain why.
12. What changes would you make in your work wardrobe, and why?
13. Name four stores in your area that carry clothing appropriate for your career image.

PROJECTS

Project 25

Create the following itinerary.

The supervisor will be attending the Communications Changes and Updates meeting which will be held in the Ballroom at the Marriott at the Capitol in Austin, Texas, September 2, 3, and 4. Travel will be from Washington Dulles airport on American Airlines flight 399, leaving at 12:36 P.M. Change planes in Dallas to flight 872, leaving at 3:44 P.M. to arrive at 4:39 P.M. The hotel confirmation number is 920342WS. The phone number for the Marriott is 512-478-1111. Return flight 1054 leaves Austin at 3:38 P.M., connecting to flight 622 in Dallas, leaving at 5:32 and arrives in Washington at 9:32 P.M.

Project 26

Set this up in an attractive format. Arrange the table in order by month.

TRAVEL PLANS
FOR NEXT YEAR

NAME	DEPARTMENT	DESTINATION	MONTH
Brian Lechner	1618	Quebec, PQ	June
Wanda McGee	1620	Des Moines, IA	September
Rodney Nuir	1620	St. Paul, MN	August
Louis Pronske	1621	Harrisburg, PA	January
Laura Schmeltz	1621	Richmond, VA	June
Ruth Eden	1621	Corpus Christi, TX	May
Mike Lezcano	1620	Louisville, KY	April
Samuel Snyder	1617	Tampa, FL	February
Janet Weinberg	1618	Miami, FL	June
Ferando Grasso	1620	Baton Rouge, LA	May

HUMAN RELATIONS SKILL DEVELOPMENT

Irritating Habits

Personal habits can be irritating to others. Some habits that may irritate co-workers are drumming fingers on the desk, chewing gum and popping it, and cracking knuckles. The best solution is to ignore the habit, but if that has become impossible, a diplomatic request to discontinue the action is required. The person with the habit may not even be aware that it is irritating to others.

- What personal habits irritate you?
- Which of your personal habits could irritate co-workers?
- What would you say to a co-worker whose gum chewing is disturbing you?

The Employee in the Middle

It is possible to have two supervisors with conflicting ideas supervising one person. Working on a project while receiving conflicting directions can be difficult. If possible, arrange a meeting with both supervisors and yourself to discuss the project. Continue to meet as a group during the project. If you find yourself meeting individually with one supervisor in a decision-making session, write a for-your-information memo for the other supervisor or talk with the other supervisor before proceeding with the project.

- What would you say to two supervisors who continually give you conflicting directions on a project?
- Describe reasons that may cause two supervisors to have opposing views on all projects.

SITUATIONS

How would you handle each of the following situations?

- You have been promoted to supervisor of your department. You are having problems with your former co-workers who are now your subordinates. They ignore your orders and decisions.
- Your supervisor informed you that next month your office will be hosting a delegation from a foreign country. How would you plan for this event?
- On your business flight to Denver, you placed your briefcase in the overhead compartment. When leaving the plane, you noticed that your briefcase was gone. A similar briefcase was found in another compartment.

PUNCTUATION REVIEW

Punctuate each of the following sentences.

1. The local government sponsored a job fair investigated child care facilities and developed public seminars
2. The office cleanup day is set for September 20 and all employees are expected to participate
3. Registration will be Friday and orientation will be Monday Tuesday and Wednesday
4. Participants gain an overview of computers graphic packages and fax machines
5. Upon successful completion of the program you will receive a certificate

6. Enclosed is a list of our clients which should be helpful to you

7. During a two month period our sales rose 25 percent but our profits fell 10 percent

8. As you may recall from my memorandum of February 12 effective March 31 our office will be implementing a Health Care Reimbursement Account Plan

9. Designed for todays mobile workforce 401(k) plans allow employees to change jobs and encourage employees to continue building on their retirement savings

10. We are happy that you have joined our club but we must remind you to pay your dues

11. Under the present tax law the amount by which you may reduce your salary is limited to 14 percent of your gross income

12. West Virginia the mountain state is near Washington DC

13. Our best friend an authority on business ethics is speaking Friday September 1

14. We are constructing a new office complex at 1400 Executive Drive Omaha Nebraska

15. When I read the book I was enchanted with it

Appendix: Review of Grammar, Punctuation, and Spelling

As an office employee, it will be important for you to use correct grammar, to punctuate sentences, and to spell correctly. These skills are used when you speak to clients, answer the telephone, write telephone messages or notes to your supervisor, write and keyboard letters and reports, and proofread your documents.

This section of the book reviews grammar, punctuation, and spelling. The objective is for you to apply knowledge, not memorize rules. A list of frequently misspelled words and a list of cities is provided so that you can improve your spelling skills. In addition, a list of similar-sounding words is provided to help increase your knowledge of word usage.

▼ GRAMMAR ▼

Capitalization

- Capitalize the first word of every sentence.

  The final draft of the report is on my desk.

- Always capitalize the pronoun *I*.

  Matthew and I are attending the convention.

- Capitalize the days of the week, months of the year, and holidays.

  We are speaking at the meeting on Monday, May 30, which is Memorial Day.

- Capitalize proper nouns and proper adjectives.

  They videotaped the Pittsburgh Business Association Conference.
  We have IBM, Xerox, Kodak, and Sharp equipment.
  The French report was translated into English, German, and Spanish.
  This year we have representatives from North Carolina, Minnesota, and New Mexico.

Subject and Verb

- The *subject* is the name of a person, place, or thing and the subject tells who performed the action. The *verb* is the action in the sentence, and it tells what was done.

  She pointed to the director.
      she   (subject)
      pointed   (verb)

Management donated the equipment.
    management   (subject)
    donated   (verb)

Subject and Verb Agreement

- The verb must agree with the subject in number and person. If the subject is singular, the verb must be singular. If the subject is plural, the verb must be plural.

  Louise writes three reports a week.
      Louise   (singular subject)
      writes   (singular verb)

  Juan and Teki write three reports a week.
      Juan and Teki   (plural subject)
      write   (plural verb)

- *Helping verbs* help the main verb.

  The following are examples of singular helping verbs:

  is, am, was, has, have

  The following are examples of plural helping verbs:

  are, were, have

  The report was read by everyone in the department.
      was   (singular helping verb)
      read   (main verb)

  Richard and Bob were delighted with the results of the sale.
      were   (plural helping verb)
      delighted   (main verb)

  The following are examples of *singular* pronouns:

  he, she, it, you, another, anybody, anyone, each, either, everybody, everyone, neither, one, somebody, someone

  Everyone in the department was late for work because of the snow.
      Everyone   (singular pronoun)
      was   (singular verb)

  The following are examples of *plural* pronouns:

  they, we, you, both, few, many, others, several
  Several were late for work because of the snow.
      Several   (plural pronoun)
      were   (plural verb)

Phrase

- A *phrase* is a group of related words not containing a subject and verb.

  black box   (phrase does not contain a verb)

Clause

- A *clause* is a group of words that contains a subject and a verb.

- An *independent clause* is a complete thought and can stand alone.

  Julie has meetings at all three locations.

- A *dependent clause* does not make sense by itself and cannot stand alone.

  If you complete the project by June, you will receive an outstanding evaluation.
      If you complete the project by June   (dependent clause)

▼ PUNCTUATION ▼

Period

- A period is used at the end of a sentence that makes a statement or issues a command.

  She attended every department meeting.

Question Mark

- A question mark is the ending punctuation for each sentence that asks a question.

  When will we have the report completed?

Exclamation Mark

- An exclamation mark is used after words or sentences to express a strong emotion.

  Our department won the contest!

Commas

- A comma is used to separate items in a series. A series must contain at least three items. The comma preceding the *and* is optional.

  Ed completed the survey, evaluation and revisions yesterday.
  Yesterday I saw demonstrations of printers, scanners, and network systems.

- A comma is used in apposition. An appositive explains the noun or pronoun that it follows.

  Ms. Halley, the director, is an enthusiastic speaker.
      Ms. Halley   (noun)
      the director   (appositive)

- A comma is placed before and after nonrestrictive clauses and phrases. Nonrestrictive clauses and phrases are words that can be removed from the sentence while keeping the clarity of the sentence. Although words have been removed, the sentence still makes sense.

  The training facility, which offers computer courses, is located at 966 Rose Tree Lane.
      which offers computer classes   (nonrestrictive clause)

- A comma is used in a direct address. Direct address indicates to whom you are speaking.

  Jane, please finish the report by 5:00 on Friday.
      Jane   (direct address to Jane)

- A comma is used in introductory expressions. An introductory expression introduces the remaining part of the sentence.

  When Larry returns from the Boston meeting, he will write a report summarizing the meeting.

  > When Larry returns from the Boston meeting   (introductory clause)

  If I am late for the meeting, do not wait for me.

  > If I am late for the meeting   (introductory clause)

- A comma is used to separate the direct quote from the remaining portion of the sentence.

  Ben said, "The guest speaker was fantastic."

- A comma is used to separate clauses in a compound sentence. A compound sentence contains two independent clauses and is joined by a coordinating conjunction—and, but, for, or, nor, and yet. If the clauses are very short, a comma is not used.

  My office bought the latest computer software, but I do not understand it.
  I like it but she doesn't. (Clause is too short.)
  Louise bought a computer, and Matthew bought a printer.

- A comma is used after yes and no when they begin the sentence.

  Yes, Richard is the reporter.

- A comma is used before and after parenthetical expressions. These are expressions that interrupt the sentence. The following words are examples of parenthetical expressions.

fortunately	*however*
as you know	*of course*
perhaps	*I think*
I believe	*in fact*

  Of course, she passed the test.
  Jung, as you know, is the most qualified applicant.
  Perhaps, the convention could be held January 12 in Florida.

- A comma is used to separate the day of the month from the year.

  The building is scheduled to be completed by January 27, XXXX.

- A comma is used to separate two adjectives describing the same noun.

  Her office was in a large, old mansion.
  The long, difficult project was completed.

- A comma is used to separate contrasting expressions.

  The briefcase is made of fine leather, not vinyl.
  The meeting began at 10:00, not 9:00.

- A comma is used to separate names from titles and degrees. Numbers in names do not use commas.

Raymond Soloman, Jr., was the guest speaker.

We are meeting Dick Madison, Ph.D., at the airport.

Donald Watkins III is my attorney.

- A comma is used to separate numbers of four or more. The comma is not used in house numbers, telephone numbers, or ZIP codes.

23,800 tons

Semicolon

- A semicolon is used to separate independent clauses not joined by a conjunction.

Michelle enjoys classical music; Nancy prefers jazz.

We stayed at the convention hotel; George stayed at the hotel across the street from the convention hotel.

- A semicolon is used to separate items in a series if the series contains commas.

They spent their vacation in Portland, Maine; San Francisco, California; and Orlando, Florida.

The seminar will be held Friday, June 16; Tuesday, August 25; Thursday, September 28; and Monday, November 5.

- A semicolon is used to separate clauses containing internal punctuation.

Marsha, my supervisor, is an effective leader; but Arleen motivates employees more quickly.

The agenda indicated that the meeting is Tuesday, October 15, XXXX; but we would like to change the meeting date to Friday, October 18, XXXX.

Colon

- The colon is used to introduce a list.

I purchased the following items: 15 legal pads, 10 computer disks, and 25 boxes of computer paper.

Dash

- The dash is used to indicate an abrupt change in thought.

Kathy, my mentor, is my best friend—at least I hope she is.

Parentheses

- Parentheses are used to set off words or phrases that are not essential to the sentence.

The chairperson of the committee (the woman from Tulsa) is receiving her doctorate this year.

Apostrophe

- The apostrophe is used to show omission of letters in contractions.

Walter can't attend the meeting.   (Contraction of *cannot*)

- The apostrophe is used when a noun is possessive.

Sara's office is small.

Hyphen

- The hyphen is used to divide syllables of words.

  scis-sors

Quotation Marks

- Quotation marks are used to enclose exactly what was said or written. Periods and commas go inside the quotation mark. Question marks are placed inside the quotation mark if only the quotation is a question. Question marks are placed outside the quotation mark if the entire sentence is a question.

  He asked, "Is the report collated?"   (Only the quotation is a question.)

  Did he ask, "Is the report collated"?   (The entire sentence is a question.)

  Tu said, "The report is completed."

▼ SPELLING ▼

Similar-Sounding Words

The following words are similar in pronunciation but have different meanings. Become familiar with the words so you can spell and use them properly.

accede	to give consent
exceed	too much; to go beyond
accept	to take
except	everything but
adapt	to fit for new use
adept	proficient
adopt	to take as a member of a family; to accept (to adopt a policy)
addition	an increase
edition	form in which a literary work is published
advice	suggestion (noun)
advise	to inform; to notify (verb)
affect	to influence (verb)
effect	end result (noun)
all ready	all prepared
already	before
all together	all in one place
altogether	completely
ascent	going up
assent	agreeing to
bear	an animal
bare	without covering

by	near
buy	to purchase something
canvas	coarse fabric
canvass	to ask or solicit
capital	money; seat of government of a state or country
capitol	building where the legislature meets
carat	unit of weight
caret	a mark indicating that something is to be inserted
carrot	vegetable
cash	money
cache	place where supplies are hidden, temporary computer memory
cereal	food made of grain
serial	published in intervals
cite	to quote an authority
sight	something seen
site	location
consul	a government official living in a foreign country
council	government body
counsel	to give advice
course	method of doing something
coarse	rough
die	cease living
dye	change the color
eminent	high esteem
imminent	going to happen
envelop	surround
envelope	container for a letter
farther	distance
further	additional
flour	ingredient used in baking
flower	blossom in a garden
grate	to make into small pieces
great	wonderful
hangar	shelter for an airplane
hanger	device to hang garments on

hour	time
our	possessive of we
immoral	contrary to public law
immortal	living forever
interstate	between different states
intrastate	within one state
new	recently received
knew	had knowledge of something; was certain
no	negative
know	to have knowledge of something; to be certain of
one	singular number
won	victorious
pair	two of the same type
pear	type of fruit
passed	met the goal; die
past	former time; ended; beyond
peace	tranquility
piece	a part of something
personal	concerning a particular person
personnel	employees in a business
precede	go before
proceed	to continue
principal	head of something; most important
principle	theory
right	correct
rite	ceremonial act
write	communication that is recorded; to inscribe
rode	past tense of ride
road	way for public or private passage
role	part that an actor takes in a play
roll	to move by turning; list of names; food
stake	support for a fence; interest in a project
steak	food
stationary	not moving
stationery	paper to write on

steal	to take illegally	
steel	metal	
their	possessive noun	
there	place	
to	a preposition meaning direction	
too	in addition	
two	a number	
vary	to change	
very	complete (as very happy)	
wait	stay in one place; inactive	
weight	unit of measure	
waive	to give up claim	
wave	to move back and forth	
ware	manufactured items	
wear	to have on as a garment	
where	in or at a place	
weather	atmospheric conditions	
whether	if that is the situation	

▼ FREQUENTLY MISSPELLED WORDS ▼

The following are lists of frequently misspelled words.

List 1

accidentally	contagious	innovation
acquittal	disbursement	interrupting
admissible	delegation	jewelry
alphabetize	description	knowledgeable
ambivalent	eliminate	license
beginning	etiquette	library
believable	facsimile	maintenance
bicycle	government	
constituent	haphazard	

List 2

assistance	expense	optimism
bequeath	independent	ostensible
bulletin	influence	peculiar
calendar	management	punctual
carte blanche	municipal	questionnaire
chronicle	ninth	rationalize
despondent	noticeable	reminisce
disappointment	official	
entrepreneur	opponent	

List 3

accountability
accreditation
additional
belligerent
beneficiary
conscious
conservation
deceive
defendant

dessert
disappear
economize
electronic
foreign
forty
genuine
guarantee
height

inevitable
occurred
outfitted
particular
perception
realization
reciprocate

List 4

adherence
advertisement
benevolence
bizarre
cancellation
capitalize
ceremony
decision
deficiency

disseminate
embarrass
endurance
flamboyant
flexible
gratuitous
guidance
habitually
movable

oblivious
observance
perpetual
personality
persuasion
rendezvous
renovate

List 5

ambiguous
antagonize
appreciation
bankruptcy
benefitted
bureaucracy
deliverance
demonstrate
embassy

embezzle
emphasize
impatient
identical
imbecile
judgment
liquidate
litigation
occurrence

ordinarily
residence
reversible
sabbatical
satellite
saturate
severance

List 6

apprehension
arbitration
architect
depreciation
despicable
encumbrance
ethical
exaggerate
friendship

frivolous
grammar
grievous
ledger
leisure
manuscript
mysterious
recommendation
reconcile

reimbursement
representative
similar
simultaneous
technical
telecommunications
utility

List 7

believe	exception	ninety
boulevard	extravagance	numerical
clientele	familiar	requisition
commence	feasibility	restaurant
compensation	harmonious	tangible
competitive	hindrance	transmittal
destructible	lieutenant	vicinity
development	likelihood	
dilemma	nineteenth	

List 8

absenteeism	continuity	guardian
arrogant	correspondent	humorous
attorney	deceitful	hypocrisy
autonomous	deference	regrettable
brochure	discretionary	relevant
friend	enthusiastic	replaceable
compliant	environment	zealous
congratulate	facilitate	
conscientious	fascinating	

List 9

abandoned	improbable	prosecution
accelerated	insolvency	rescind
accessible	itinerary	ridiculous
accommodation	jeopardize	sincerity
acquaintance	justifiable	sophisticate
affidavit	obvious	specialize
affluent	occasionally	transferred
equipped	perquisite	
extraordinary	proprietor	

List 10

amateur	mediocre	strategy
character	merger	subpoena
eighth	necessary	substantial
eliminate	neighbor	useful
execute	nuisance	vacillate
illegible	perseverance	weird
immediately	prosperous	Xerox
inventory	psychology	
malicious	statistical	

List 11

abdicated	February	pamphlet
abeyance	interfered	precede
abhorrent	interrupt	predominance
analysis	irrevocable	souvenir
annoyance	minimize	successor
applicable	miscellaneous	sufficient
approximately	mischievous	suspicious
endorsement	misdemeanor	
erroneous	negation	

List 12

absence	counsel	secretary
advantage	credibility	seize
advise	criticism	separate
agenda	monopolize	stationery
arbitrary	mortgage	subsidy
argument	occurring	sympathy
assignment	omitted	synonymous
barricade	organize	
council	remembrance	

List 13

anecdote	generation	logistics
autumn	geographical	longevity
cafeteria	germane	sympathize
camouflage	glossary	transparent
changeable	gorgeous	tremendous
collateral	gubernatorial	triplicate
congratulate	legislation	waiver
contribution	lethargic	
controlling	liaison	

Cities and States

Akron, Ohio	Boston, Massachusetts
Albuquerque, New Mexico	Buffalo, New York
Amarillo, Texas	Charlotte, North Carolina
Anaheim, California	Chattanooga, Tennessee
Anchorage, Alaska	Chicago, Illinois
Atlanta, Georgia	Cincinnati, Ohio
Baltimore, Maryland	Cleveland, Ohio
Baton Rouge, Louisiana	Columbus, Ohio
Birmingham, Alabama	Corpus Christi, Texas

Dallas, Texas
Denver, Colorado
Detroit, Michigan
El Paso, Texas
Honolulu, Hawaii
Houston, Texas
Indianapolis, Indiana
Jacksonville, Florida
Kansas City, Missouri
Knoxville, Tennessee
Lexington, Kentucky
Los Angeles, California
Louisville, Kentucky
Madison, Wisconsin
Memphis, Tennessee
Miami, Florida
Milwaukee, Wisconsin
Minneapolis, Minnesota
Nashville, Tennessee
New Orleans, Louisiana
Newark, New Jersey
Norfolk, Virginia
Oklahoma City, Oklahoma
Omaha, Nebraska
Philadelphia, Pennsylvania
Phoenix, Arizona
Pittsburgh, Pennsylvania
Portland, Oregon
Raleigh, North Carolina

Rochester, New York
Sacramento, California
San Antonio, Texas
San Diego, California
San Francisco, California
San Jose, California
Seattle, Washington
Shreveport, Louisiana
Spokane, Washington
St. Louis, Missouri
St. Petersburg, Florida
Syracuse, New York
Tampa, Florida
Toledo, Ohio
Tucson, Arizona
Tulsa, Oklahoma
Wichita, Kansas

Calgary, Alberta
Edmonton, Alberta
Halifax, Nova Scotia
Montreal, Quebec
Toronto, Ontario
Vancouver, British Columbia
Windsor, Ontario
Winnipeg, Manitoba

Index